Acquiring Metaphorical Expressions in a Second Language

Also available from Bloomsbury

Language Acquisition and the Multilingual Ideal, by Toshiyuki Nakamura
Reflective Language Teaching, by Thomas S. C. Farrell
Second Language Acquisition in Action, by Andrea Nava and Luciana Pedrazzini
Teaching and Learning the English Language, by Richard Badger
The Cultural Memory of Language, by Susan Samata

Acquiring Metaphorical Expressions in a Second Language

Performance by Chinese Learners of English

Chris Mengying Xia

BLOOMSBURY ACADEMIC
LONDON • NEW YORK • OXFORD • NEW DELHI • SYDNEY

BLOOMSBURY ACADEMIC
Bloomsbury Publishing Plc
50 Bedford Square, London, WC1B 3DP, UK
1385 Broadway, New York, NY 10018, USA
29 Earlsfort Terrace, Dublin 2, Ireland

BLOOMSBURY, BLOOMSBURY ACADEMIC and the Diana logo
are trademarks of Bloomsbury Publishing Plc

First published in Great Britain 2019
Paperback edition published 2021

Copyright © Chris Mengying Xia, 2019

Chris Mengying Xia has asserted her right under the Copyright,
Designs and Patents Act, 1988, to be identified as Author of this work.

For legal purposes the Acknowledgements on p. x constitute
an extension of this copyright page.

All rights reserved. No part of this publication may be reproduced or
transmitted in any form or by any means, electronic or mechanical,
including photocopying, recording, or any information storage or retrieval
system, without prior permission in writing from the publishers.

Bloomsbury Publishing Plc does not have any control over, or responsibility for,
any third-party websites referred to or in this book. All internet addresses given
in this book were correct at the time of going to press. The author and publisher
regret any inconvenience caused if addresses have changed or sites have
ceased to exist, but can accept no responsibility for any such changes.

A catalogue record for this book is available from the British Library.

Library of Congress Cataloging-in-Publication Data
Names: Mengying Xia, Chris, author.
Title: Acquiring metaphorical expressions in a second language:
performance by chinese learners of english / Chris Mengying Xia.
Description: New York, NY: Bloomsbury Academic, 2019. |
Includes bibliographical references and index. |
Identifiers: LCCN 2019020793 (print) | LCCN 2019021466 (ebook) |
ISBN 9781350071803 (epdf) | ISBN 9781350071810 (epub) | ISBN 9781350071797 (hb)
Subjects: LCSH: Metaphor–Study and teaching. | Language and languages–Study
and teaching. | Phraseology–Study and teaching. | Figures of speech. |
Idioms. | Second language acquisition–Study and teaching.
Classification: LCC P301.5.M48 (ebook) | LCC P301.5.M48 M385 2019 (print) |
DDC 401/.43071–dc23
LC record available at https://lccn.loc.gov/2019020793

ISBN: HB: 978-1-3500-7179-7
PB: 978-1-3502-4449-8
ePDF: 978-1-3500-7180-3
eBook: 978-1-3500-7181-0

Typeset by Newgen KnowledgeWorks Pvt. Ltd., Chennai, India

To find out more about our authors and books visit
www.bloomsbury.com and sign up for our newsletters.

Contents

List of Illustrations	viii
Acknowledgements	x

1. Introduction — 1
   1.1 Questions and objectives — 1
   1.2 Terminological remarks — 4
   1.3 The overall structure of the book — 8
2. Metaphorical expressions: A historical review — 13
   2.1 Introduction — 13
   2.2 Metaphorical expressions in (post-)Gricean philosophy of language — 14
   2.3 Metaphor in cognitive semantics and lexical semantics — 22
   2.4 Summary — 26
3. Metaphorical expressions under cross-linguistic influence — 29
   3.1 Introduction: A short overview of studies on cross-linguistic influence — 29
   3.2 Lemmatic transfer: A general review — 32
      3.2.1 Defining and delimiting lemmatic transfer — 32
      3.2.2 Types of realization of lemmatic transfer — 34
      3.2.3 Lemmatic transfer in the acquisition of figurative language — 39
   3.3 Factors influencing cross-linguistic influence — 45
      3.3.1 Markedness — 46
      3.3.2 Learners' knowledge — 50
   3.4 Summary — 53
4. Processing metaphorical expressions by native speakers and learners — 55
   4.1 Introduction — 55
   4.2 The processing of metaphorical expressions by native speakers — 56
   4.3 The processing of figurative expressions by second language learners — 65
   4.4 Summary and loose ends — 71

5.	Placing metaphorical expressions in a bilingual mental lexicon	73
	5.1 Introduction	73
	5.2 Storing concrete and abstract words and meanings in a bilingual mental lexicon	74
	5.3 Bilingual mental lexicon in a developmental view	82
	5.4 Acquiring different meanings in a classroom setting	89
	5.5 Hypotheses for the status of metaphorical expressions in a bilingual lexicon	93
	5.6 Summary	99
6.	Methodologies in second language metaphor research	101
	6.1 Introduction	101
	6.2 Formulating specific research questions on the acquisition of metaphorical expressions	102
	6.3 Possible experimental instruments to test the acquisition of metaphorical expressions	104
	6.3.1 Productive experiments	104
	6.3.2 Receptive experiments	107
	6.4 Selection of research participants	120
	6.5 Selection, construction and classification of metaphorical expressions for an experiment	122
	6.6 Possible supplementary experiment instruments	125
	6.6.1 Lexical evaluation survey	125
	6.6.2 Proficiency test	128
	6.6.3 Vocabulary size test	129
	6.6.4 Working memory capacity test	129
	6.7 Summary	130
7.	Two experiments on the acquisition of metaphorical expressions	133
	7.1 Introduction	133
	7.2 Judging metaphorical expressions	134
	7.2.1 Participants	134
	7.2.2 Materials	134
	7.2.3 Method	136
	7.2.4 Procedure	137
	7.2.5 Data adjustment	138
	7.2.6 Results	139
	7.3 Processing metaphorical expressions	156
	7.3.1 Participants	156
	7.3.2 Materials	157

		7.3.3 Method	159
		7.3.4 Procedure	160
		7.3.5 Data adjustment and analysis	160
		7.3.6 Results	161
	7.4	Summary and loose ends	171
8.	Acquiring and teaching metaphorical expressions in a second language		173
	8.1	Introduction	173
	8.2	The acquisition of metaphorical expressions with different availability in a second language: What can be achieved and what cannot	174
	8.3	Factors influencing the transferability and transfer of metaphorical expressions	182
	8.4	Learning and teaching metaphorical expressions in a second language	185
	8.5	Summary and loose ends	191

Appendix 1: Instruction and sentences used in the acceptability judgement task	193
Appendix 2: Instruction, sentences and questions used in the self-paced reading task	196
Appendix 3: Lexical property scores for the critical lexical items	201
Notes	204
Bibliography	205
Index	213

Illustrations

Figures

5.1	The Distributed Conceptual Feature Model	76
5.2	The Sense Model	78
5.3	The Revised Hierarchical Model	84
5.4	The structure of *gongji*, attack and relevant concepts in an RHM fashion presentation	86
5.5	The Modified Hierarchical Model	88
5.6	A simplified model of bilingual lexicon with literal and metaphorical distinctions	94
6.1	An excerpt of an acceptability judgement task for research on acquisition of metaphorical expressions	111
6.2	A simplified illustration of a self-paced reading task	117
6.3	A simplified illustration of a maze task	119
6.4	An excerpt from an online lexical evaluation survey	127
7.1	Acceptability scores for literal and metaphorical expressions by group	140
7.2	Confidence scores for the six target types for each group	142
7.3	Distribution of coreness scores for the MB and MS expressions in the AJT, as perceived by Chinese native speakers	147
7.4	Distribution of the coreness scores of the LB and MB expressions in the AJT, as perceived by Chinese native speakers	147
7.5	Segment-by-segment reading time pattern for the native group	162
7.6	Segment-by-segment reading time pattern for the learner groups	164
7.7	Reaction times (left axis) and mean scores for answers for the native group	167
7.8	Reaction times (left axis) and mean scores for answers for the learner groups	169

Tables

5.1	Possible routes for the retrieval of the literal meaning of an L2 word	95
5.2	Possible routes for the retrieval of the metaphorical meaning shared between the L1 and the L2	96
5.3	Possible routes for the retrieval of the L2-specific metaphorical meaning of an L2 word	97
5.4	Possible routes for the retrieval of the L1-specific metaphorical meaning from the L2 word form	98
5.5	Different bundles of possible routes of metaphorical meaning retrieval in L2	98
7.1	Linguistic backgrounds of the learner participants in the acceptability judgement task	134
7.2	Availability of different types of expression in Chinese and English	136
7.3	Identification of traces of transfer in the judgements of MB expressions	144
7.4	Identification of traces of transfer in the judgements of MS expressions	145
7.5	Identification of traces of transfer in the judgements of MT expressions	145
7.6	Estimated percentage of traces of transfer of different metaphorical expressions in the learner groups	145
7.7	Distribution of traces of transfer on LB and MB expressions across learners' proficiency	148
7.8	Distribution of relevant feedback sentences provided by each group of participants across different metaphorical conditions	151
7.9	Distribution of the types of reaction across different proficiency groups	152
7.10	Examples of types of strategies adopted by participants in the sentence correction section	154
7.11	Average number of relevant feedback sentences with different strategies provided by individual participants at different proficiency levels	154
7.12	All 16 relevant feedback sentences for 'My mother said that these books would be *food* for thought' given by different groups of participants	156
7.13	Linguistic backgrounds of the learner participants	157
7.14	A pair of sample test sentences and their structure	159

Acknowledgements

This book is based on my research project conducted at University of Cambridge between 2015 and 2018. I wish to show my deepest gratitude to my supervisor, Dr Henriëtte Hendriks, without whom I could not have completed it. I would also like to thank all of the people at the Section of Theoretical and Applied Linguistics, University of Cambridge, for their support, discussions and comments made and given throughout the whole project, as well as for allowing me to occupy a desk when I wrote the book.

I am grateful to the current and former members at Bloomsbury Academic, especially Gurdeep Mattu, who encouraged me to start a book of my own, and Andrew Wardell, who was always there to keep me on the right track. Special thanks go to three anonymous reviewers for their comments on the proposal of the book, and two anonymous reviewers for their valuable opinions on the first draft.

I would like to thank my parents Yilin Xia and Yun Huang, my boyfriend Zhiyi Yang, my kittens Coffee and Milk, and all my friends for helping me to deal with the difficulties and cheering me up when I had a headache about how to transform my thesis into this book. I also want to thank those who have participated in my experiments – your participation was indeed crucial for both the study and my thoughts.

And finally, I would like to thank you, the reader, for making the existence of the book meaningful.

Part of the materials presented in Section 7.3, 'Processing metaphorical expressions', was first published as 'Processing L2 Metaphorical Expressions by Chinese Learners of English', in *Selected Proceedings of the 2017 Second Language Research Forum (SLRF)*, ed. N. King et al., Somerville, MA: Cascadilla Press.

1

Introduction

1.1 Questions and objectives

This book aims to discuss the acquisition of conventional metaphorical expressions in a second language, both from a theoretical perspective and from an empirical view. While the content of the book is, I presume, applicable to any situation of second language acquisition, some of the examples and experiments reported in this book have a primary focus on Chinese native speakers who acquire English as a second language, mostly in a classroom setting. As the readers shall see in this book, the choice of Chinese and English is not arbitrary, but a practicality due to a lack of relevant studies and discussions on this topic. In fact, when talking about the acquisition of L2 metaphorical expressions, one needs to start by defining the very basic concepts: metaphors and metaphorical expressions.

This chapter, being the very beginning of the book, serves as an overview of the whole book. Specifically, it aims to delimit the target of this book, namely 'metaphorical expressions'. While a further theoretical discussion on metaphors and metaphorical expressions will be presented in Chapter 2, this chapter will provide the first taste of those metaphorical expressions discussed later in the book. Section 1.2 clarifies the definitions of all the key terminologies, and the last section includes an overview of the following chapters.

The concept of metaphor, as well as the theoretical account associated with the concept, has been extensively debated in contemporary linguistics. In the past few decades, an agreement has been reached in at least one area; metaphors, or to be more precise, metaphorical expressions are more than the decoration of daily language use. Metaphorical expressions are widely used in all types of discourse, written or spoken, consciously or subconsciously, and have formed a great number of conventional collocations in almost every language. One can observe metaphorical expressions even in the title of this book; I can *acquire* a book or a house by paying money to the bookstore or the owner, and I can touch and feel what I have acquired. However, I can also 'acquire' a language, or 'acquire' a particular skill, and I can do so probably without any financial cost, and certainly without knowing the shape of the language or the colour of the skill. The expansion of the meaning of 'acquire' is therefore metaphorical, although this may not be realized by those people who understand the word, or those who have researched second language acquisition for years. It is difficult, then, to separate metaphorical expressions from other parts of language use and to assert that metaphorical expressions are simply a decoration of the language.

Metaphorical expressions, based on their description, are expressions that convey certain metaphorical meanings. Most languages, if not all, have their own metaphorical expressions. They can be conventionalized and lexicalized as an established part of the language, or be novel and creative for any language user. Chinese, as described by Liu (2002) and Link (2013), is renowned for using 'eat' in depiction of all the sufferings you can imagine: you 'eat the loss' when you lose your wealth, 'eat the bitterness' when you encounter some hardship, 'eat a lawsuit' when you are sued by your enemy, and 'eat a bullet' when you, unfortunately, are sentenced to death. Such metaphorical expressions based on 'eat' are somehow beyond the understanding of English native speakers who do not have any prior knowledge of Chinese. Similarly, as a Chinese learner of English, I also experienced such a 'metaphorical shock' in my life in an English-speaking environment. I never thought that a person could 'buy' an idea, or that a country could 'buy' its peace. Even though I have a first language which uses 'eat' for all sorts of life experiences, I still had no idea what 'food for thought' meant, before I was told. Despite those dramatic differences, however, Chinese and English also share a large number of metaphorical expressions; people both 'lay the foundation' and 'build the structure' of an article, as if the article was a skyscraper; and people both try to make the argument 'clear' and the evidence 'strong', as if they could visually perceive an argument or physically touch a piece of evidence. The diversity of metaphorical expressions across languages, as well as the common members between the languages, provides material for theoretical linguists to analyse how languages can reflect cultural variations and cognitive universals, which, at the same time, creates problems for people who wish to master a second language.

To understand how metaphorical expressions work in second language acquisition, and thus help language learners to understand their strengths and weaknesses in terms of metaphorical expressions, three major comparisons should be made, which leads to three main research questions in this book. The first comparison is between literal expressions and metaphorical expressions. Is there any difference between these two types of expressions? Are learners, in general, better at one or are they actually good at both? Since metaphorical expressions are always considered to be 'secondary' due to the influence of literary metaphors, such 'secondariness' may also be reflected in the learner's receptive and productive performance regarding such expressions. The second comparison is between the metaphorical expressions of learners in L1 and L2. As exemplified above, a pair of languages do not only share metaphorical expressions, they also have their own language-specific expressions. However, does such difference of availability have a significant impact in terms of the outcome of the acquisition? This comparison can be further connected to the general impact of cross-linguistic influence on second language acquisition, as cross-linguistic influence has been discovered pervasively in almost all aspects of language acquisition (see Odlin 1989 for a classic summary) it is natural to assume that metaphorical expressions cannot escape the impact of cross-linguistic influence either. In this book, I will examine cross-linguistic influence on the acquisition of metaphorical expressions using the framework proposed by Jordens and Kellerman (1981; see also Kellerman 1983). The third comparison is between native speakers and the reaction of learners to metaphorical expressions. Both theoretical and experimental semantics have established a good knowledge of the ability of native speakers to use metaphorical expressions in daily language, which provides a baseline to investigate the learners' use of metaphorical expressions. Could it possibly be the case that learners can achieve native-like results without much effort? Or, will it be the case that metaphorical expressions are something that non-native speakers can never fully master? The entire book, especially the experiment part, aims to answer the research questions coming from the three comparisons.

Furthermore, this book intends to establish the importance of conventional metaphorical expressions as a proper topic in second language acquisition and to associate the topic with other widely-surveyed aspects in second language acquisition, including cross-linguistic influence, bilingual vocabulary and non-literal language processing in a second language. In the domain of theoretical semantics and pragmatics, metaphorical expressions receive no less attention than other members of non-literal language. Theoretical proposals have been raised concerning the creation, semantic construction, derivation, conventionalization and usage of non-literal language. However, in terms of second language acquisition, the research on conventional metaphorical expressions and other types of non-literal language is out of balance, which is reflected by a well-established research history of the acquisition of other non-literal language phenomena (particularly idioms and phrasal verbs) and a lack of in-depth, systematic investigation on the acquisition of conventional metaphorical expressions. It seems that, while idioms and phrasal verbs are generally recognized as linguistic elements which require additional instruction, there is little research on the question of whether conventional metaphorical expressions can be acquired autonomously by L2 learners. However, the results in this book reveal that metaphorical expressions are not taken for granted when a second language is acquired in a classroom setting. I expect this book to provide some insights to different groups of people: to researchers of second language acquisition, in order to understand metaphorical expressions and their status in the bilingual mental lexicon; to researchers of (theoretical) semantics and pragmatics, in order to understand the universality and cross-linguistic variability of metaphorical expressions and the influence of such cross-linguistic variation on individual language users; to instructors of a second language, in order to understand the importance of metaphorical expressions and design appropriate contents based on the results; and to learners of a second language, in order to understand the strength and weakness of oneself in this area.

1.2 Terminological remarks

The topic of this book is 'metaphorical expressions', which essentially means that I will focus on the linguistic elements like, 'I *see* what you mean' which carry metaphorical senses, rather than conceptual metaphors like SEEING IS UNDERSTANDING. Here, I would like to define a 'metaphorical expression' as a grammatical multi-word phrasal structure (such as a grammatically complete verb phrase or noun phrase) in which one, and only one, of the lexical items should be interpreted as a conventionalized metaphorical meaning to make the phrase meaningful. While a metaphorical expression is defined in terms of syntactic structure, such a view is essentially from formal semantics as a Principle of Compositionality, a common formal semantic theory which states that the meaning of a phrasal structure is determined by both: (1) the meanings of individual lexical items in the structure and (2) the structural organization (Frege 1991). In this sense, a metaphorical expression is a multi-word phrase in which one, and only one, word contributes to the compositional meaning using its metaphorical sense.

Similar to other figurative expressions, a metaphorical expression has a semi-fixed structure. For example, expressions like 'attack the proposal', 'attack the argument' and 'attack the idea' can all be combined as one semi-fixed metaphorical expression [attack [NP]], while a noun phrase should fall into the semantic domain of 'ideas and thoughts' to trigger the intended metaphorical result by the collocation of that lexical item. Words that: (1) fall into the semantic domain of required collocation; and (2) can form valid conventional expressions can all be filled into the blank part of the semi-fixed structure. Compared to idioms, conventional metaphorical expressions allow a higher degree of flexibility of wording, which makes them less idiomatic and more semantically compositional; metaphorical expressions are in the form of a loose collocation, since the words collocating with the metaphorically used lexical item can be changed, while a strict collocation, like an idiom, does not allow any change of words in the collocation.

The metaphorical expressions under discussion in this book are all conventionalized, and it is usual to find these expressions in a dictionary. A pair of simple examples indicating the contrast between a literal expression and a conventionalized metaphorical expression is demonstrated below:

(1) a. John <u>attacked</u> Mary with a stick.

    b. John <u>attacked</u> Mary's proposal in the meeting.

The literally used and the metaphorically used words are marked by underlining. The core and fundamental meaning of the word 'attack' is reflected in (1a) as 'to try to hurt or defeat using violence' (Wehmeier 2000), and it could be seen that the meaning of 'attack' in (1a) clearly involves physical contact and conflict. If we look at (1b), this makes use of the metaphorical meaning of 'attack', which is defined as 'to criticize someone strongly' (Wehmeier, 2000), and the action of 'attacking a proposal' obviously does not involve any physical conflict, for sometimes there is not a physical entity for 'a proposal'. However, even a naïve language user could sense the 'similarity' between 'attack' in (1a) and 'attack' in (1b); they both involve some sudden, harsh, violent attitude, causing negative results. As in Chapter 2, the metaphorical meaning of 'attack' is a historical deviation of the literal meaning of that word. Even if one does not sense the usual metaphorical meaning of 'attack' in (1b), the close relation between the expression and its literal meaning still qualifies it as a metaphorical expression. Moreover, by the time one acquires this metaphorical meaning, either in one's L1 or L2, it has already become highly conventionalized. With both criteria fulfilled, 'attack the proposal' can be recognized as a conventionalized metaphorical expression, which falls into a category of discussion in this book.

Due to the complicated use of 'metaphor' in the literature, which will be presented in Chapter 2, the term 'metaphor' is largely avoided in this book. On the few occasions where the exact term 'metaphor' appears, it refers only to a conceptual metaphor that is not linguistically expressed but is conceptually embedded. When it comes to the subject of the book, that is, the conventionalized linguistic realization of metaphor, a series of terminologies are used: 'metaphorical expressions'; 'metaphorical meanings' (of a lexical item); 'metaphorically used lexical items'; and 'metaphoricalness'. The central terminology among the four is 'metaphorical meanings' (of a lexical item); following the MIP paradigm developed by the Pragglejaz Group (2007), all meanings that are a departure from the core, fundamental meaning(s), but are associated with the core meaning(s), are defined as 'metaphorical meanings' of that lexical item. Since there is a set of criteria in the MIP paradigm to define metaphorical meanings, the concept of 'metaphorical meanings' is stable and objective, and one can distinguish the conventionalized metaphorical meaning from the literal meaning in a dictionary entry of one particular lexical item. In fact, all the metaphorical meanings surveyed in this study have been identified in several mainstream dictionaries as non-core meanings of polysemous words.

The concept of 'metaphorical expressions' has developed, based on the concept of 'metaphorical meanings'. The basic idea is that a single lexical item without any context can neither be literal nor metaphorical, as the literal or metaphorical meanings of that lexical item can only be activated by the collocation of that lexical item. A 'metaphorical expression' is a multi-word expression in which the metaphorical meaning of (at least) one lexical item is activated. In example (1b), the word 'attack' should be interpreted as 'to criticize someone strongly', which is a conventionalized metaphorical meaning of 'attack'. Based on that, 'attack' is a metaphorically used word and the whole expression 'attack one's proposal', as the activator of the metaphorical meaning of 'attack', is a metaphorical expression, and the fact that 'attack one's proposal' is a metaphorical expression confirms the metaphorical nature of 'attack' in that expression. While the ultimate aim of a study on the acquisition of metaphorical expressions is to explore the acquisition of the metaphorical meanings of lexical items, it is more practical to look at the learners' reaction to metaphorical expressions, since a metaphorical meaning cannot be activated without a metaphorical expression. Meanwhile, when considering metaphorical expressions from an experimental view, it is difficult to examine all the possibilities of a semi-fixed metaphorical expression at the same time. Therefore, the experiments in this book only examine some instances of semi-fixed metaphorical expressions, and I hope to use these instances to represent all the instances in which other lexical items or phrases are filled into the blank part of a semi-fixed metaphorical expression. When describing a 'metaphorical expression' in an experimental condition, this refers only to a specific instance of that semi-fixed structure used in the experiment.

The term 'conventional' in 'a conventional metaphorical expression' in this book expresses a twofold convention: first, the metaphorical meaning activated by the metaphorical expression is conventional; second, and more importantly, the expression itself, or collocation of words, is also conventional and frequently seen in daily language use. Therefore, two possible types of metaphorical expression are ruled out from the target of the research; expressions like 'Chris is a cactus', in which 'an unapproachable person', as the intended meaning of 'cactus', is not conventional and thus 'above the threshold'; and, expressions like 'attack the product', in which 'attack' is intended to mean 'to criticize someone strongly', since the expression is less conventional than other uses of 'attack' listed in the last paragraph. The focus of this book concentrates exclusively on the acquisition of conventional expressions that contain a lexical item that expresses its conventional metaphorical meaning.

As mentioned in Section 1.1, one of the focuses of this book is to compare metaphorical expressions and literal expressions, which indicate that literal expressions, though not the focus of the current investigation, are treated as a baseline of learners' acquisition, and thus an essential counterpart of metaphorical expressions. Terminologies used for literal expressions are constructed and defined in a way similar to the terms for metaphorical expressions above. The 'literal meaning' of a lexical item is the core and fundamental meaning of that lexical item, usually the meaning with the longest history (Nacey 2014); most of the time, a lexical item only has one literal meaning, but in the case of homonyms there can be more than one literal meaning for a word. In a literal expression, the literal meaning of the critical lexical item is activated, such as 'attacked Mary (with a stick)', in (1a), since the word 'attack' in the expression displays its literal meaning, or at least a meaning that is not a clear departure from the literal meaning 'to try to hurt or defeat using violence'. The word 'attack' in (1a), then, is a literally used lexical item, and 'attack Mary' shows its literalness by using the literal meaning of 'attack'.

Throughout the book, 'being metaphorical' is defined as a binary parameter, which means that 'literalness' and 'metaphoricalness' are used as a pair, or an antonym; all the expressions in the experiments or discussions can be either literal or metaphorical, but not both. That definition is rather an idealization of language use, no matter whether in one's L1 or L2. From a contextualist, semantic view, daily language use allows the flexibility of interpretation and literalness, or metaphoricalness, of a particular expression or sentence, which can be achieved by the manipulation of the greater context. It is possible, and sometimes feasible, that an expression can be interpreted both literally and metaphorically, as the example of (2) below, in which both (2a) and (2b) can be valid interpretations of (2):

(2) John attacked Mary in the meeting.
  a. John beat Mary fiercely in the meeting.
  b. John criticized Mary harshly in the meeting.

Such ambiguity expressed in (2) has been extensively discussed in the indexicalist account of metaphor, as shown in Chapter 2, and is recognized as inevitable language use by both native speakers and learners. However, ambiguous expressions like 'attack' in (2) are excluded from the current discussion, since the knowledge involved in comprehending (2) and generating the metaphorical interpretation as (2b) is not related only to the acquisition of the metaphorical meaning of a lexical item, but more to the ability of making contextual inferences. In the studies of metaphorical expressions in this book, none of them discussed such kinds of ambiguous expressions. When a lexical item is under investigation, *either* the literal meaning of a critical lexical item *or* one of the metaphorical meanings of that lexical item is investigated.

1.3 The overall structure of the book

Starting from Chapter 2, this book can be roughly divided into three parts. The first part, from Chapters 2 to 5, presents different theoretical arguments of the acquisition of metaphorical expressions from several perspectives. The second part, including Chapters 6 and 7, serves as an empirical study guide on the acquisition of metaphorical expressions. In this part, general research methodologies are demonstrated and the results of some existing studies are provided as examples. In the meantime, readers can observe from this first-hand data how second language learners deal with metaphorical expressions in reality, and whether they follow the patterns discussed in the first part. The last part, which is the last chapter of the book, focuses on learners' behaviours and teacher strategies regarding metaphorical expressions.

Before moving to the acquisition of metaphorical expressions, which is the core of the book, the first issue I need to discuss is the linguistic element being acquired – what counts as metaphorical expressions? Although I have already presented a first taste of conventional metaphorical expressions, I still need a well-established theoretical review to delimit metaphorical expressions and, at the same time, formally build up the connection between metaphorical expressions and literal expressions. Chapter 2, as a chapter exclusively focusing on the semantic properties of metaphorical expressions, illustrates several semantic accounts. Some of these accounts emphasize the difference between literal and metaphorical expressions, while others tend to stress the internal connections. Whether similarities or differences, these theoretical views will help to predict how metaphorical expressions can be integrated in one's vocabulary knowledge, which serves as the foundation of the discussion.

After the discussion of semantic theories, I will step into the field of 'acquiring' metaphorical expressions. As proposed in Section 1.1, two major aspects of language acquisition can be associated with the acquisition of metaphorical expressions: first, cross-linguistic influence; and second, the structure of the bilingual lexicon. Chapter 3 is a review of cross-linguistic influence, in which I show the details of transfer in vocabulary acquisition and acquisition of other types of figurative language, such as idioms, proverbs and phrasal verbs. This chapter also includes an analysis of how cross-linguistic influence might be affected by a language-internal factor, namely the degree of markedness of a linguistic element, as well as a language-external factor, namely the learner's proficiency – following the seminal work by Jordens and Kellerman (1981) on cross-linguistic influence.

Chapters 4 and 5 together discuss the second aspect of acquisition of metaphorical expressions, that is, the status of metaphorical expressions in a bilingual lexicon, which still have separate emphases. Chapter 4 reviews the psycholinguistic studies on the processing of different figurative language by both native speakers and second language learners. Since few studies exclusively work on the processing of metaphorical expressions by learners, I need to refer both to the reaction of native speakers to metaphorical expressions and to the learners' processing patterns of other figurative expressions to build up a series of assumptions regarding the processing of metaphorical expressions by learners. Chapter 5 attempts to connect the acquisition of metaphorical meanings of words to the construction of a bilingual lexicon, since a metaphorical expression is regarded as fully acquired only when it is fully integrated into a learner's mental lexicon. This chapter reviews several possible frameworks of bilingual lexicon, showing their strengths and weaknesses by applying them to explain the acquisition of the metaphorical meanings of a lexical item. At the end of Chapter 5 a framework of processing metaphorical expressions is constructed as part of the research hypotheses.

Moving to the experimental part, Chapter 6 explores the possible methodologies that can be used for research on the acquisition of metaphorical expressions. While this topic has not been examined to the same degree in previous research, there is an opportunity for researchers to investigate this issue from different perspectives. This chapter provides an illustration of the possible tasks that can be used in experiments, including productive and receptive tasks and online and offline methodologies. It also provides additional information about possible supplementary tasks and the criteria for the selection of participants and test materials.

Chapter 7 presents a series of experiments on the outcome of acquisition of metaphorical expressions by Chinese learners of English, which I intend to use as: (1) a practical realization of the research methodologies listed in Chapter 6 and (2) examples of research on the acquisition of L2 metaphorical expressions. In this chapter, I will show how Chinese learners of English at different proficiency levels judge the degree of acceptability of different types of metaphorical expression, and how these learners process metaphorical expressions that appear in sentences. All the analyses aim to answer the three questions in Section 1.1; therefore, the results are reported following the three comparisons: between literal and metaphorical expressions, between shared and language-specific expressions, and between native and learner speakers. The influencing factors on transferability are also included in the report. This chapter also includes a qualitative analysis of the learners' production of metaphorical expressions and the literal counterparts of metaphorical expressions, and an analysis on successful retrieval by learners of the intended metaphorical meanings, based on their performance in comprehension questions.

Chapter 8, as the final chapter of this book, is a general discussion on the topic, from the perspective of both second language acquisition and second language teaching. It can be seen as a bridge between the research results, the learners' behaviours and possible strategies that can be used in second language education, especially in a classroom setting. An overall picture will be presented in the chapter about learners' strengths and weaknesses in their acquisition of metaphorical expressions, particularly from two aspects: (1) learners' developmental curves of their knowledge of metaphorical expressions; and (2) the impact of cross-linguistic influence on the acquisition of metaphorical expressions. By comparing the outcome of learners and the ideal picture (as presented by native speakers), I will then set up to find some ways to both teach metaphorical expressions and learn metaphorical expressions better.

2

Metaphorical expressions: A historical review

2.1 Introduction

Metaphor, no matter what definitions this word is used to refer to, has caused a large scale of linguistic debate since the middle of the previous century. The discussion on metaphors can be divided into two large categories: (1) the nature of metaphor, that is, whether metaphor is a purely linguistic phenomenon or whether it is actually embedded in both the linguistic and cognitive systems of human beings; and (2) the interpretation of metaphor, that is, whether metaphorical expressions should be interpreted semantically or pragmatically, and how a language user could derive the metaphorical meaning. These two large categories, however, are not fully separated from each other. Theoretical views that regard metaphor as a purely linguistic phenomenon are more likely to discuss the interpretation of metaphorical expressions as the derivation of certain pragmatic inference (e.g. Grice 1989; Sperber and Wilson 1995), while in the area of cognitive semantics, where metaphor is seen as both linguistic and cognitive, the interpretation of metaphorical expressions come from the modification of concepts without traditional without pragmatic enrichment (e.g. Fauconnier and Turner 2008; Lakoff and Johnson 1980).

The key objective of this chapter is to provide a historical review of the theoretical arguments that shed some light on the acquisition of conventional metaphorical expressions in a second language. Particularly, two types of theoretical accounts are focused. The first has the basis of truth-conditional semantics, in which semantic or pragmatic inference (as per individual theories) is crucial for the interpretation of metaphorical expressions. This category is led by the well-known Gricean account of conversational implicature (Grice 1989), while, subsequently, several theoretical arguments depart from the implicature view and gradually recognize metaphorical meanings as a type of semantic meaning. The second comes from the stream of cognitive semantics, led by Lakoff and Johnson's Conceptual Metaphor Theory and Fauconnier's Blending Theory. I will also show how lexical semantics can cater for the conventionalization of metaphorical expressions. It should be noted that while, intuitively, the approaches based on truth-conditional semantics and the theories of cognitive semantics seem to contradict to each other, there is space for the co-existence or even integration of the two branches of the tree of metaphor research. As I will show later in this chapter, a truth-conditional semantic approach can always take a cognitive semantic theory as one of the premises; even though cognitive semantic theories in lexical semantics are utilized, I can still assume that a sentence should be interpreted as a compositional, truth-conditional way.

2.2 Metaphorical expressions in (post-)Gricean philosophy of language

Linguistic theories regarding the linguistic realization of metaphor began to flourish in late 1960s when Grice (1967) first proposed the concept of implicature, together with the four well-known conversational maxims: quantity, quality, relevance and manner. Grice's theory emerges with a background of compositional semantics, which suggests that the meaning of a sentence is essentially derived from the composition of the meaning of each constituent of that sentence. Compositional semantics, however, fail to explain how interlocutors 'read between lines' and get the intended meanings that are not expressed by the compositional meaning. Grice aims to provide an explanation to this question by positing the idea of conversational implicature.

Grice intends to establish a dichotomy between 'what is said' and 'what is implicated'. The former is 'the meaning of a sentence', which should be directly derived from the composition of the meaning of each constituent of a sentence, while the context only provides referential assignment. The latter is 'the meaning of an utterance', which is the meaning intended by the speaker when their intention and the contextual information are all taken into consideration. In this framework, an utterance 'the room is hot' can be a simple statement that a particular room is hot (as 'what is said') or, in a particular context, a request from the speaker about opening the window or turning on the air conditioner (as 'what is implicated'). Grice suggests that the implicature of an utterance can be deduced from what is said using one or more conversational maxims: quantity, quality, relevance and manner.

Metaphorical utterances, according to the original proposal of Grice, should be interpreted using the maxim of quality: when producing a metaphorical utterance and the speaker says something that is blatantly incorrect, what is said cannot be the meaning intended by them. Grice (1989: 34) provides an example of how 'what is implicated' of a metaphorical utterance can be derived based on his maxim of quality; when a speaker says 'you are the cream in my coffee', the hearer would know immediately that the speaker does not mean that literally, because a person can never be the cream in one's coffee. Therefore, what is said is blatantly false, and the hearer needs to derive the implicature of that utterance by thinking about the speaker's attitude towards 'cream in my coffee'; then the hearer would know that they are either the speaker's pride or their bane.

Grice's theory of implicature leads to several suggestions or hidden assumptions, to name but a few important ones: (1) the meaning of linguistic realization of metaphor is essentially from implicature and (2) there should be a literal-first processing pattern, so that a hearer can be led to the derivation of conversational implicature when he finds the literal interpretation not possible. Different from previous theories focusing on the semantic aspects of metaphor (e.g. Beardsley 1962; Black 1962), Grice was among the first who defined the meaning of metaphorical expressions as a pragmatic meaning, not a semantic meaning. That is, understanding metaphorical expression not only requires the use of semantic knowledge (in a Gricean view, such semantic knowledge can only be used to retrieve the literal meaning of a lexical item in a metaphorical expression) but also, more importantly, the use of pragmatic knowledge and the ability to draw inferences. The assumptions mentioned above have greatly impacted the investigation of metaphor from different perspectives; while philosophy of language continues to debate on the nature of metaphorical meaning, psycholinguistic research begins to explore whether a literal-first processing pattern exists (see Chapter 4 for the evolution of research on the processing of metaphorical expressions).

Although the Gricean account of metaphor is primarily about the pragmatics of a native speaker's language, it may have a very limited effect on the acquisition of metaphorical expressions in a second language, nevertheless some possible assumptions can still be derived from Grice's claim. The most prominent idea is that, for Grice, metaphorical meanings of an expression, like other figures, assumes that speech is secondary in both memory and processing. This assumption eventually leads to an argument that there should not be any distinction between conventional and unconventional metaphorical expressions in theory, since both of them involve a secondary meaning and should always be processed through the retrieval of the literal meaning of any lexical items involved. If that is the case for native speakers, then there is no reason to assume that any second language learner would bypass the literal meaning when processing both conventional and unconventional metaphorical expressions. I would expect a second language learner to spend significantly more time when reading a conventional metaphorical expression than when reading a literal expression in the same way as native speakers. Also, I would expect that the ability to understand metaphorical expressions, even by the second language learners, is not from the knowledge of lexical items, but from general pragmatic abilities. Therefore, if learners are able to understand metaphorical expressions in their L1, there should no difficulty for them in their L2.

Further discussions on the nature of metaphorical meanings in philosophy of language, no matter what suggestions arise, are constantly under the influence of the Gricean framework. Here they are categorized as post-Gricean approaches under the convention of philosophy of language (mainly including formal semantics, truth-conditional semantics and theoretical pragmatics, but excluding cognitive semantics). This subsection will briefly introduce three major accounts that have great impact on the discussion of understanding metaphorical expressions: the relevance-theoretical view (Carston 2002; Sperber and Wilson 1995), the indexicalist view (Leezenberg 2001; Stern, 2000), and the threshold of literal meaning (Recanati 2004). The three theoretical accounts all depart from the original Gricean statement that literal meanings are processed prior to figurative meanings, but they continue to investigate the origin of metaphorical meanings and the relationship between metaphorical meanings and literal meanings under the tradition of philosophy of language.

Relevance Theory, as proposed by Sperber and Wilson, aims to explain the mechanism of pragmatic inference by referring to a specific cognitive ability of humans which is generally used within and outside communication, namely seeking the relevance between objects or activities. Sperber and Wilson suggest that, while language and gestures with communicative intentions are explicitly used to evoke communication ('ostensive phenomena' in their terminology), the hearer or recipient of an ostensive phenomenon is also prone to the communicative intention behind the phenomenon, as well as the mental representation of the speaker or communicator. A capable hearer can integrate the information in an ostensive phenomenon and the context of that phenomenon and can derive the 'hidden messages' of an ostensive phenomenon by: (1) seeking the relevance between that ostensive phenomenon and other contextual information and (2) inferring the potential mental representation of the communicator. For example, if a bartender sees a customer next to the bar raising an empty glass to them, they would treat 'raising an empty glass' as a piece of ostensive phenomenon even if no language is involved. Then, they would integrate the information of someone raising a glass together with the context of that information (in a bar, the glass is empty, the speaker is a customer, the hearer is a bartender, etc.) to seek a valid mental representation of the speaker, and then reach the most relevant interpretation, which is that the customer needs another glass of beer.

Relevance Theory further distinguishes between implicit and explicit information communicated by an utterance. It allows a certain degree of pragmatic enrichment and views all the assumptions that can be directly derived from the logical form of an utterance as explicitly communicated assumptions, under the name of 'explicature' (Sperber and Wilson 1995); on the other hand, any assumptions that cannot be directly derived from the logical form are implicit, under the name of 'implicature'. The sense of implicature in Relevance Theory already departs from the original Gricean notion; the Gricean implicature has now been split into two parts; directly or indirectly associated with the logical form of an utterance. The features of explicature could explain why metaphorical meanings behave differently from other typical conversational implicatures. For example, conversational implicatures can be cancelled, while metaphorical meanings, once established, cannot simply be negated or cancelled. Furthermore, slightly different from implicature, that could be a secondary inference from an utterance, the metaphorical meaning of a metaphorical expression is always the primary inference of an utterance, and it is always the message being communicated between the speaker and the hearer. This feature makes the metaphorical meaning of an utterance closer to an explicature, since the metaphorical meaning is explicitly intended and communicated by the speaker.

If metaphorical meanings are treated as explicature, then one should be able to find a stable way to compute the explicature from the logical form of a metaphorical utterance. In Relevance Theory, metaphorical utterances, as well as some other tropes such as metonymy and hyperbole, are treated in the same line as an everyday, mundane loose use of words. In that sense, the metaphorical utterance 'Chris is a cactus' is processed and comprehended in the same mechanism as utterances like 'France is a hexagon'. The way to derive a pragmatically enriched meaning of a metaphorically used word and a loosely used word involves concept broadening, and sometimes concept narrowing. Such adjustment of the concept of an individual lexical item is based on

Barsalou's (1983, 1987) discovery on the change of concept in language comprehension: a hearer is able to, in different contexts and communicative purposes, retrieve different encyclopedic information to construct distinct concepts for one entity. Similarly, when a hearer understands a metaphorical utterance (or a loose utterance), he or she would: (1) retrieve several different properties of the conventional concept of the metaphorical or loosely used word, and such aspects include both core logical properties and stereotypical properties; (2) select one or more defining properties of the modified concept, and these can also be either core logical or stereotypical properties; (3) construct a new concept of that metaphorical or loosely used word, which exclusively includes the properties that are useful in the context; and (4) finally integrate the new concept in the interpretation of that metaphorical or loose utterance to form the explicature of that utterance (Carston 2002). The newly constructed concept of such a metaphorical or loosely used word is called an 'ad hoc concept'. It should be noted that since the context of an utterance is always required when a hearer constructs an ad hoc concept, such pragmatic enrichment of a metaphorical utterance should be seen as a top-down process, that is, the hearer first gets hold of the full context of that utterance and then selects an appropriate interpretation of an individual lexical item based on the context.

Carston, among other relevance theorists, also proposes a theory of word meaning in comprehension that is compatible with the processing of metaphorical expressions and the computation of explicature. She suggests that the 'concept' of a lexical item is not directly accessed, but is always constructed with a selective procedure. When a hearer comes across a lexical item she would first access all the possible properties, or, in Carston's description, a 'package of information' associated with that lexical item, and then selectively keep some information from the packaging. This proposal unifies the mechanism of comprehension of literal meaning, loose meaning and metaphorical meaning of a lexical item, even for the comprehension of the literal meaning, that is, the construction of the concept that represents one or more literal meanings of a lexical item, where a hearer should select from the properties associated with that lexical item, where it is necessary to either narrow or broaden a concept before putting the word meaning into the explicature. Carston uses this proposal to illustrate that semantic under-determinacy is inevitable in everyday communication and pragmatic enrichment is always required, which is an argument against any minimalist theories on semantics (i.e. the view that some utterances could deliver their intended messages without any pragmatic enrichment). Meanwhile, I can use this proposal to show that the literal and metaphorical meanings of a lexical item can be selected and activated in a parallel way. Whether a meaning is more accessible, using Carston's proposal, is about: (1) whether there is a valid context to trigger a top-down pragmatic enrichment and (2) whether a concept is conventional enough that it does not require extra time and cognitive effort for concept broadening and narrowing. In this case, when researching conventional metaphorical meanings in comparison to literal meanings, I can roughly treat the two types of meaning as highly conventional, and thus I should finely control the context of that word to ensure that a metaphorical meaning is readily accessible, or as accessible as the literal meaning of the same word.

While Relevance Theory emphasizes the importance of pragmatic enrichment triggered by a broader context and suggests that all the meanings are processed through the construction of ad hoc concepts, other theories of the philosophy of language tend to argue that it is a narrow context, that is, the collocation of a lexical item rather than a general context that contributes to the activation of a specific meaning of a word, whether literal or metaphorical. In these theories, concepts or meanings are not constructed in an *ad hoc* manner but are readily accessible as they are. The narrow context, such as the collocation of a word or the surrounding environment of a particular utterance, helps to select the most appropriate meaning among several. One representative of this type of theory is the indexicalist view of metaphor. It originates from the philosophical discussions of indexical expressions such as 'I', 'here' and 'now' (Kaplan 1989). Kaplan argues that those indexical expressions do not have any content that resembles the dictionary meaning, but only have 'characters' like *Dthat* to help the interlocutors to resolve the reference of the expression. The fundamental idea is that the reference of an indexical expression is selected in a 'bottom-up' fashion; the character of an indexical expression leads the interlocutor to survey the possible references in the local context and assign the indexical expression to the most appropriate reference. The extension of the indexicalist view to the interpretation of metaphors treats metaphors as a special type of indexical and suggests that the meaning of a metaphorical expression is determined by a local context. Therefore, an alteration of local context, such as an adjacent constituent of a lexical item, can change the meaning of that lexical item and lead to the formation of a metaphorical meaning of a word. Stern (2000) proposes that a metaphorical expression always has a metaphorical character, *Mthat*, which resembles Kaplan's *Dthat*. A metaphorical expression can have several stereotypical metaphorical properties; for example, the action of 'attack' can involve properties like fierceness, suddenness and intention to defeat someone. The function of *Mthat*, according to Stern, is to remind the interlocutors to select one or more of the metaphorical properties, and then construct a new meaning as the 'appropriate metaphorical reference'. Leezenberg (2001), argues instead that a metaphor has neither a content nor a character; he suggests that a metaphorical expression will evoke a set of 'salient properties' based on the literal concept of that metaphor, and an interlocutor will combine all the salient properties to construct the meaning of that metaphor.

From the two indexicalist views, it can be seen that, although they have minor differences when talking about how to select the properties involved in a metaphorical expression, they all suggest that local contextual information, especially the collocation of the metaphorically used lexical items, manipulates the meaning of the metaphor – higher level contexts do not play a further role to decide the semantic meaning of the metaphor. The indexicalist approach has a special advantage which explains why a hearer can identify and comprehend a conventionalized metaphorical expression without difficulty: she only needs to select the most appropriate meaning of a lexical item from a collection of meanings, and there is no need to construct the meaning from the literal meaning of that lexical item and the broad context. That means it is *possible* for a hearer to comprehend a conventionalized metaphorical expression as fast as comprehending a literal expression. The indexicalist approach is rather important for language acquisition, since it suggests that the (conventional) metaphorical meaning and literal meaning of a lexical item can be distinguished by a pair of different collocations. I will show how this idea can be further utilized in the experiments.

The last post-Gricean view worth mentioning here is from Recanati's (2004) book *Literal Meaning*; in that book Recanati discusses the different types and levels of literalness and analyses how literalness could affect the derivation process. He suggests that although all metaphors involve departure from the literal meaning of a word, some metaphors are not 'far' enough from the literal meaning to be called 'non-literal', while others may be a far departure from the literal meaning and should be seen as definitely 'non-literal'. Recanati proposes three layers of literalness, mainly depending on the distance between the intended meaning and the compositional meaning of a sentence: (1) 'm-literal' for minimal-literal, that is, the intended meaning is exactly the same as the compositional meaning of a sentence, and (2) 'p-literal' for primary-literal, that is, the intended meaning of the sentence only involves minimal departure from the compositional meaning of the sentence. The two types of literalness lead to a three-way categorization of all sentences. In the first type, the sentences are both m-literal and p-literal, such as literal sentences like 'Chris swallowed the candy'. In the second type, the sentences are neither m-literal nor p-literal, such as novel metaphorical sentences like 'Chris is a cactus'. In this sentence, the meaning of 'cactus' in the sentence clearly departs from the literal meaning as a species of plant, and the intended meaning of the whole sentence is also a clear departure from the compositional meaning of 'Chris is a cactus'. The third type includes sentences that are p-literal but not m-literal, which includes the target of the book – conventional metaphorical sentences. A good example is 'the ATM swallowed my debit card'; the meaning of 'swallowed' in the sentence clearly departs from the literal meaning of that word, but the meaning of the entire sentence can still be derived from the composition of each constituent. Recanati argues that, although both conventional metaphors and novel metaphors belong to metaphor, they can be distinguished in this paradigm, because conventional metaphors are less 'non-literal' than novel metaphors. He suggests that such a distinction implies that there is a threshold of non-literalness, with a novel metaphor above the threshold and a conventional metaphor below it. The idea of non-literal threshold is borrowed and used in the discussions to refine the metaphorical expressions under investigation.

Going back to the definition of metaphorical expressions in Chapter 1, all of these (post-)Gricean accounts of metaphorical expressions have a prominent focus; they all treat a metaphorical expression as a structurally-complex semantic composition, and they all somehow assume that each component of that semantic composition corresponds to a concept, or several properties of a concept. In this way, all these theories turn the question of 'metaphorical meaning' into 'how one can derive the new compositional meaning from several word meanings that do not strictly lead to the compositional meaning, and why?' This is definitely an important question for metaphor research, as language is essentially compositional, and a metaphorical meaning can only be triggered within certain specific collocations. However, none of these theories can answer the question, why do people develop such a metaphorical meaning, but not another one, for a lexical item? Why do people tend to describe argument as a war by saying 'he attacked my ideas' but are less likely to describe a war as an argument'? (Post-)Gricean semantic views do not aim to answer these questions, but, fortunately, there are still other approaches to this more basic question on metaphor – the cognitive approach.

2.3 Metaphor in cognitive semantics and lexical semantics

Most, if not all, of the theories of metaphor before the Gricean account, including the seminal works by Beardsley (1962), Black (1962) and Grice himself, take one premise for their discussion of metaphors – metaphors should have a strong sense of non-literalness. In other words, as described in the previous theories, metaphors should always be above Recanati's p-literalness threshold in order to qualify as metaphors. Since metaphors are believed to be always above the threshold, they are also believed to be marked, creative, deliberate and uncommon in daily language use, therefore most of the theories of metaphor before the Gricean era have a clear focus on the literary use of metaphor. The theories of metaphor, based on cognitive semantics, including the Conceptual Metaphor Theory (henceforth CMT) of Lakoff and Johnson (1980; see also Lakoff 1987; Lakoff & Turner 1989) and the Blending Theory (Fauconnier 1994) have drastically changed the view that metaphors are marked in natural language.

In the foundational work *Metaphors We Live By*, Lakoff and Johnson redefine the concept of metaphor in two ways. First, they suggest that metaphor is not only a linguistic phenomenon, it is also a cognitive phenomenon – humans constantly use metaphor in their perception of the world, and it is a general cognitive pattern to map a concrete, familiar, touchable entity to the concept of an abstract, unfamiliar, less perceivable entity. Two levels of metaphor are clearly differentiated in CMT: conceptual metaphors, which exist in human thought and are an essential mechanism for individuals to acquire new knowledge, concepts and linguistic metaphors, which are the linguistic realization of the conceptual metaphorical mappings. Second, since conceptual metaphors are widely available in human thought, and language is regarded as the essential reflection of human thought, the linguistic realization of conceptual metaphors is also inevitable in human language. Linguistic metaphors are not necessarily 'deliberate' or 'creative', as is the case with the examples found in literary works; rather, any departure from the core meaning of a lexical item can be seen as 'used metaphorically'. Therefore, everyday expressions like 'I see what you mean' are metaphorical, because 'what you mean' is an abstract entity and cannot be visually perceived, and the use of 'see' in that sentence is metaphorical in the sense of CMT. CMT has become one of the most influential theories of metaphors in linguistics, contributing to the understanding and construction of metaphor in individual languages (see Yu 1998 for Chinese examples) and the universality and cross-linguistic variation of conceptual and linguistic metaphors (e.g.

Kövecses 2005). CMT is also frequently adopted in other domains of linguistic research, including pragmatics, language acquisition and psycholinguistics. The philosophical accounts of metaphor mentioned in the last section also allow for CMT to co-exist. For instance, Recanati (2004), although not explicitly stating it, treats the 'everyday linguistic metaphors' in CMT as examples of metaphors. In the case of 'the ATM' mentioned above, he regards it as a conventional metaphorical expression; meanwhile, from a CMT perspective, it can be seen as the linguistic realization of personification, which is a specific type of conceptual metaphor.

Current research on metaphor in the field of cognitive semantics, although still under the influence of the original proposal of CMT in 1980s, has departed substantially from Lakoff and Johnson's account. The original CMT received criticism, such as circular reasoning and lack of support for context-sensitivity, heavily relying on constructed examples rather than natural language evidence and the like (see Kövecses 2017 for a list of criticism), and is no longer favoured in recent studies on metaphor. Meanwhile, scholars have been establishing new theoretical views of metaphor based on CMT, making modifications and providing empirical supports to it. For instance, a clear contrast has been observed between the original CMT proposal in the 1980s and a more contemporary, dynamical view of metaphor. While the original CMT proposal has focused more on the formulaic construction of linguistic metaphors and the conceptual mappings behind them, the dynamical view can be seen as a convergence between a cognitive semantic convention and a post-Gricean view on the function of contexts. Instead of assuming that linguistic metaphors are always formulaic and stable, the dynamical view recognizes both the regularities of metaphorical expressions based on conceptual metaphors and the influence of context-sensitivity when constructing metaphorical expressions in a piece of discourse (Gibbs 2017). The conceptual root of linguistic metaphor being recognized, recent theories begin to focus more on how metaphorical expressions are created, used and evolved.

One criticism of CMT is about the concepts and conceptual domains involved in a metaphorical mapping. It has been questioned whether the conceptual domains mentioned in CMT, such as WAR, BUILDING, or SEEING and JOURNEY, are valid categories. While the proposal of conceptual mapping is intuitively plausible, it is somehow difficult to clear up the boundaries, if any, of a conceptual domain like WAR. Specifically for metaphorical expressions, people know that 'attack' in a war and 'attack' in an argument are essentially different; instead of copying the concept of 'attack' in a war directly to the domain of argument, 'attack' in an argument may sound more like a combination of some manners that resemble 'attack in a war' and some manners that belong to argument – a competing theory that could explain such 'combination' – the Blending Theory of metaphor – was expressed by Fauconnier (1994).

The Blending Theory suggests that, unlike any direct mapping or transfer between different conceptual domains, new concepts and metaphorical concepts can be formed by the blending of two conceptual domains. That means, if one would like to construct the meaning of 'attack' in an argument, one should take certain features of the prototypical attack from the concept of WAR and some other features from arguments, and then create a new blending space for them. Blending, similar to blending a drink, means that language users coordinate features from the two sides to make sure that they can form a unified new concept without conflicting and contradiction. The new concept therefore hosts the features from both the source and the target conceptual domains. A blending space can become the source of a new blending, thus allowing further creation of new concepts from a blended concept. Compared with CMT, although both being cognitive semantic theories on metaphor, Blending Theory receives relatively less attention from linguistics; however, the use of a frame-like structure for conceptual domains and the combination of frames for blending are welcomed in computational sciences.

The cognitive semantic view of metaphor, particularly CMT, has also been used in lexical semantics to interpret the emergence of some types of polysemy. Sweetser (1990), who uses 'see' as the material of her case study, proposes the idea that the different polysemous senses of 'see' originate from conventional linguistic metaphors. With the conventionalization of these linguistic metaphors, the metaphorically constructed meanings have been accepted by language users and have become part of the dictionary meanings of a lexical item. This process is also suggested by Traugott (2004) from the perspective of historical pragmatics; the metaphorical meanings of a lexical item could originally be understood as conversational implicature, which, as in the Gricean account, is derived through the literal meaning and the context, but gradually these become conventional metaphorical expressions, stabilized and lexicalized after frequent use, and, finally, the properties of conversational implicature disappear and the metaphorical interpretations become encoded meanings rather than ad hoc implicatures. It has been widely recognized (cf. Gibbs 1995; Lakoff 1987; Sweetser 1990) that the metaphorical meaning(s) and the literal meaning(s) of a lexical item are closely related, and lexical items that can be interpreted both literally and metaphorically should be treated as polysemy.

In recent years, there has been an initial attempt to put cognitive semantics, particularly CMT, into methodologies of second language teaching. While this book will partly relate the acquisition of metaphorical expressions with cognitive semantics, I decided to introduce the theories of cognitive semantics in a minimal manner, and restricted them to linguistic analysis. That means, I observed a clear boundary between linguistic metaphor and conceptual metaphor, and simply adopted the conventional terminologies of cognitive semantics when discussing the linguistic phenomenon. The experimental materials were selected from the discussions of metaphorical expressions in the approach to CMT, and the lexical semantic theory was based on that. However, when talking about learning and teaching strategies, or discussing a possible role of cognitive semantics in second language education, I have tried not to rigidly connect the two aspects. Cognitive semantics, either CMT or Blending Theory, are essentially *semantic* approaches to metaphor, and do not aim to provide a clear explanation for the acquisition of metaphorical expressions (but see Littlemore and Low (2006) for the use of the CMT in teaching metaphorical expressions). At the same time, this fails to explain a number of features of metaphorical expressions discussed in this book. First, CMT cannot provide a convincing account of the cross-linguistic diversity of metaphorical expressions; particularly, it has been observed that the same underlying conceptual metaphor does not always lead to the same conventionalized metaphorical expressions across languages. For instance, when the conceptual metaphor SEEING IS UNDERSTANDING is assumed universally, both Chinese and English allow the expression 'a clear idea' for an idea that is easy to understand ('clear' is originally used to describe visual perception), but only English allows the conventional use of the verb 'see' as 'understand', such as 'I see what you mean'. Considering this phenomenon, it is difficult to attribute the cross-linguistic diversity of the conventional metaphorical expressions to CMT, and thus can hardly use CMT to explain how a learner perceives and understands such cross-linguistic diversity. Second, and more importantly, even if CMT is well-established, it is questionable whether the learner understands the concept of conceptual metaphor when they acquire a second language, not to mention whether they could utilize their knowledge of conceptual metaphor in the acquisition of metaphorical expressions. Not all learners surveyed in the current study have a substantial knowledge of CMT or other semantic theories of metaphor; moreover, such semantic theories are not available in the environment of research, namely a classroom setting in secondary and tertiary education in China where English is treated as a 'second' or 'foreign language'. Meanwhile, the metaphorical expressions researched in this book are all 'below the threshold', so that neither native speakers nor learners will identify those expressions as 'metaphorical'. It is therefore questionable whether: (1) a learner could know that a conventional metaphorical expression in her L2 is 'metaphorical' in terms of the definition of CMT, (2) she knows about the relation between metaphorical expressions and conceptual metaphor and (3) she makes use of this knowledge. Taking these two factors into consideration, I am relatively pessimistic about the acquisition of the conventional metaphorical expressions under the framework of CMT. While I do not thoroughly discuss the theoretical plausibility of cognitive semantics in the field of second language acquisition in most of this book, I simply maintain the use of terminologies of cognitive semantics as a handy reference to the linguistic phenomenon.

2.4 Summary

To understand the acquisition of metaphorical expressions, the first thing to understand is how metaphorical expressions function in a language. As a semantic phenomenon, how the meaning of a metaphorical expression comes into existence is crucial for both researchers and learners; without understanding the mechanisms behind them, metaphorical expressions are no different to arbitrary strings of words. So, this chapter has provided a systematic review from the perspective of theoretical semantics, and showed that: (1) metaphorical expressions follow the Principle of Compositionality in a similar yet slightly different way from literal expressions and (2) metaphorical meanings can be traced historically and conceptually back to the literal meanings of lexical items.

The two points above could always contribute to research and the application of acquisition of metaphorical expressions. If one knows that an alternation of context, either the broad, top-down context or the narrow, bottom-up context, could help the reader to distinguish between literal and metaphorical meanings, one can manipulate the context of a lexical item to trigger its literal or metaphorical meaning in both experimental studies and learning materials. For the link between literal and metaphorical meanings of the same lexical item, a conclusion can be drawn which makes it is possible for language users to infer the metaphorical meaning from the literal meaning of a lexical item. When a metaphorical meaning is conventionalized, it is also possible for native speakers to skip the inferencing process. This conclusion can then be used as a baseline for second language research: would learners have the same ability to derive metaphorical meanings from literal meanings? Or, if a metaphorical expression is available in the learners' L1 and L2, would the learners be able to use their knowledge of L1 metaphorical expressions when they acquire the same expression in L2? I will continue this discussion in the next few chapters on some possible cross-linguistic and inter-lexical differences between metaphorical expressions.

3

Metaphorical expressions under cross-linguistic influence

3.1 Introduction: A short overview of studies on cross-linguistic influence

For a book on second language acquisition, it is somewhat inevitable to talk about a prominent phenomenon in this process, namely cross-linguistic influence. As a long-standing research topic in second language acquisition, cross-linguistic influence has been subject to comprehensive discussion since the 1950s, even if some aspects of it still await further exploration. The phenomenon of cross-linguistic influence is referred to in SLA research literature using a number of different terms at different times. These include 'transfer', 'native language influence' and, sometimes, 'interference'. Despite the variation in terminologies, the definition is clear: it is a phenomenon involving a bilingual speaker, usually a second language learner, incorporating certain elements of at least one previously known language in the production and/or comprehension of another language. In this book, I use 'cross-linguistic influence' and 'transfer' interchangeably. When cross-linguistic influence on the acquisition of word meaning is discussed, the term 'lemmatic transfer' (as per Jarvis 2009) is used.

The reason that a whole chapter is devoted to cross-linguistic influence is that it may have a decisive influence on the acquisition of metaphorical expressions. In this chapter, cross-linguistic influence will be restricted to the influence of learners in L1 on L2. As I will show in the following subsections, cross-linguistic influence occurs not only in the process of the acquisition of individual lexical items but also in the process of the acquisition of other figurative expressions, particularly idioms. I maintain the practice of other mainstream studies in second language acquisition in regarding cross-linguistic influence as a specific phenomenon in second language acquisition. The presence of cross-linguistic influence on a linguistic element, no matter what form it takes, indicates that a learner has not yet fully acquired the linguistic element. Cross-linguistic influence often takes the form of non-native-like production, perception or metalinguistic judgements (e.g. self-rating of confidence level by learners). When learners show a native-like production, perception or metalinguistic judgements it may be considered that, unless a linguistic element is shared between learners' L1 and L2, cross-linguistic influence, particularly negative influence, does not appear and learners are very likely to have acquired the linguistic element.

Early investigations of cross-linguistic influence between L1 and L2 are best represented by the Contrastive Analysis hypothesis (henceforth 'CA') proposed by Lado (1957). Lado examined the phenomenon from the perspective of behaviourism, as developed for language by Skinner. It was widely believed at that time that knowledge of an L1 would be internalized as part of the learner's habits, and such habits would intrude into the production of L2 and lead to errors. Lado suggested that such influences were more likely to lead to production errors if there was a clear difference between the grammar of L1 and that of L2; therefore, a CA between L1 and L2 could reveal the linguistic elements that were most susceptible to error in the acquisition of the L2.

Such views, even though they could provide a relatively clear view of a proportion of cross-linguistic influence, have been shown to be problematic from several perspectives. The first difficulty concerns the assumption of behaviourism itself. It has been discovered that individuals do not acquire a language, either the first or the second, as a set of habits. Children acquiring their first language and learners of a second language produce errors that are not found in the input, which means that they do not directly copy from adults or native speakers when they receive the input (see Meisel 2011 for a full historical review). Moreover, if it is assumed that a grammar is a 'habit', then cross-linguistic influence should only happen unidirectionally from L1 to L2 because only grammar acquired earlier can become a 'habit'. The discovery of bidirectional influence at a relatively early stage of acquisition, namely the co-existence of L1–L2 and L2–L1 influences, contradicts the major prediction of the CA hypothesis. Therefore, since the mid-1970s, attitudes towards cross-linguistic influence have gradually shifted to a more developmental view, which has become mainstream.

With progress in relevant research and a better understanding of cross-linguistic influence, it has further been discovered that grammatical differences between L1 and L2 do not necessarily lead to difficulties and 'errors' in L2 production by learners, and similarities do not always lead to the correct output (see Odlin 1989 for a summary). It seems that an L2 learner of language

'A' will also replicate some errors produced by children when acquiring 'A' as their first language, regardless of the similarities and differences between that learner's L1 and L2. Also, even if an element in L2 is similar to the learner's L1, the learner might still make errors, and such errors cannot be predicted by the CA hypothesis. It therefore needs to be concluded that the acquisition of an L2 cannot be simply seen as being influenced by learners' behaviour. Instead, the developmental path of L2 acquisition should be considered and explained, by considering influence not only from the source language, but also from the target language.

Furthermore, cross-linguistic influence based on a CA tends to be seen negatively, while positive aspects of the phenomenon are largely ignored. Such bias originates from a flawed methodology; if only the differences between two grammars are emphasized and compared, the results are naturally regard 'errors' and 'interference' as being due to the influence of L1. While these 'errors' are generally more prominent in observation, it is logically feasible, as has since been shown, that the elements shared between L1 and L2 might show cross-linguistic influence as well. Influences on the same or similar elements in L1 and L2 are less 'observable', as often such influence leads to appropriate use of the L2 (but cf. the phenomenon of *false friends*).

To investigate cross-linguistic influence in a comprehensive way, one should be aware that cross-linguistic influence appears in various forms with different frequencies in the acquisition of an L2. Not only can the appearance of L1 structures in the production of the L2 be seen as transfer, but it has been discovered that the avoidance of certain structures in the L2 can also reflect the influence of L1 (Kellerman 1983). If a particular structure appears in L2 but is absent in L1, a learner may use other structures to express the same meaning while dismissing the L2-only structure so as to preserve L1 grammar in the production of L2 utterances – such a learner may be less confident about the L2-only structure. A recorded case is the overuse of 'make' by Taiwanese learners of English: they prefer using 'make someone upset' rather than the direct verb form 'upset someone', because 'upset' cannot be used as a verb in Chinese and these learners follow Chinese grammar in adding the verb 'make' (Wong 1983). It is difficult to record all the possible influences that an L1 has on L2 production just by investigating the interlanguage of a group of learners with similar linguistic and educational backgrounds. If possible, a comparison should be made between L2 learners with different L1 backgrounds, or between learners of a language and native speakers of that language, since both comparisons can capture the influence from a specific L1.

In this chapter, I will discuss cross-linguistic influence from two main perspectives closely related to the acquisition of metaphorical expressions. Following Jordens and Kellerman's (1981) discussions in Section 3.2, I shall discuss cross-linguistic influence in the acquisition of different lexical items and figurative expressions.Section 3.3 concerns several factors that influence cross-linguistic influence. The above authors cover the main topic cover the main topic: that the acquisition of metaphorical expressions should be seen as the acquisition of a particular kind of lexical item, and cross-linguistic influence in the process of acquisition may vary depending on learners' perception and proficiency as well as the material to be acquired. The final section is a short summary of existing findings and some gaps in these studies.

3.2 Lemmatic transfer: A general review

3.2.1 Defining and delimiting lemmatic transfer

While the transfer of lexical items, or lexical transfer, can generally be defined as the presence of cross-linguistic influence during vocabulary acquisition in a second language, it is important to clarify what types of lexical transfer one may expect to observe. In particular, with deeper understanding of cross-linguistic influence, the delicate boundary between cross-linguistic influence based simply on word meanings versus influence involving conceptual change has been gradually discovered. Therefore, it is also important to clarify the scope of the term *lexical transfer*, and to establish what scope transfer of metaphorical meanings of lexical items falls within.

Jarvis (2009) argues that lexical transfer can happen on two different levels: lexeme level and lemma level. At lexeme level, the morphological and phonological features of a lexical item can be transferred to the L2, while at lemma level, the syntactic and semantic features can be transferred. Transfer at lexeme level is also referred to as 'formal transfer' (Ringbom, 2006), since what is transferred in the process are the formal features, particularly morphological features, of a lexical item. Lexemic transfer, or formal transfer, is more likely to happen between cognates; on the other hand, transfer at lemma level is referred to as 'semantic transfer' by Ringbom in the same article, because the most prominent transfer observed at that level is related to word meanings. Unlike lexemic transfer, lemmatic or semantic transfer can happen between cognates or non-cognates; a similarity in form between the two words in the two languages is not always required.

In a pair of languages, it is possible to find both cognates and non-cognates; the case of non-cognates may be more prominent if the two languages are barely related historically and typologically, such as Chinese and English. However, it is easy to recognize that the issue of transfer of metaphorical expressions may exist in both cognates and non-cognates, as this is essentially a part of the semantic properties of lexical items, no matter what the word form (e.g. the phonological or orthographical form) looks like. It is possible that a pair of non-cognate translation equivalents share the same metaphorical meaning, while a pair of cognates have a different conventionalized metaphorical meaning. Since the semantic aspect of a lexical item is usually seen as the link between the word form and the concept it represents, the discussion in this chapter is essentially to investigate whether *such a link between the word form and a metaphorical concept* is transferable from a learner's first language to a second language. This may vary slightly between cognates and non-cognates, but it can be largely ignored due to the emphasis on the meaning aspect of lexical items.

It should be noted that a more fine-grained borderline should be drawn between lemmatic transfer and concept transfer, the latter having drawn the attention of researchers in recent years. Language-specific concepts and the transfer caused thereby frequently appear in the language of bilingual speakers, as discussed in detail by Pavlenko (2009). To provide an example, *chashka* in Russian and *cup* in English are generally seen as translation equivalents, but *chashka* cannot be used to refer to cups made of paper or plastic; instead, these are called *stakanchiki*, or 'small glasses'. When an English learner of Russian misuses the word *chashka* to refer to a paper cup, not only are two lexical items 'mixed up', but there is also a direct transfer of the concept of CUP to Russian. While in Russian CHASHKA contains the concept of ceramic cups and STAKANCHIKI contains the concept of paper cups, a new category CHASHKA may be created by an English learner of Russian that includes both CERAMIC CUPS and PAPER CUPS; as a result, the form STAKANCHIKI may not be used to refer to paper cups. In this case, what is transferred is the way in which a learner categorizes the individual items and formulates the conceptual categories. Hence, this phenomenon is termed 'concept transfer' and is subsequently distinguished from lemmatic transfer. To summarize briefly, lemmatic transfer affects whether a lexical item can be linked to an established concept, such as whether 'glass' can mean a paper cup, while concept transfer affects how different concepts in the L2, according to a learner's knowledge of L1, such as whether the glass and cup are intended to be 'the same thing'.

It is not only literally-used words that may be linked to language-specific concepts, but also metaphorical meanings. For example, *chi* in Chinese can either describe the action 'eat' or be used to describe bad experiences involving 'suffering', because when one experiences a loss, one can only endure it by 'swallowing/ eating the experience'. The meaning of 'suffering' is clearly not covered by 'eat' in English, and thus *chi* 'suffering' should be regarded as a language-specific link and any use of *eat* by a Chinese learner of English to express SUFFERING clearly reflects some type of transfer. At first glance, one might think that such a transfer of metaphorical meaning might belong to concept transfer, since it is related to concepts in general. However, when comparing the examples of *chashka* and *chi*, the case of *chashka* involves recategorizing paper cups in that system, which leads a learner to change the concept of *chashka*. In the case of *chi*, a learner is still fully aware that eating and suffering are two distinct concepts and does not add or remove any subordinate concepts from the superordinate concept 'eating'; what has happened is that a link has been created between *eat* and 'suffering'. In this case, the transfer of metaphorical meaning is a case of an ordinary lemmatic transfer, therefore it seems that the transfer of a metaphorical expression is a form of lemmatic transfer rather than a concept transfer.

Pavlenko herself has also analysed the type of transfer to which metaphorical expressions belong. She suggests that knowledge of metaphorical expressions belongs not to concept representation but to semantic representation, which includes implicit knowledge of 'the mapping between words and concepts determining how many concepts, and which particular concepts, are expressed by a word via polysemy or metaphoric extension' (2009: 148). This means that she regards the metaphorical concept and the literal concept, represented by a single lexical item, as if they were two unrelated, independent concepts. Whether this statement is feasible from the perspective of metaphor will be discussed further in Chapter 5, but it is at least recognized by other researchers that transfer of metaphorical expressions is semantic, and thus can be discussed in parallel with other phenomena of lemmatic transfer and the transfer of other types of figurative language.

3.2.2 Types of realization of lemmatic transfer

Having assumed that transfer of metaphorical expressions belongs to lemmatic transfer, the next step is to survey the possible outcomes of lemmatic transfer, whether it is beneficial or obstructive to the acquisition of vocabulary. Various types of realization and the outcome of lemmatic transfers will be analysed and summarized in this section to show how lexical transfer can facilitate, complicate, or have no significant impact on, the acquisition of L2 lexical items.

Positive transfer with regards to lemmatic transfer mainly comes from a transfer between cognates; however, cognates involve not only lemmatic transfer, but also lexemic transfer. The shared phonetic/orthographic form, as well as identical or similar meanings, in a pair of cognates can effectively facilitate the acquisition of L2 lexical items. With a proper knowledge of L1 vocabulary, a learner will easily identify the cognates in L2 and transfer relevant knowledge to the acquisition of these lexical items. Then, a further assumption can be drawn; when a learner observes a large number of cognates, L1 and L2 may be perceived as relatively close in that learner's psychotypology, which, as discussed in Section 2.3, may boost both positive and negative transfer from L1 to L2. A series of investigations into the acquisition of an L3 by bilinguals (e.g. Bardel & Lindqvist 2006; Leung 2005; Ringbom, 1978; Sjöholm, 1976) reveals that when learners make use of their lexical knowledge of two languages to acquire L3 words, they will select the language that shares more cognates with L3.

Although positive transfer is widely observed between cognates, it can also occur between non-cognates, even if this has been not been discussed to such an extent in previous studies. A positive transfer between non-cognates may happen when a learner, who attempts to acquire an L2 phrase based on lexical items that have already been acquired, assumes that a phrase that is available in L1 is also available in the L2, if: (1) the lexical items involved in the phrase have the same meaning across the L1 and L2, (2) that phrase is also available in L1, and (3) that phrase is not typically idiomatic, that is, can be interpreted by compositing the semantic meanings of each lexical item.

As discussed at the beginning of this chapter, cross-linguistic influence is generally less observable when it comes in the form of positive transfer. This is reflected in the current research on lemmatic transfer; most discussions observe a wide range of negative transfer and emphasize errors in word use due to interference from L1 vocabulary knowledge. Common problems due to negative lemmatic transfer include the phenomenon of false friends and semantic overextension. False friends involve L1 and L2 lexical items with a certain degree of morphological similarity, but different meanings; a typical example is the word *sensible*, which means 'reasonable' in English, but 'sensitive' in French. Odlin (1989), however, proposes another type of false friend that is less typical but widely observable. This type does not involve morphological similarities, but only semantic similarities, which can be seen as the overextension of partial translation equivalents. In order to be classified as 'translation equivalents', a pair of lexical items in two languages need to share at least (part of) the lexical meaning, but it is not necessary for them to share all their meanings (for example, if both words in the pair are polysemous). As a result, a learner might wrongly infer that all the meanings of the (partial) translation equivalents are shared when they are not, and then mistakenly transfer the non-shared meanings. For instance, a Finnish learner of English might use 'spin' to describe the 'purring' of a cat, because the Finnish word *kehrätä* is polysemous and corresponds to the meanings of both 'spin' and 'purr' in English (Jarvis 2009).

The misuse of polysemous false friends in a second language, especially the incorrect inference that the L2 lexical item is also polysemous, might indicate an assumption that a given lexical item in a learner's L1 and L2 forms a one-to-one correspondence. As shown in the example described above, the misuse of 'spin' is more like a mismatch between the word and the context in which it appears. While this can occur when the collocation is loosely formed, as in the case of 'the purring of a cat', it can also occur when the collocation is a fixed multi-word expression, such as an idiom. Metaphorical expressions, while residing between a loose, flexible collocation and a fixed idiom, might also encounter such false friends in the process of acquisition. It is possible for learners to assume that, if a metaphorical meaning, such as 'suffering' in the case of the lexical item 'chi/eat' is available in Chinese, it may also be available in English. In such cases, the misuse of 'eat' in 'eat some loss' (meaning *suffer a loss*) is indeed comparable to the misuse of 'the spinning of a cat'.

However, lemmatic transfer is not the only cause of errors. It has been proposed that the frequency of certain structures in L2 production may be different from the frequency of those structures in a native speakers' speech. Unlike qualitative differences that can be easily observed by looking for errors in L2 learners' production, frequency differences can only be captured by a more delicate comparison between the production of L2 learners and that of native speakers. Generally, such differences include both overproduction and underproduction (Odlin 1989). The reasons for over- and underproduction might be a lack of knowledge of appropriate L2 lexical items, or possibly the transfer of peripheral features of L1 lexical items, such as the frequency of a word or expression in L1. While the frequent appearance of an L1 word may lead to the overproduction of its translation equivalent in L2, the lack of translation equivalents of an L2 word in a learner's L1 can result in underproduction. Sometimes, even if a learner has acquired a new expression in L2, it may not be selected due to a lack of translation equivalents in L1.

In the same article, Odlin suggests that both overproduction and underproduction should be seen as negative transfer in much the same way as the impact of false friends, since both lead to production differences between learners and native speakers. Nevertheless, I argue that overproduction and underproduction are not 'negative' examples of the false friends mentioned above because: (1) they do not directly lead to any significant semantic errors or breakdown in communication and (2) they involve quantitative rather than qualitative differences between learners and native speakers. Although it is possible that overproduction and underproduction might make learners sound less native-like, the production influenced by them is not 'wrong'. It is not the case that a learner is not able to learn or produce a structure or expression, but it is difficult to master the more peripheral features, such as the frequency of that structure or expression.

Other cases of lemmatic transfer that do not affect semantic meaning, as listed below, have also been observed, although sometimes it is debatable whether they are authentic cases of lemmatic transfer. While false friends are a typical case of inappropriate semantic overextension, semantic overextension may also happen without the presence of a pair of (partial) translation equivalents, and sometimes without leading to any significant semantic errors. For instance, Bamgbose (1982) reports an example of semantic overextension in Nigerian L2 English: 'being away' can be phrased as 'travel', and a sentence like 'My father has travelled' can mean 'my father is away'. In such situations of semantic overextension, a lexical item can be used in L2 production to represent a meaning that is generally relevant to its original meaning, especially when a learner fails to select an appropriate L2 word and faces a lexical gap (Bamgbose 1982). This phenomenon is alternatively referred to as 'approximation' (see Blum & Levenston 1978). It should be noted that, even though a learner may use semantic extension to fill a lexical gap, this does not indicate an inability to differentiate between the two concepts. In a case where an Apache learner of English uses 'dead food' to refer to 'rotting food', there is no evidence to show that that learner has mixed the concept of 'death' and 'rot', and it is possible that that the learner is fully aware that food does not have a life and thus can never 'die'. Therefore, semantic extension and approximation should be classified as semantic transfer rather than concept transfer.

The semantic overextension or approximation described above, as in the case of 'travel', does not necessarily lead to significant communication breakdown, as in the case of 'the spinning of a cat'. Odlin (1989) shows reluctance to classify such semantic overextension as 'lexical transfer'; he suggests that this type of overextension is not attached to any specific language, but is universally possible between any language pairs, even within a language. Since neither semantic overextension nor approximation are direct reflections of the structures of either L1 or the L2, it cannot be categorized as 'transfer from L1 to L2'. This author would suggest, however, that such semantic overextension should be seen as lexical transfer from another perspective. The use of semantic overextension is, and must be, accompanied by a certain degree of underproduction, because the appearance of an overextended expression in a particular context always indicates that a learner has not yet fully acquired an 'appropriate' L2 expression which should be used in that context. A learner who does not know the 'appropriate' L2 expression is faced with the choice of either using the more radical strategy of transferring an L1 expression, which might lead to semantic errors, or using a language-neutral strategy and adopting an approximation, which might seem to be safer. Both of these strategies do, in fact, show that a learner is utilizing *knowledge of L1* to fill a 'lexical gap' in L2 knowledge in different ways, and thus they should both be seen as cross-linguistic influence. The strategy of semantic overextension and approximation, as well as other language-neutral strategies (such as the use of literal expressions instead of figurative expressions), might be especially favoured when a learner finds that the intended L2 meaning is less available in L1.

This section has briefly introduced different realizations for lemmatic transfer that have been discussed in previous research. Lemmatic transfer may lead to semantic errors in production (as in the case of false friends), as well as differences in frequency, and, possibly, a sense of non-nativeness (as in the case of overproduction and underproduction) – and sometimes to a less precise paraphrase of the intended meaning (as in the case of semantic overextension and approximation). All these possible types of realization of lexical transfer are expected in the acquisition of metaphorical expressions; the transfer between shared metaphorical expressions will lead to the facilitation of the acquisition of metaphorical expressions, even if what is transferred are non-cognates, while the transfer between different metaphorical expressions in L1 and L2 will lead to semantic errors in production. Furthermore, some semantic extension or paraphrasing of metaphorical expressions may happen when knowledge of L2 metaphorical expressions is absent from the learners' knowledge. Although semantic extension or paraphrasing is not likely to lead to any significant errors in production and comprehension, its occurrence with metaphorical expressions only may indicate that metaphorical expressions are more difficult to acquire than literal expressions, and thus need more attention from both learners and instructors.

3.2.3 Lemmatic transfer in the acquisition of figurative language

Several features of figurative language have further complicated transfer of these expressions: (1) figurative language often appears in multi-word structures, such as phrasal verbs and idioms; (2) figurative language (especially idioms) is generally semantically opaque, which means it is difficult to infer the meaning of a figurative expression from its components; and (3) figurative language is usually language-specific, or at least perceived as being language-specific. It should be noted that in some studies the term 'formulaic expressions' may be used as an alternative to refer to some figurative expressions, especially idioms (see Cieślicka 2008 for an example). The phrase 'formulaic expression' indicates that such expressions consist of multiple words with a fixed order and a stable meaning across different contexts. However, the two concepts are essentially different, since a formulaic expression is not required to be figurative and, in some cases, the component that is identified as 'figurative' in an expression may be only one word, which happens to be the case in this book. The transferability of several types of figurative language, predominantly idioms, has been subject to intensive investigation in past decades; this section is devoted to a review of the progress in that area, starting with idioms.

Idioms demonstrate almost all the prominent features of figurative language mentioned above (see Grant & Bauer 2004 for a comprehensive redefinition of idioms), and that makes them seemingly less transferable from one language to another. The actual transferability of idioms has long been a focus of studies on cross-linguistic influence in the acquisition of lexical items; idioms have been the subject of well-organized surveys that investigated transferability and acquisition, while other types of figurative language, including metaphorical expressions, have generally received less discussion. The transferability of idioms may, however, shed some light on the transferability of metaphorical expressions; on the one hand, with both being examples of figurative language, the two types of expression may share some similarities in terms of their figurativeness, while the distinction between these expressions and the literal uses of lexical items may predict similar patterns of transfer in an L2 acquisition. On the other hand, metaphorical expressions in the current discussion do not significantly overlap with idioms, which means that the features of the acquisition of idioms in a second language can only be seen as a reference point when I formulate hypotheses and design experiments to investigate the acquisition of metaphorical expressions.

In the view of Jordens and Kellerman (1981), idioms are mostly language-specific and semantically opaque. As a result, learners are not always aware of the corresponding expression in L2, and consequently will avoid transferring known idioms from L1 to L2. While Kellerman (1983) points out that his initial proposal did not indicate that idioms are not transferable, he suggests that idioms are indeed less transferable than the literal use of lexical items and other semantically transparent expressions. Kellerman's conclusion, however, is a rather general one that ignores differences between idiomatic expressions, and is only applicable in the comparison between the acquisition of idioms and that of other elements in second language acquisition. Within the category of idioms, it is possible that the transferability of individual idioms will still vary according to certain principles. Furthermore, the key factor, measured by Jordens and Kellerman (1981), is the grammaticality of the idiomatic expressions as perceived by L2 learners; however, the acquisition of idioms does not depend only on the grammaticality issue, the more important factor is the semantic aspect of the idiom. A grammaticality judgement test cannot fully capture whether learners transfer their knowledge of semantics in the processing and production of idioms; an experiment should, therefore, be designed to detect learners' understanding of those expressions. This need also exists for other types of figurative language, for which I expect semantic transfer to happen.

Regarding the exact transferability of different types of idiomatic expression, Irujo (1986a, 1986b, 1993) has investigated the influence of the degree of cross-linguistic formal similarity of idioms on their transferability among advanced Spanish learners of English. She formalizes the translation equivalents of idioms into three major categories: (1) idioms that share an identical form between L1 and L2, that is, L2 idioms which can be seen as a word-to-word translation of L1 idioms; (2) idioms that share a similarity in form between L1 and L2, that is, the L2 idioms, although not exact word-to-word translations of L1 idioms, make use of most of the words in L1 idioms, with one or two words altered; and (3) idioms that are totally different in their L1 and L2 forms. Such a categorization leads to a continuum of formal similarity when semantic similarity is controlled; the first category is strictly similar in form, and the third not similar at all. This categorization thus makes it possible to investigate the influence of the formal similarity of idioms on cross-linguistic influence. Irujo (1986b) then compares the learners' comprehension and production of different categories of idioms in multiple choice questions: a definition task, a discourse completion task and a translation task. In particular, the participants are asked to complete English paragraphs with appropriate English idioms, with the Spanish text given, and in the instruction and example sessions they are encouraged to use English idioms. When the proficiency of participants is controlled, they perform best when they encounter *identical* idioms; they demonstrate greater accuracy in both the comprehension and the production of such idioms, which indicates that they can make use of positive transfer to acquire the idioms. When the participants acquire *similar* idioms, they can comprehend them as well as they comprehend identical idioms; however, the production of these idioms is influenced by L1, so that negative transfer can be observed. No transfer is detected when the idioms are in different forms, and the different idioms are more difficult to comprehend and produce, which means that difficulty in acquisition is greater for idioms that share some elements. From these results, Irujo proposes the so-called 'Transfer Theory' of idiom acquisition, which suggests that idioms are more likely to be acquired if they are both formally and semantically identical between L1 and L2 learners.

Based on the methodology and the results of previous studies (Irujo 1986b; Kellerman 1983), Irujo (1993) further explores whether highly-advanced learners would avoid using idioms in L2 production if they were free to do so. She targets her study at fluent Spanish-English bilinguals who began the acquisition of English in adulthood and reside in an English-speaking environment, which means that they possess a fair knowledge of figurative language and have received sufficient exposure to native speakers' English production. The participants were required to translate Spanish text containing idioms into English, but they were not instructed to use idioms in the translation, contrary to the previous study. However, as with the previous studies, incorrect word-to-word translation from L1 idioms was observed in the experiment, thereby showing a trace of L1 transfer in the production of L2 idioms. Moreover, the results showed that, while fluent bilinguals were able to produce correct idioms (both intended and not intended by the experimenter) most of the time, they also made use of non-idiomatic paraphrases. A non-idiomatic paraphrase is the second method frequently used by the learners and is widely used in situations in which L1 and L2 idioms are different in form. Among these non-idioms, literal paraphrasing is used more frequently than metaphorical non-idiomatic paraphrasing. In other cases, the participants failed to produce the English idioms entirely, by omitting them or giving up translating them. Irujo identifies failure of production as instances of avoidance and points out that avoidance of L2 idioms can happen among advanced L2 learners and even fluent bilinguals living in an L2 environment.

However, she suggests that the paraphrasing of idioms in the translation task did not indicate that the fluent bilinguals avoided using idioms, because such paraphrasing is regarded as an alternative means to express the same meaning, and the participants may have chosen paraphrasing for reasons other than communication requirements.

As well as the formal similarities between L1 and L2 idioms, other factors that may influence the acquisition of idioms were also taken into consideration. A prominent feature that may greatly contribute to the discussion of figurative language acquisition is the degree of semantic transparency of an expression. The semantic transparency of an expression is the possibility of inferring the meaning of that expression from the meaning of each component item (Vega-Moreno 2007). For example, Vega-Moreno argues that language users may be able to derive the meaning of 'spill the beans' by composing the meaning of each component together, and thus 'spill the beans' is semantically transparent. On the other hand, they may fail to do the same with 'kick the bucket', which means that 'kick the bucket' is semantically opaque. Irujo (1993) has already found that the degree of semantic transparency of an idiom can influence the outcome of acquisition. Overall, semantically transparent idioms are better acquired and produced by learners than semantically opaque ones. It can be further inferred that semantically transparent idioms may be more likely to be transferred from L1 to L2 than semantically opaque idioms, because learners might believe that a transparent idiom in their L1 may also be semantically transparent in the L2.

The concept of semantic transparency is crucial here because it may influence the acquisition of different types of figurative language. Regardless of their exact degree of semantic transparency, idioms are generally seen as semantically opaque, and such a view of opacity is observed among both native speakers and L2 learners. Therefore, unless individuals receive sufficient exposure to such opaque idioms, they may fail to understand them; both native speakers and learners need sufficient input, be it through observation (native speakers and learners) or through explicit instruction (L2 learners). Metaphorical expressions, however, are figurative even if they are not always semantically opaque. As discussed in Chapter 2, the figurativeness of metaphorical expressions comes from a departure from the core, literal meaning of the lexical item. When a metaphorical meaning is seen as a meaning of a polysemous lexical item, the meaning of a larger constituent containing a metaphorically-used word can be derived in a compositional manner, and the only difference is the replacement of the literal meaning of that lexical item with the metaphorical meaning. This higher degree of semantic transparency in metaphorical expressions may actually ease the process of acquiring these expressions for both L1 and L2 users. According to Sweetser (1990), a native speaker is capable of deriving the metaphorical meaning(s) of a lexical item when given the contexts and the literal meaning of that lexical item, since the metaphorical meaning(s) are closely connected to the literal meaning. In a similar fashion, in a situation in which: (1) a learner has acquired the literal meaning of a lexical item and (2) that same lexical item is presented metaphorically with appropriate contexts (i.e. a collocation that is biased towards the metaphorical interpretation), it may be possible to infer the correct metaphorical meaning of that lexical item, even if the metaphorical meaning has never been encountered before. Hence, compared with idioms, it may be easier for learners to acquire and accept metaphorical expressions, and it is possible that some learners can acquire metaphorical expressions even without guidance from instructors.[1]

The categorization of idioms by Irujo has become a standard categorization in studies of L2 idiom acquisition. The methodology used by Irujo has been applied to research on the acquisition and processing of idioms between different pairs of L1 and L2 (e.g. Liontas 2002; Zhang 2008; see Bortfeld 2003 and Laufer 2000 for two similar paradigms. One of the weaknesses of the experimental methodology is obvious, particularly in the investigation of cross-linguistic influence. The production task is actually a translation task, since the text in L1 is provided to the participants and the participants must refer to the L1 text in order to know how to complete the L2 paragraph, even if they are not told in the instructions that they should translate the idioms. The presence of L1 idioms may draw additional attention from participants to the form of L1 idioms, which may result in a greater effect from transfer in the production of L2 idioms. Therefore, alternative offline tasks have been developed and applied in this area, including a sentence completion task that is only administered in L2 (Cieślicka 2006) and a discourse completion task in L2 conversations (e.g. Türker 2016a).

Further offline experiments on the acquisition of figurative language and the transfer thereof include the investigations of the use of phrasal verbs (Matlock & Heredia 2002), the interpretation of sentential metaphors (Littlemore 2010), and the interpretation of the linguistic realizations of HAPPY, SAD, and ANGER metaphors (Türker 2016b). Matlock and Heredia (2002) asked English learners from a variety of L1 backgrounds to complete sentences with a phrasal verb that was semantically opaque, and then compared the results with the production of native English speakers. Phrasal verbs are generally not available to learners in L1s; in their L1, a combination of a verb and a prepositional particle is more likely to be interpreted simply as a verb and a preposition; for instance, while the phrasal verb 'sleep in' is available in English as 'to sleep longer than usual', non-native English speakers may interpret it as 'to sleep in a location'. The result of the sentence completion task shows that learners are significantly less willing to interpret a phrasal verb like 'sleep in' as an entire structure; instead, they tend to interpret it as verb + preposition, and produce 'sleep in his own bedroom'. That result indicates that learners are less likely to go for the non-literal meaning of a combination of a verb and a prepositional particle. However, Matlock and Heredia also reported that proficient English learners were able to recognize and use phrasal verbs in the experiment, since this learner group interpreted the given expressions more as phrasal verbs than as combinations of a verb and a preposition. Türker's (2016b) study is among the first to investigate the acquisition of conventional metaphorical expressions. In his experiment, English learners of Korean were asked to interpret the meaning of fifty-four Korean conventional metaphorical expressions into three categories: (1) same conceptual mapping and same linguistic expression, (2) same conceptual mapping but different linguistic expression and (3) different conceptual mapping and different linguistic expression. The results showed that, in general, learners gave the most accurate interpretation to metaphorical expressions that were both conceptually and linguistically shared between English and Korean, and the smallest number of accurate interpretations to metaphorical expressions that were both conceptually and linguistically different in English and Korean. These experiments reflect the fact that cross-linguistic similarities facilitate the acquisition not only of idioms but also of other types of figurative language, while cross-linguistic differences may create obstacles in the process of acquisition, which is exactly the same as for the acquisition of ordinary lexical items and literal expressions.

While Irujo's experimental paradigm is also applicable to research on the acquisition of metaphorical expressions, some modifications should be made to capture possible cross-linguistic influence accurately. First, as discussed earlier, a translation task such as that of Irujo (1986b), or any task involving reading in one language and writing in another (e.g. Türker 2016b), may bias a learner and lead to a more significant effect from cross-linguistic influence. Such bias can be largely eliminated if the experimental task is conducted monolingually; that is, if learners receive the metaphorical expression and produce feedback in the same language, namely L2. Second, although metaphorical expressions in the two languages can be divided into categories according to the form and meaning of those expressions, it should be noted that the definition of 'identical/similar' for metaphorical expressions must be different from Irujo's classification. According to her classification, two idioms are cross-linguistically 'identical' only when they can be translated in an exact word-to-word fashion. Therefore, the English idiom 'a needle in a haystack' and its Chinese counterpart 'a needle in the sea' are not identical, but only similar, because there is a mismatch between the word 'haystack' and 'sea', even if other words in the multi-word constituents are all the same. As for metaphorical expressions, since only one word is interpreted metaphorically in the expressions, there is no requirement for the context also to be a word-for-word equivalent. If a pair of translation equivalents shares the same metaphorical meaning in the same collocation or context, they can be seen as identical metaphorical expressions, otherwise, they are essentially different. A status of 'similar metaphorical expression' does not exist in the current study.

Following Irujo's design (with some modifications), I expect to see different effects from cross-linguistic influence in the acquisition of metaphorical expressions, which will be in line with Irujo (1986b) and will follow studies of figurative language more generally. Thus, when a lexical item can only be interpreted metaphorically in one language, I propose that the following cross-linguistic influence can be observed: if the metaphorical expression is L1-specific, when a learner is asked to judge a word-to-word translation of such an L1 expression, I expect to observe acceptance of the expression due to L1 interference; if the metaphorical expression is L2-specific, I expect to see underproduction or avoidance of the L2-specific metaphorical expression, such as rejection in acceptability judgement, omission of the expression, and, possibly, different types of paraphrase.

3.3 Factors influencing cross-linguistic influence

In a series of studies from the late 1970s to the mid-1980s, Jordens and Kellerman investigated the strategies of transfer adopted by second language learners, particularly the conditions in which learners were more willing to transfer elements from their L1. It should be noted that, if a 'strategy of transfer' is being investigated, then 'transfer' is assumed to be consciously controlled rather than subconsciously used. Within such a framework, we must clearly differentiate two types of transferability. One is the binary, objective transferability of a linguistic element, which is decided by the linguistic elements available in L1 and L2 to learners. If a linguistic element is available at the same time in both L1 and L2, then it is objectively transferable from L1 to L2. The other is the subjective transferability of a linguistic element as perceived by the individual learner in the form of a continuum. This subjective transferability of a linguistic element varies between individual learners; it is probable that, for the same pair of languages, learner A may perceive a linguistic element as fully transferable while learner B may perceive it as not transferable at all. The focus of the studies by Kellerman and his colleagues, then, can be seen as an attempt to identify the possible factors that influence the subjective transferability of a certain linguistic element among different learners.

In the seminal works on the influential factors on transfer (or cross-linguistic influence), Jordens and Kellerman proposed three main factors and their possible effects, namely: psychotypology (the distance between L1 and L2 as perceived by learners), markedness of a linguistic element, and learners' knowledge. The three factors were discussed and delimited in subsequent studies, although some of them still remain debatable and even controversial. In this subsection, I will survey the factors that are: (1) closely related to acquisition of metaphorical expressions and (2) 'universally applicable' without considering the specific L1s and L2s of learners. That means I am not able to discuss psychotypology extensively (see M. Xia 2017 for an initial discussion of the relationship between psychotypology and the outcome of acquisition of metaphorical expressions); I mainly focus on the two other factors, that is, markedness of a linguistic element and learners' knowledge.

3.3.1 Markedness

The term *markedness* is often only loosely defined in research on cross-linguistic comparison, not only in second language acquisition but also in other relevant areas. The problem continues in Jordens and Kellerman (1981), as well as in the following research by others. The 'looseness' of the definition comes from two aspects, the scope of markedness and its nature. When I speak of the *scope* of markedness, I mean whether markedness is defined intralingually or interlingually. The terminology is mostly used intralingually, referring to the property of an element that is 'marked' within one language; at the same time, it can also be used interlingually to refer to the 'cross-linguistic rarity or frequency' of an element (Haspelmath 2006: 26). A more problematic issue is what 'markedness' usually refers to in linguistic investigation. Haspelmath concludes that there are twelve different definitions of 'markedness', including complexity, difficulty and abnormality (i.e. rarity) in all aspects of a linguistic system; all twelve types of 'markedness' are defined linguistically and within linguistic system(s). The definitions, however, are not fully overlapping; that an element may be morphologically complicated, such as an overt plural marker, does not indicate its rarity in daily language use; on the other hand, a rarely used expression may only be an individual word, which is not 'marked' structurally. The loose definition of markedness creates obstacles to quantifying it and investigating its cross-linguistic influence in a quantitative manner; one must identify the 'marked' elements as per the definition, evaluate how marked they are, and then see how 'markedness' interacts with other factors in language acquisition.

If the definition used by Jordens and Kellerman (1981; see also Kellerman 1983) is closely examined, it is slightly different from the linguistic definition of markedness. They describe 'markedness' as 'the degree of specialness to [sic] NL (=Dutch) elements within their various NL subsystems' (Jordens & Kellerman 1981: 196). This is more like one of the *intralingual* definitions of 'markedness' mentioned in Haspelmath (2006), or at least a combination of several *intralingual* definitions. Unlike other linguistic definitions of 'markedness' summarized in Haspelmath (2006), Jordens and Kellerman's markedness is a psycholinguistic rather than linguistic concept (see interpretation by Rutherford 1982); the 'markedness' of an element in a learner's mind is decided by that learner rather than being based on the structure of the linguistic element itself. This distinction is similar to the distinction between psychotypology and linguistic typology discussed in the last subsection; the former is perceptual and subjective, while the latter is actual and objective.

The subjectivity of markedness in Jordens and Kellerman (1981) does not simplify the question though. If 'markedness' here is defined as the specialness of an L1 element as perceived by a learner, the next question quickly emerges, where does the sense of markedness come from? They do not provide any hint in their work, so I must make my own inference on the assumption that the native speakers of one language do not show great variation in terms of their perception of the degree of markedness of an element. In their original work, they provided three examples to justify their argument: (1) an expression involving less productive syntactic rules is more marked than another expression that expresses the same semantic content but does not involve less productive rules; (2) an idiom, particularly a semantically opaque one, is more marked than a semantically decomposable expression; and (3) a peripheral meaning of a polysemous word is more marked than a core meaning. While some examples may correspond to certain individual definitions of markedness, as described in Haspelmath (2006), it is difficult to cover all the marked elements they mention using one single criterion, for example, conceptual complexity or frequency, particularly in light of the overlapping concepts that 'markedness' stands for (as discussed before). For instance, a less productive syntactic rule may appear less frequently than a more productive syntactic rule but is, perhaps, no more conceptually complex; on the other hand, an idiom may be semantically more opaque than a literal expression but is, possibly, as frequently used as the literal expression. This may eventually correspond to what Haspelmath defines as the final case of markedness – a multi-dimensional correlation without further specification. While it is difficult to strictly define the concept of markedness by Jordens and Kellerman in the experiments described in this book, the methodology used to measure the degree of markedness of a linguistic element is similar to the one used by Jordens and Kellerman in order to best follow their original proposal of markedness.

After discussing what is marked in a language (in a loose way), Jordens and Kellerman further suggest that the markedness of a linguistic element may have an impact on the subjective transferability of that element to a second language. They conclude that if an element is marked in a learner's L1, that learner may be less willing to transfer it to their L2. Here, an indication of a shift from intralingual markedness to interlingual markedness can be observed; if an element is marked in L1, a learner may believe either that it is difficult to find an identical counterpart in L2, or that an alternative element is available in L2. Therefore, the learner will not transfer the linguistic element from L1. In other words, an element that is marked intralingually may also be marked interlingually from the point of view of a learner. Although this statement does not always hold true in cross-linguistic comparison, for it is always possible for an element to be marked in language A but unmarked in language B, one should bear in mind that the definition of markedness in the current discussion is psychological rather than linguistic, and it is natural for a learner who does not have sufficient materials to make precise inferences to transfer a perception.

The markedness and subjective transferability of idioms has been extensively discussed in work by Kellerman and Jordens (see Jordens 1986; Jordens & Kellerman 1981; Kellerman 1979, 1983), who takes idioms as good exemplars of marked elements in a language. He briefly introduces possible influential factors on the transferability of idioms, particularly semantic transparency. If an idiom is semantically opaque, it is less likely to be transferred. This may initially sound contradictory when comparing Kellerman's result with the Transfer Theory by Irujo (1986b, 1993), which indicates that a learner may selectively transfer certain idioms from L1 to L2 depending on the availability of idioms, but the two results are internally connected. The selective transfer of L1 idioms can still be interpreted by the degree of markedness; it is simple and feasible to assume that not all the idioms are perceived as marked to the same degree in L1, and less marked idioms may be perceived as being more transferable between L1 and L2. How the degree of markedness varies between individual idioms is, nevertheless, still unknown. It may be the case, following Kellerman himself, that semantic transparency is decisive or, following Irujo (1986b), that the similarity of forms in two languages may be important or, if applicable, the frequency of an idiom in L1 use may have a certain impact.

Jordens and Kellerman also try to implement the concept of markedness in the acquisition of different meanings of the polysemous word 'break'. That research is similar to the topic of this book, namely the acquisition of the metaphorical meaning of words. Before they investigated the subjective transferability of each meaning of 'break', they first measured the degree of markedness of each meaning, which at least provided a way to quantify and evaluate the degree of markedness. The result of a card-sorting experiment (in the manner of Miller 1969) reveals that the properties of the meanings of 'break' can be reduced to two dimensions: *coreness* and *concreteness*, where coreness is the degree of prototypicality of the meaning and concreteness refers to the literalness or imaginability of the meaning. They state that between the two dimensions, coreness or prototypicality should be used to indicate the (un)markedness of a meaning. More importantly, from the perspective of the study of metaphor, they point out that the coreness and concreteness of a meaning does not *always* correlate; an abstract meaning, such as 'break one's heart', can be core, while a concrete meaning, such as 'someone's voice breaks', can be peripheral. The follow-up examination of subjective transferability also shows that it is the core meanings and not the concrete meanings that are more likely to be transferred from Dutch to English by Dutch learners of English. They then conclude that the core meanings of a polysemous word are less marked and more likely to be transferred, while peripheral meanings are more marked and learners tend not to transfer them. They also argue that a learner knows intuitively that some meanings of a lexical item seem to be more 'universal' than other meanings and will rely on such intuition in forming a personal perception of the transferability of a meaning.

At first glance, the result above may easily be interpreted as implying that abstractness/metaphoricalness does not play a significant role in influencing the subjective transferability of the meaning of a polysemous word, but a cautious examination is always required to confirm that point. The most prominent problem with the statement, which is essential to my discussion, is the degree of correlation between metaphoricalness and coreness, if I follow Jordens and Kellerman in taking coreness as the indicator of markedness. Jordens and Kellerman divide the meanings of 'break' into two ranks to show that there are clear differences between the rank of coreness and that of concreteness, but it seems that coreness and concreteness are indeed weakly correlated in the survey since both the concrete-but-peripheral meanings and the abstract-but-core meanings are relatively rare (see Figure 1, Jordens & Kellerman 1981: 210). Without further detail, it is difficult to assert that coreness and concreteness are two independent factors, and that concreteness (or, in the current study, metaphoricalness) does not influence the subjective transferability of any meaning at all. As I will show in the experiments in Chapter 7, the methods used by Jordens and Kellerman were adopted selectively to investigate whether: (1) there is any correlation between markedness (indicated by the degree of coreness) and literalness and (2) markedness can be used to predict the subjective transferability of metaphorical expressions and the outcome of the acquisition of metaphorical expressions.

3.3.2 Learners' knowledge

Another influential factor in the transfer strategy proposed by Jordens and Kellerman is the so-called 'knowledge of the L2 learner'; although in a later revision Kellerman abandoned it as a major influential factor (Spolsky 1985), this factor is nevertheless an important one in second language acquisition. The logic of this factor is very straightforward; if learners possess, or believe that they possess, knowledge of an element in L2, they no longer need to adopt strategies to deal with it. The 'knowledge' defined here includes two parts: the actual knowledge that has already been acquired and the 'assumed knowledge' that is believed by the learner to have been acquired. Acquired knowledge can be achieved from either intentional or incidental learning, while assumed knowledge can come from a learner's guess, deduction, inference or 'intuitional guess'. Although the role of assumed knowledge is not confirmed by a learner in the process of acquisition, it is likely that the assumed knowledge is derived from some acquired knowledge of the learner; for a piece of knowledge, even 'assumed', cannot come out of nowhere. The advantage of defining 'knowledge' this way, as already discussed by Jordens and Kellerman (1981), is that a learner cannot fully differentiate the two parts of the acquisition process. While current methodologies of assessment can largely differentiate implicit and explicit knowledge (Ellis 2005), it is still difficult to differentiate actual and assumed knowledge, even if a learner's metalinguistic knowledge was assessed (i.e. asked for an explanation for particular judgements); therefore, a good way is to combine the two parts of knowledge, as proposed by Jordens and Kellerman.

To continue with Jordens and Kellerman's proposal, I predict that the effect of cross-linguistic influence from L1 will be generally weakened throughout the process of second language acquisition. This remains in line with the general description of cross-linguistic influence at the beginning of this chapter; if a learner has fully mastered a linguistic element, cross-linguistic influence from L1 will eventually disappear. However, considering the different types of cross-linguistic influence (or transfer), the 'weakened' effect is not always universally observable. On the one hand, a learner is less likely to make any mistakes that originate from the grammar of L1, and it would be methodologically easy to observe the disappearance of negative transfer. On the other hand, it is not known whether positive transfer still plays a role when that learner reaches a higher level of proficiency, because the effect of positive transfer and the reflection of knowledge are similar in linguistic form, if one *only* examines the learner's linguistic output. It can be seen from the analysis above that evidence for 'knowledge' (including both actual and assumed) and positive transfer is not clearly separated; when a learner correctly produces a linguistic element shared between L1 and L2, it may evince knowledge that the linguistic element has been acquired, or simply that what is known from L1 has been mapped to L2, unless justification is required for the production. The boundary between 'the utilization of transfer strategy' and 'the adoption of (assumed) knowledge', therefore, cannot be effectively reflected solely by the output of a learner. In fact, Jordens and Kellerman realized this problem, and they tried to blur the boundary by pointing out that the transfer strategy always departs from some type of knowledge. It seems to be difficult for them, as well, to establish a definite boundary between knowledge and transfer in their experiments without referring to the metalinguistic descriptions provided by the learners. At a later stage, Kellerman eliminates this factor from his discussion, which might ultimately indicate that the borderline between '(assumed) knowledge' and 'transfer' is not definable for him.

However, from the perspective of a learner, transfer only happens when a person does not have the relevant knowledge, or at least assumes this to be the case, and the difference between '(assumed) knowledge' and 'transfer' can eventually be reduced to the difference between the 'existence' and 'non-existence' of that knowledge; this means that even a naïve learner might make a distinction between the existence and non-existence of knowledge. Therefore, if a metalinguistic description of a learner, especially in terms of their confidence level in producing a linguistic element, is included in an analysis of output, it may be possible to establish what knowledge is already acquired or assumed to have been acquired by the learner, and what comes from transfer. If a learner is confident in judging or producing a linguistic element, and is able to justify the output that is produced, then that judgement or production is more likely to come from (assumed) knowledge; on the other hand, if that learner is not confident in judging or producing a linguistic element and cannot refer to metalinguistic knowledge to explain the output, this may suggest a reliance on cross-linguistic influence when producing the output.

As well as the problem of the blurred borderline between positive transfer and (assumed) knowledge, another problem can be identified when considering the methodology used to examine a learner's knowledge. In existing studies, a learner's knowledge is often reflected by L2 proficiency, and it is generally assumed that the higher a learner's proficiency is, the more knowledge is possessed and assumed. While that measurement is feasible, proficiency itself is occasionally measured by the length of exposure to L2 in a classroom setting (see Experiment 1 of Jordens & Kellerman 1981) or, in some cases, the major of a group of college student participants (e.g. Zhang 2008). It seems that, when developing the original proposal, Kellerman aimed to establish a correlation between three factors: a learner's knowledge (both acquired and assumed); the proficiency level; and the length of L2 instruction received. In a strict sense, such correlation cannot provide a full picture of a learner's knowledge, although it can be a fallback if a more accurate test is not applicable. The use of the length of L2 instruction to reflect a learner's knowledge is rather problematic. Longer exposure to L2 classroom instruction can only reflect that a learner has been taught more, whereas a learner's knowledge from non-guided acquisition, as well as assumed knowledge, is left unevaluated. If 'knowledge' here is defined as a combination of acquired and assumed knowledge, a measurement of acquired knowledge exclusively does not provide a strong foundation for the entire argument. To take a further step and to associate it with the topic of acquisition of metaphorical expressions, different aspects of L2 knowledge may develop in an imbalanced way as proficiency rises, which may not be accounted for in the correlation. It is probable that some L2 knowledge is less accessible, or even less learnable, in the process of acquisition, and it may remain underdeveloped even though a learner has received years of L2 instruction and achieved a relatively high proficiency. Therefore, it cannot be simply hypothesized that, with a rise in general L2 proficiency, a learner will gradually give up strategies of transfer in all aspects of L2. While currently the knowledge of the learner is still considered to be one of the major factors that influence strategies of transfer, whether the rise of proficiency will lead to the development of knowledge of metaphorical expressions will be one of the focuses of the experiments in this book. At the same time, it is also possible to propose a methodological solution to differentiate positive transfer and (assumed) knowledge in a learner's judgement.

3.4 Summary

In this chapter, I have discussed in detail the phenomenon of cross-linguistic influence in the acquisition of lexical items and how such discussions can be extended to include the acquisition of metaphorical expressions. While there is a lack of comprehensive discussion on the acquisition of metaphorical expressions in L2 in the current literature, I refer to previous studies on the acquisition of ordinary lexical items and idioms, since metaphorical expressions seem to reside between the two in a continuum of semantic transparency. The general predictions of cross-linguistic influence on metaphorical expressions seem to be in line with other studies on lemmatic transfer in general. Overall, one expects to see both positive and negative lemmatic transfer in the acquisition of metaphorical expressions, depending on the cross-linguistic availability of metaphorical expressions with learners in L1 and L2. While learners can acquire the shared metaphorical expressions better, they may misuse the metaphorical expressions only available in their L1, in a fashion similar to false friends.

Some factors influencing cross-linguistic influence were also discussed in this chapter. The proposal of Jordens and Kellerman, together with follow-up studies, shows that cross-linguistic influence is subject to factors other than cross-linguistic similarity (or difference) in expressions, and these factors, including markedness and a learner's knowledge, should also be taken into account for a full exploration of possible cross-linguistic influence on the acquisition of metaphorical expressions. In the meantime, I also observe a lack of proper methodology to estimate these influential factors in previous research, which may intricate the current discussion. I will investigate further the influence of these factors in the experiments in Chapter 7; I will also provide some possible methodological solutions in Chapter 6 as possible supplementary tasks for an experiment design.

4

Processing metaphorical expressions by native speakers and learners

4.1 Introduction

The online processing of metaphorical and other figurative expressions has been a central research topic in psychology, pragmatics and psycholinguistics, following the theoretical discussions of figurative language from the late 1970s. As discussed in Chapter 2, under a Gricean convention it has long been a tradition to regard metaphorical expressions and other figurative language as 'secondary' and inferior to literal expressions. This view was only abandoned after a breakthrough in psycholinguistics which showed that native speakers of a language do not spend more time processing metaphorical expressions than they do processing literal expressions.

In this chapter I will focus on extant psycholinguistic and other experimental studies on the processing of metaphorical expressions. Again, considering that there has been a general lack of study on the processing of metaphorical expressions by second language learners, I will approach this issue in a roundabout, peripheral way; I will review the processing of metaphorical expressions by native speakers as well as the processing of other figurative expressions (e.g. idioms, phrasal verbs, etc.) by second language learners or bilingual speakers, respectively. Such a review will create a more comprehensive picture of the processing of different types of non-literal expressions. Then, I will draw inferences from the processing of conventional, metaphorical expressions by second language learners from these joint evidences. If there is a systematic difference between the processing pattern of native speakers and that of second language learners in terms of other figurative expressions, then it is very likely that the same patterns will be observed when native speakers and second language learners process conventionalized metaphorical expressions. Then I can test, by empirical evidence, whether the assumptions are valid.

4.2 The processing of metaphorical expressions by native speakers

The investigation on the processing of linguistic metaphors has been developing since the emergence of two competing theories on the construction of metaphorical meanings. The first, which became widely spread well after Grice's proposal of conversational maxims, is the 'literal-first' hypothesis. To give a brief reminder, Grice regards metaphorical meaning as a type of conversational implicature, and suggests that one should always compute the literal meaning of an utterance prior to the derivation of a metaphorical meaning. The 'literal-first' hypothesis hypothesizes that a hearer can only proceed to the non-literal meaning of a sentence if the literal meaning of the sentence does not make any sense. Therefore, a direct inference of the hypothesis is that it will take more time for a hearer to process the metaphorical meaning than to process the literal meaning. Additionally, since metaphorical meanings are regarded as 'secondary' and can only be derived after an attempt to derive the literal meaning, one can also assume that a reader could stop in the middle of processing if they do not want to derive the metaphorical meaning of an expression. In that sense, metaphorical meanings can be optional and ignored, which is different from literal meanings that are compulsory.

The second proposal originates from Conceptual Metaphor Theory (CMT). Although one can simply assume that the 'literal-first' hypothesis does not stand if the experimental results show that metaphorical expressions do not require a longer time to process, a theoretical background for such a prediction will still be needed. The emergence of CMT provides an excellent chance to explore the possibilities outside the 'literal-first' hypothesis. From the perspective of CMT, if a reader perceives the whole world in a 'metaphorical' manner and constantly maps concrete concepts onto abstract conceptual domains to understand the world, then they should not encounter any difficulty when understanding the linguistic realization of metaphorical thoughts and conceptual metaphors, namely metaphorical expressions. Although, as discussed in Chapter 2, there has not yet been a series of solid evidence for conceptual metaphors, CMT did allow one to pose a prediction of metaphor processing when it was first proposed in 1980s. CMT is also the very first theory that backs up a prediction against the literal-first hypothesis, while other theories only contributed to the issue after the first experiments based on it.

Research on the processing of linguistic metaphors was initiated by Glucksberg and colleagues (Gildea & Glucksberg 1983; Glucksberg, Gildea & Bookin 1982), who compared the reading time of conventional sentential metaphors like 'my lawyer is a shark' and literal sentences in a similar structure like 'my lawyer is a man'. They based their experiment design on CMT, assuming that, when comprehending the metaphorical meaning of 'shark', readers would be able to reach the metaphorical meaning without any additional processing time. They also conducted a literal meaning judgement task to see if metaphorical meanings can be ignored; in this task, participants were given metaphorical sentences that were literally false, such as 'some jobs are jails', and they were asked to judge whether the sentences were *literally* true or false. Participants took a significantly longer time to reject metaphorical sentences than the so-called 'scrambled metaphorical sentences' that are not readily interpretable, such as 'some jobs are birds'. The intended meaning of a metaphorical sentence can be easily derived without hesitation if the context provides solid support. It seems that the processing of metaphorical meanings is at least parallel to the processing of literal meanings among native speakers; that is, metaphorical meanings never 'depend on' or 'follow after' the derivation of literal meaning. Later experiments by McElree and Nordlie (1999) further reveal that the metaphorical interpretation of a sentence can interfere with the processing of the literal meaning. When the contextual information of a target sentence shows incongruence between a true literal meaning and a false metaphorical meaning, for instance, calling a magic performer who cannot manage his finance well 'a magician', participants will take longer to agree that the person is literally a magician. Such a delay disappears when the literal meaning and metaphorical meaning are both true. All the experiments reflect that native speakers process the metaphorical meaning of a conventional metaphorical sentence parallel to the literal meaning in general. This leads to the so-called 'direct access view', which suggests that, just the same as literal meanings, metaphorical meanings of expressions can be directly accessed by language users. If both types of meaning are directly accessible, then it is natural that there is no difference in processing speed or effort between them. Another theory similar to the direct access view is the parallel activation view, which suggests that literal and metaphorical meanings are activated in parallel, until the reader selects the intended meaning according to the context of that expression.

A naïve language user, however, may feel that metaphorical sentences are different in terms of processing difficulty. Some sentences, such as 'some jobs are jails', are very easy to process and the metaphorical interpretation can be reached after a simple glance; on the other hand, some sentences are more difficult to comprehend, such as scrambled metaphorical sentences like 'some jobs are birds'. In some cases, for example, sentences that can be interpreted either literally or metaphorically, a naïve language user may provide different interpretations; it seems to them that some sentences are more readily interpreted metaphorically while others are more readily interpreted literally. CMT, as a theoretical framework on semantics, does not aim to explain such processing differences; it cannot explain whether all metaphorical expressions are regarded equally as linguistic realizations of conceptual metaphor. Particularly, it can be clearly observed that different metaphorical expressions can evoke drastically different patterns, even though they are the realization of the same underlying conceptual metaphor. For example, 'the girl is a rose' is easy and straightforward to understand, while one may take some time to work out the meaning of 'the girl is a tulip', although both roses and tulips are common flowers and the two sentences both illustrate HUMAN IS PLANT. Then, given all of the other conditions, what could influence the processing speed and the process outcome of a metaphorical expression by native speakers?

When entering this stage of an investigation, psycholinguistic explanations are proposed to analyse differences between the processing of individual metaphorical expressions. Most of the explanations are beyond any analysis of semantics and, indeed, do not favour any specific semantic theory of metaphor, for they do not intend to show how the meaning of a metaphorical expression or sentence can be derived at an abstract level via compositionality or conceptual metaphors. Instead, their focus becomes 'why': why language users react differently to different metaphorical expressions, despite all the expressions being classified as metaphorical. Nevertheless, some psycholinguistic explanations of metaphor processing do coincide with the semantic proposals mentioned in Chapter 2, especially the Relevance Theory. That is mainly because the Relevance Theory predicts the same results as these psycholinguistic explanations.

One of the most prominent models that deals with both the parallel between literal and metaphorical meanings and the potential distinction between different meanings (both literal and metaphorical) is the Graded Salience Hypothesis by Giora and colleagues (see Giora 2002 for a full analysis). The Graded Salience Hypothesis is not used exclusively for the processing of metaphorical expressions; instead, it provides a counterpart to the general literal-first view based on the Gricean pragmatic notions, and can be used to analyse all types of figures of speech, including metaphor, irony and metonymy. In their view, the order and speed of meaning access are not purely based on the literalness of an expression but are decided by the relative degree of salience of that meaning. If the literal meaning and figurative meaning of an expression are both salient in a context, then they can be activated simultaneously. However, if the literal meaning of an expression is more salient than the figurative meaning, then there is usually a literal-first processing pattern; that is not because the first meaning is literal but because it is more salient.

At first glance, the Graded Salience Hypothesis proposes a powerful tool to explain the two problems described above. On the one hand, by suggesting that the sequence of processing is largely due to the degree of salience, it can be used to illustrate why in some cases a metaphorical meaning comes no later than a literal meaning, probably due to the same or similar degree of salience. On the other hand, it also avoids the problems of the Direct Access View, namely assuming that all the metaphorical meanings are accessed directly and ignore the discrepancies between different metaphorical expressions. Particularly, it deals with the apparent difference of processing speed between conventionalized and novel metaphorical expressions; conventionalized metaphorical expressions are easy to be processed because they are already salient enough, while novel metaphorical expressions take a longer time to process precisely because of their lack of salience.

However, considering the issue of salience and the development of metaphorical meanings as described in lexical semantics, there remains an important question in the proposal of the Graded Salience Hypothesis; how is salience defined? If I simply use Giora's original proposal of salient senses and suggest that a salient sense of an expression is 'the one directly computable from the mental lexicon' regardless of the context of that expression, I then simply fall into a circular argument without explaining where the salient meaning comes from. Similar to the issue of markedness in Chapter 3, there is a problem of definition as well as the quantification of that criterion. Gibbs and Coulson (2012) advise that salience can be measured in a multi-dimensional way by taking into consideration relative frequency, relative familiarity, conventionality and/or prototypicality. But if I take this approach to analyse metaphorical expressions, the results may fall outside of my expectations. As illustrated in Chapter 2, while literal meanings are already conventional, metaphorical meanings are gradually 'conventionalized', and would this order of conventionality play a role in deciding the degree of salience? Also, problems emerge when considering prototypicality; conventionalized metaphorical expressions are constructed in such a way that people map a concrete conceptual domain onto an abstract domain, and it is easy to take for granted that the meaning from the original conceptual domain is more prototypical than the meaning from the other domain. That said, the literal meaning of a word should be more prototypical than the metaphorical meaning of that word, unless people come across the situation when the literal meaning of a word becomes obsolete. Furthermore, Giora, in her original proposal, argues that the literal meaning and a salient figurative meaning should both be activated, even if the given context is biased to the figurative meaning. As seen in the experiments, when tapping into the sequence of meaning activation it can be assumed that, under such circumstances, the literal meaning and the figurative meaning are indeed activated at the same time. Such 'activation at the same time', however, cannot hold without any limit; one expects to see that the less salient meaning will be activated later at the point when there is a clear difference between the degree of salience of literal and figurative meanings. However, the threshold itself is unknown. Will any difference of degree of salience trigger a processing sequence, or only if the difference 'large enough'? If it is the latter, how large should the difference be? Neither question has been fully answered yet. In short, it is difficult to clearly define the degree of salience and account for the difference of processing patterns triggered by salience.

An alternative to the Graded Salience Hypothesis that focuses on the processing mechanism of figurative meaning is the so-called 'Underspecification Hypothesis'. This theory is particularly relevant to the form of metaphorical expression I target in this book because its primary goal is to deal with the processing of 'words with related polysemous senses', which fits perfectly with the discussion of conventional metaphorical expression; it can also be easily connected to the theoretical arguments on the context and metaphorical meanings in Chapter 2. The Underspecification Hypothesis by Frisson and Pickering (2001) suggests that no matter what type of expressions or sentences a reader processes, whether literal or metaphorical, the first meaning to be activated is an underspecified schematic meaning rather than a definite word or expression-specific meaning. For example, while 'attack the enemy' and 'attack the argument' involve different types of 'attack', the first meaning activated by a reader after reading the word 'attack' is biased to neither the physical conflict nor the verbal conflict. Instead, the meaning is 'underspecified', with a sense of 'conflict' solely. Only when the full collocation is presented to the reader will she select the final meaning of 'attack' and continue to process the rest of the sentence.

Frisson and Pickering make use of eye-tracking experiments to examine native English speakers' processing of sentences containing metaphorical expressions. They use a paradigm involving conflicting contexts and polysemous word meanings to reveal whether a reader would activate the meaning closely related to context, even before the presentation of the rest of the collocation. They discovered that, even though the preceding context is biased to the metaphorical (or literal) meaning of the target word, participants do not activate the context-specific meaning until after seeing the target word. The presence of the context preceding the target word does not fully determine the target meaning, but simply helps with a process that resembles ambiguity resolution. Frisson and Pickering therefore suggest that the processing of literal and metaphorical expressions does not involve any sequential activation (cf. the literal-first hypothesis or the Direct Access View); instead, it should be seen as ambiguity resolution in which a general, schematic meaning becomes literal or metaphorical based on the information given in the context.

As the processing of metaphorical expressions is converted to the problem of ambiguity resolution in the Underspecification Hypothesis, it comes with several issues which are either unaddressed or unavoidable. This hypothesis mainly focuses on the processing of conventionalized metaphorical expressions, since it assumes that the meanings to be activated should be fully established in the reader's mental lexicon. That means that this hypothesis is not designed to explain unconventional figurative meanings because these are not included in the mental lexicon of a native speaker. While it is possible to provide other examples that show that unconventional figurative meanings need a longer time to process, exactly because they cannot be activated as their conventionalized counterparts in the process of ambiguity resolution, this point was not explicitly argued in the original hypothesis. It should be noted that the absence of discussion on unconventional metaphorical expressions does not harm the integrity of the whole hypothesis; when the hypothesis was proposed, Frisson and Pickering explicitly stressed that this theory is for conventionalized figurative expressions only.

Nevertheless, the proposal of the Underspecification Hypothesis faces a greater threat from the problem of one of its core definitions, the so-called 'underspecified meaning'. It is questionable, from both lexical semantics and psycholinguistics, what the 'underspecified meaning' is and what concept it should include. From Frisson and Pickering's description, it is easy to interpret such 'underspecified meaning' as an umbrella, albeit in a highly abstract sense that covers the essence of both literal and metaphorical meanings of a lexical item. It should be an umbrella which should be able to easily collapse into the context-specific meanings in the process of ambiguity resolution without any further processing effort; this feature, in turn, requires the meaning to be highly abstract. But does such a meaning exist naturally, and is such a meaning included in one's mental lexicon? I am very pessimistic as to the existence of such a meaning, especially considering the emergence of a metaphorical meaning and its distinction from the literal meaning of that word. Taking a CMT approach to the creation of a metaphorical meaning, either conventional or not, one directly maps the domain of a concrete concept to another domain of an abstract concept, and then realizes such mapping in language. This process can go without any type of abstraction, which can be reflected by the presence of rich embodied and ontological metaphorical expressions. If abstraction does not appear in the creation of a metaphorical meaning, then it would be redundant to assume its appearance after the creation of a metaphorical meaning, and even further redundant to assume its position in one's mental lexicon. From another perspective, if such an underspecified meaning exists it should be regarded semantically as the primary meaning of a word because all other meanings, literal and metaphorical, are only the instantiation of that meaning in different contexts. Such 'primary meaning', as seen in Chapter 2, is far from a feasible account for both theoretical semantics and a valid representation of one's mental lexicon. Although the Underspecification Hypothesis can explain the same processing cost of literal and metaphorical expressions superficially, it does not provide a better underlying processing mechanism than the parallel hypothesis.

Apart from the systematic psycholinguistic explanations of figurative languages above, theories focusing exclusively on the processing of metaphorical expressions have also been proposed. A number of them aim to discuss the potential influencing factors of the processing of metaphorical expressions, and the focuses fall into two major categories: (1) the relationship between the 'properties' of metaphorical expressions and the processing cost and (2) the similarities and differences between the processing of metaphors and that of similes. Although they seem to be irrelevant at the first glance, the two topics are related in terms of a common borderline between two possible types of metaphorical expressions. It has long been assumed, possibly due to the formal similarity between metaphorical sentences and simile sentences, that at least some metaphorical expressions are processed in the same way as simile, since both involve the reader's effort to find the similarity between the tenor and the vehicle words of a metaphorical expression. If I intend to argue that some metaphorical expressions are processed differently from simile expressions, then a border between these metaphorical expressions and others is naturally posed according to certain criteria. The two research topics can thus be reduced to one, namely an internal classification of metaphorical expressions: those more 'metaphor-like' expressions and those more 'simile-like' expression.

The potential influence of the properties of metaphorical expressions were systematically investigated by Chiappe and Kennedy (1999, 2001; see also Chiappe, Kennedy & Chiappe 2003) in a series of online and offline comprehension experiments. Among several candidates, they identified aptness of a metaphorical expression as the most important factor that influenced the processing speed of metaphorical expressions and the reader's preference for metaphorical or simile expressions. Aptness can be defined as whether a metaphorical expression can capture the important features of the topic being described, regardless of the conventionality of the expression. They found that when a metaphorical expression was rated higher in degree of aptness, it was processed faster by the participants and, in a recall task, the metaphorical expression was more likely to be recalled correctly in the form of linguistic metaphor rather than simile.

Other than aptness, other potential factors have been identified and discussed in Glucksberg and Haught (2006) as well as Gentner and Bowdle (2008), including familiarity and conventionality of a metaphorical expression. In these studies, familiarity and conventionality were defined differently; familiarity referred to the frequency of co-occurrence of the tenor and vehicle expressions in daily language use, that is, whether a specific metaphorical expression appeared frequently in everyday use; conventionality, on the other hand, focused on the use of the vehicle expressions only, and a conventional metaphorical expression means that the use of the vehicle word in the expression is frequent and accepted by most language users (see Roncero 2013 for a detailed explanation). Among the three factors, researchers consider familiarity to be the least important one, while aptness and conventionality can be more decisive in the processing speed of a metaphorical expression. The reason is rather straightforward: a rare metaphorical expression, which means it has a low degree of familiarity, can still be processed quickly if it 'is easy to understand', that is, either it is highly apt or it uses a highly conventional vehicle expression. A study by Jones and Estes (2005) further suggests that aptness is more important than conventionality when deciding the processing time of a metaphorical expression, but Roncero (2013) did not find any significant influence of both factors on the reading time of the vehicle of a metaphorical expression.

The discussion of the potential influencing factors, particularly the impact of conventionality of the vehicle expressions and the metaphorical expressions as a whole, is often connected with the comparison between the processing of metaphorical and simile expressions. Such connections originated from a proposal of metaphor processing raised by Glucksberg and Keysar (1993), namely the categorical inclusion theory. Based on Barsalou's (1983) research on emergent properties of concepts, they suggest that a metaphorical sentence, or more generally a metaphorical expression, should be comprehended as an expression of categorical inclusion. This processing strategy distinguishes metaphorical expressions from simile expressions that utilize comparison strategy. According to the categorical inclusion proposal, when one processes the metaphorical sentence 'the girl is a rose', one needs to understand that 'the girl' referred in the sentence is a member of a larger category '(metaphorical) roses', and one can then infer the properties of the girl based on one's understanding of the properties of roses. This idea is further introduced into the Relevance Theory to illustrate the composition of meaning of a metaphorical expression; the meaning of 'rose' in the sentence is modified by conceptual broadening and loosening before it enters the process of compositionality, thus creating an explicature 'the girl is a ROSE*' for that sentence (see Carston 2002 for details).

Bowdle and Gentner's *The Career of Metaphor* (2005) – see also Gentner and Bowdle (2008) – takes Glucksberg's categorical inclusion proposal and develops it further to become a developmental account of processing of metaphorical expressions. The name of the theory, specifically the metaphorical use of 'career', aims to reflect the importance of conventionalization of metaphorical expressions and the change of processing patterns led by such conventionalization. Bowdle and Gentner propose that, when an expression is less conventional, a metaphorical category may be yet to be established, and then readers are more likely to: (1) favour the simile version (e.g. 'the girl is like a tulip') more than the metaphorical version (e.g. 'the girl is a tulip') and (2) draw a comparison between the tenor and the vehicle rather than seeing the vehicle as a category in which the tenor is included as a member. Thus, in the sentence 'the girl is a tulip', readers are more likely to compare the girl to a tulip to find out if they have any features in common. On the other hand, when a metaphorical expression becomes conventional, particularly when a vehicle expression is closely associated with an established metaphorical category, then readers are more likely to favour the metaphorical version more than the simile version, and are also more likely to interpret the metaphorical expression as a relationship of categorical inclusion.

The difference between the processing mechanism of conventionalized and unconventional metaphorical expressions, as illustrated in *The Career of Metaphor* proposal, could help to explain the difference of processing speed and cost when readers encounter different metaphorical expressions; comparison may take more time to process since it involves searching for similarities, while categorical inclusion with an established metaphorical category can be directly processed, precisely the same as the processing of categorical inclusion with an established literal category. This proposal, as well as empirical evidences supporting it, together help to establish a baseline for the processing of conventional metaphorical expressions; for native speakers of a language, there is no additional time cost or cognitive effort to process a conventional linguistic metaphor, no matter which form it is in. That means a native speaker will spend the same time, whether reading a literal sentence or a conventional metaphorical sentence of the same length and grammatical structure.

Finally, neurolinguistic evidences reveal that, even though conventional metaphorical expressions are metaphorical by definition, they may not evoke the 'feeling of metaphoricalness' or any comprehension difficulty as novel metaphorical expressions do in real-time processing. In experiments using event-related potentials (ERPs) as indicators, the N400 response, namely a negative potential appearing 400 ms after the presentation of the critical stimulus, generally indicates that the reader or listener experiences some type of semantic anomaly. Recent studies utilizing EEG monitoring shows that less conventional metaphors trigger an N400 response in the reading process, which means that the readers feel a semantic anomaly at the beginning of the processing, while more conventional metaphors and literal expressions do not evoke any N400 response in the processing, indicating that the readers do not feel any semantic anomaly (Lai, Curran & Menn 2009). That said, conventional metaphorical expressions are regarded as 'literal-like' by native speakers, both in terms of the processing pattern and the feeling of semantic anomaly. This result can be used as a baseline for research on both the processing of novel metaphorical expressions by native speakers and the processing of conventional metaphorical expressions by second language learners.

4.3 The processing of figurative expressions by second language learners

While in the last subsection I focused exclusively on the processing of metaphorical expressions by native speakers, as I said at the very beginning of this chapter it is unfortunate that I cannot do the same for second language learners; therefore I should consider an alternative approach to this problem.

If I investigate how second language learners process figurative expressions in general, I may find those aspects which they share certain similarities with, or behave drastically different from native speakers. Such similarities and differences are also likely to appear in the case of processing of conventional metaphorical expressions, since conventional metaphorical expressions are essentially a type of figurative language. In this subsection, I will look into the processing of different figurative expressions by both native speakers and second language learners and attempt to derive a general assumption for figurative language processing by second language learners. This leads to further discussion in Chapter 5 on bilingual lexicons and word meaning retrieval, as well as providing a potential model for the processing of metaphorical expressions by second language learners.

The processing of figurative language – including metaphors, idioms and phrasal verbs – by second language learners has been stressed only recently, although the transferability of figurative language in second language acquisition and learners general performance of the acquisition of L2 figurative expressions has been studied extensively over the past decades. The study of figurative language processing includes two major topics: (1) how figurative language is stored in a learner's mind and (2) whether a learner can achieve a native-like processing pattern when processing figurative language. I aim to provide a brief review of previous research on figurative language processing in L2, emphasizing the possible patterns of figurative language acquisition and processing by L2 learners.

Similar to the case of first language processing, the reading time of an expression or a sentence structure is regarded as an effective indicator of processing difficulties in second language processing (Clahsen & Felser 2006); a longer reading time usually indicates that a learner may experience some difficulties, which possibly including complex syntactic structures, lexical retrieval difficulties, ambiguity resolution, and so on. In this subsection, the processing difficulty of different types of figurative language is generally reflected by a prolonged reading or reaction time. As I will show in the rest of this subsection, the reading time of a figurative expression is associated with the way of 'meaning-making' of that expression. In a broader sense, the meaning of a multi-word figurative expression can be either constructed or accessed. 'Constructing' here refers to a more complicated process of meaning-making, involving searching, selecting and adjusting the meanings of individual constituents of a figurative expression. 'Accessing' refers to a more direct process, which means that a figurative meaning is readily available and a reader can get the meaning without complicated selection, activation and possibly inhibition of incorrect meanings. Although, from its description, it could be concluded that accessing should be faster than constructing, they can form a continuum of processing time; some people can quickly construct the meaning of a figurative expression, while others may take longer. One could then connect reading times to different processing patterns; a longer reading time is more likely to involve construction and a shorter reading time is more likely to involve direct access.

When discussing figurative language processing, whether L1 or L2, it is inevitable to start with the validity of the 'literal-first' hypothesis. If I associate the literal-first hypothesis with the meaning-making process above, then clearly the literal-first view is a typical process of meaning construction, which involves the selection of figurative meaning and the inhibition of literal meaning after the first stage of processing. In the last subsection, I denied its validity in the processing of conventional metaphorical expressions in one's first language; meanwhile, this hypothesis is also rejected in terms of the processing of other conventional figurative expressions, particularly idioms. When the reading times of an idiomatic expression in a biased literal context and a biased idiomatic context were compared, it was discovered that native speakers spend a significantly shorter time reading and understanding the idiomatic use than the literal use (see Glucksberg, 2001 for extended discussions). If the processing of idioms does not involve a process of (figurative meaning) selection and (literal meaning) inhibition, then it is natural to assume that native speakers do not decompose idioms into individual lexical items and construct their meanings from scratch. Thus, idioms are widely assumed to be memorized in a holistic manner by native speakers, and native speakers prefer accessing the idiomatic meaning to the literal meaning when they see a string of words that can be interpreted idiomatically. The literal-first hypothesis is also rejected in the processing of familiar proverbs, phrasal verbs and other conventional figurative expressions.

Nevertheless, due to the differences between L1 and L2, and particularly the lack of metaphorical competence of L2 learners (Kecskés 2000; Littlemore & Low 2006), one may conclude that L2 learners are not as sensitive as native speakers in terms of access to non-literal meanings. While 'literal-first' may not be the case in figurative language processing among native speakers of a language, one may still conclude that L2 learners need to spend more time reading and understanding the figurative meaning of an expression in their L2, including idioms, proverbs, phrasal verbs and metaphorical expressions. At the same time, the reading time of L2 figurative language might be influenced by factors other than figurativeness. If the assumptions of idiom acquisition is considered, particularly the Transfer Theory (Irujo, 1986b, 1993), one may see that learners have varied reading times for idioms; learners may take a shorter time to read the idioms, whether identical or similar, between their L1 and L2, while they may take a longer time to read idioms that differ between their L1 and L2. The proficiency of an L2 learner is also expected to influence the processing of figurative language, which is the same as the influence of proficiency on the processing of other structures in an L2; more proficient learners are expected to process figurative language faster than less proficient learners.

Previous studies on figurative language processing by L2 learners show conflicting patterns in different situations. Cieślicka (2006) investigates the processing of English idioms by Polish learners of English in a lexical priming test; the result indicated that learners favoured the literal meaning of English idioms when they first heard them in the experiment. She reports that learners show a faster reaction to a target if its primer is a literal expression, while they take longer time to react to the target after hearing an idiom. Cieślicka also suggests that the longer reaction time after the presentation of an idiom is due to the activation of the literal meaning of that string before learners finally arrive at the idiomatic meaning; the result of her experiment largely stays in line with the 'literal-first' assumption of idiom processing (e.g. Gibbs & Nayak 1989; Glucksberg 2001). She then argues that, different from native speakers who can directly access the idiomatic meaning, the literal meaning of an expression is always more salient among L2 learners, and L2 learners always need to construct the idiomatic meaning. Similar results have been observed in other studies (see Siyanova-Chanturia, Conklin & Schmitt 2011 for eye-tracking evidence), which show that L2 learners demonstrate a pattern of idiom processing distinct from native speakers; they treat idioms in the same line as novel expressions, and tend to derive the compositional meaning of an idiom before accessing the figurative interpretation.

However, a series of studies by Heredia and his colleagues on the processing of phrasal verbs and idioms by English learners reveal that learners are able to show a reading pattern similar to native speakers of English, and that they access the figurative meaning of an expression first. In their research, phrasal verbs are defined as a combination of verb and a prepositional particle from which the meaning cannot be directly deduced from the meaning of the verb and the meaning of the particle. Matlock and Heredia (2002) examined the reading time of English idiomatic phrasal verbs and literal verb phrases (both in the form of verb + preposition) by native speakers of English and early and late English learners. They found that learners of English, especially learners who started learning before the age of twelve, showed a reading pattern similar to that of the native speaker group, and spent significantly less time reading the idiomatic phrasal verbs. Heredia et al. (2007) examined the processing of different types of idioms in isolation and in literal, figurative and unbiased contexts by Spanish learners of English – to check the validity of Irujo's Transfer Theory in real-time idiom processing. While Transfer Theory indicates that identical or similar idioms will be processed faster by L2 learners than different idioms, the results of Heredia and others showed a contrary pattern. The different idioms in English and Spanish actually trigger faster reaction among the learners when: (1) they appear in isolation, (2) the context is not biased or (3) the context is biased to the figurative interpretation of the string. The identical or similar idioms are processed more slowly than the different idioms in the three conditions above. They then argue that idioms are stored differently in the learner's mind, depending on the form of the idioms. The idioms with different forms in L1 and L2 are stored separately and holistically in the learner's mind, which resembles the storage of idioms of native speakers, and learners can directly access the idiomatic meanings when processing those phrases. In contrast, identical or similar idioms require learners to reconstruct them in the access, which may trigger inter-language competition and ultimately slow down the processing (Heredia et al. 2007). The observations by Heredia et al. indicate that L2 learners do not always adopt the 'literal-first' strategy in the processing of figurative language, while highly proficient learners are able to identify the figurative uses of language immediately, and show a native-like processing pattern.

The conflicting results in different studies reveal that figurative language processing is a complicated phenomenon involving multiple factors; the tasks used in the studies, the test items and even the participants' native language can affect the results. The survey by Titone et al. (2015) on idiom processing by English-French bilinguals show that the figurativeness of an idiom, general familiarity to an idiom, as well as cross-linguistic similarity of an idiom between learners L1 and L2 can all influence the speed of idiom processing and the accuracy of the results, but the decomposability of an idiom does not directly influence the processing of an idiom. It should be noted that these factors are not independent from one another; a pre-test survey showed that the cross-linguistic similarity of an idiom between two languages positively correlates with the familiarity of that idiom significantly, and both of the two factors positively correlate with the decomposability of that idiom significantly. That means if an idiom is a familiar one to learners, it is usually semantically more decomposable, that is, learners find it easier to derive the meaning of the idiom from its semantic composition, and the idiom looks similar cross-linguistically between learners L1 and L2 (see also Libben & Titone 2008). The correlation between these factors might be used to explain why learners show conflicting performances across different experiments; idioms with a higher degree of cross-linguistic similarity are semantically more decomposable so a learner may be more willing to use the literal meaning of each component to derive the figurative meaning of the idiom, which leads to the early activation of the literal meanings in a string. On the other hand, less familiar idioms are not always decomposable and learners may need to memorize the idiomatic meanings separately and holistically, which may result in the direct retrieval of the figurative meaning of those idioms.

While idiom comprehension by L2 speakers has been widely surveyed in online experiments, few of the past studies have focused on the processing of conventionalized metaphorical expressions. García et al. (2015) point out that the mechanism of metaphor and idiom comprehension might be essentially different. According to García et al., the comprehension of metaphor may require more contextual information, because it is possible that metaphorical expressions, either conventional or unconventional, are not stored in the learner's mind in a holistic way, and learners may need ad hoc construction in order to get the meaning of the metaphorical expressions. On the other hand, metaphorical expressions are semantically more decomposable than some of the idioms, and learners are indeed able to rely on the compositional meaning to construct the metaphorical meaning of those expressions. Even for the metaphorical meaning itself, learners may be able to derive this from the basis of the literal meaning of the word, which might be similar to the manner native speakers process less conventional metaphorical expressions.

Finally, when comparing the results of the studies on the processing of figurative expressions mentioned above and those of the studies on the judgement or production of figurative expressions in the previous chapter, the results somehow seem to be clearly different. There is a general trend that, while learners are able to achieve a certain degree of native-like performance in a processing study, their behaviour deviates more from native speakers in an offline judgement or production study. Such a difference does not indicate that one type of study is more accurate than the other, for both are indeed able to capture the learner's performance from different perspectives. Such difference is likely to be caused by a certain degree of task-specific effect when L2 acquisition is observed in different experiments. One noticeable effect is the so-called online/offline difference, which may be used to explain the distinction between online experiments measuring the reaction time and offline experiments that examine the judgements provided by the learners. Offline tasks are generally considered to be methods that examine the explicit knowledge of learners (Sanford et al. 2004), and if an offline task involves production, it also requires the learner's active vocabulary. Online tasks, on the other hand, are believed to tap into the learner's implicit knowledge (Mitchell 2004); usually online tasks involve perception but not production, and that only requires the learner's passive vocabulary. Different results between online and offline tasks may not necessarily be conflicting; it is possible that learners can understand figurative language intuitively, but lack the confidence or enough explicit knowledge to make an active judgement, or even deliberately avoid figurative language when they are given sufficient time to produce an utterance. I will show in the second part of this book how to use both online and offline methodologies to investigate the acquisition of metaphorical expressions.

4.4 Summary and loose ends

In this chapter, I have gone through the history of psycholinguistic studies on the processing of metaphorical expressions and other figurative expressions by both native speakers of a language and second language learners. After a fine contrast between native speakers and learners processing of different types of figurative expressions, there are now some clues as to where the processing of metaphorical expressions by second language learners may fall. It is possible that second language learners can directly access the figurative meaning of a metaphorical expression without any intermediate steps, which is similar to native speakers processing patterns and closer to the processing of figurative phrasal verbs by learners. Meanwhile, considering a wider picture of learners processing of other figurative expressions, a more probable proposal is that learners may still need to access the literal meaning prior to the figurative meaning of a metaphorical expression, which leads to a 'literal-first' pattern and is distinct from a native speaker's reaction to a metaphorical expression. These discussions will all help to build and test the assumptions central to this book, how learners process and understand conventional expressions.

There is, however, a third possibility for certain learners, or if one takes a lexical semantic argument; what if learners acquire the conventionalized metaphorical meaning of a lexical item not as the 'figurative expressions' in the usual classification, but simply as a type of word meaning that is different from the literal meaning of that lexical item? Should we always convert the question of acquiring metaphorical expressions to the question of acquiring a new word meaning? If so, how do learners store this type of meaning in their mental lexicon, and do they store the two types of meaning in the same or different ways? I will deal with this problem in the next chapter from a perspective of bilingual mental lexicon.

5

Placing metaphorical expressions in a bilingual mental lexicon

5.1 Introduction

Looking at the acquisition of figurative language in a second language, either in a static offline view (as in Chapter 3) or in a dynamic online view (as in Chapter 4), it is somewhat astonishing that few studies try to connect the acquisition of figurative meanings of L2 words to the establishment and development of a bilingual lexicon. Not because the acquisition of L2 figurative language no longer forms part of the discussion on lexical acquisition, nor because people no longer investigate lexical acquisition or develop the possible frameworks of bilingual mental lexicon; I would like to attribute the lack of relevant discussion to a failure or difficulty to connect the two parts. It has been a long tradition that discussions on bilingual mental lexicons focus on: (1) single-unit lexical items, namely individual words and (2) literal meaning(s) of lexical items. One can have a clear view of such a preference in the following review of different frameworks; however, fitting metaphorical expressions or other figurative language into an established framework of a bilingual mental lexicon seems to be more difficult. In order to reach a developmental view of how metaphorical meanings of lexical items are acquired by second language learners, it is almost inevitable that one must investigate the issue in the context of bilingual lexicons. After all, people all recognize that learners successfully acquire an L2 lexical item only when they are able to associate the word form in L2 with the concept that the word represents, and there should not be any exception for metaphorical expressions.

According to the discussions in Chapter 2, the conventionalized metaphorical meanings of a lexical item are already regarded as a particular type of word meaning. In the view of lexical semantics based on the cognitive approach of metaphor, both the metaphorical meaning(s) and the literal meaning(s) of a lexical item essentially share equal status as word meaning; none of them is treated as implicature. Such an argument, however, is only established at the level of theoretical semantics. If this argument stands, the equality between the status of literal and conventional metaphorical meanings can and should be reflected in a model of word acquisition and retrieval. In order to acquire a conventional metaphorical meaning of an L2 lexical item, the learner must establish the link between the metaphorical concept and the L2 expression; also, to understand a metaphorically used word, they need to go through the link between the word form and the metaphorical meaning.

In this chapter, I will focus on several existing models of bilingual lexicons and the possibilities of fitting metaphorical meanings into these models. It should be noted that while all these frameworks focus on the links between the L1 and L2 lexicon and concepts, and some of them on the differences between the access to abstract and concrete words, few works have investigated how a metaphorical meaning can be stored in a mental lexicon and accessed in the reading process. Still, I hope to gain some insights from a combination of some of these frameworks and, possibly, get a more precise prediction to the status of metaphorical meanings and expressions in the learner's lexical knowledge. Additionally, I will discuss in detail how a classroom setting can impact upon the acquisition of metaphorical expressions. As an example, I will illustrate this issue using Chinese students learning, but similar situations can be observed across the world where students of a second or foreign language receive only limited exposure to a classroom setting.

At the end of this chapter, I will derive a developmental framework of a bilingual lexicon for both literal and metaphorical meanings. This framework aims to capture the semantic connection between the literal and metaphorical meanings of a single lexical item, as well as the influence of cross-linguistic availability of metaphorical expressions on the storage of metaphorical meanings in a bilingual lexicon (while literal expressions are assumed to be shared between the learner's two languages). This framework will be used to provide hypotheses on the acquisition of metaphorical expressions, which will be examined in Chapter 7.

5.2 Storing concrete and abstract words and meanings in a bilingual mental lexicon

As discussed in Chapter 2, in lexical semantics one of the decisive differences between the literal and metaphorical meanings of a lexical item is that the former is usually concrete while the latter is more abstract. Such difference of concreteness, according to the CMT, is based on the different conceptual domain in which a meaning is constructed; the literal meaning is constructed in a concrete conceptual domain, while the metaphorical meaning is established in an abstract conceptual domain. If a conceptual blending approach is adopted, then the literal meaning represents a 'pure' concept, but the metaphorical meaning is a blend of several concepts. Although learners sometimes do not feel the difference of concreteness, such a difference may impact on the way of storing meaning in the learner's mental lexicon, especially when the mental lexicon involves more than one language. In this section I will first look at whether concrete and abstract lexical items are stored differently in a mental lexicon, and then move to question whether concrete and abstract meanings of the same lexical item are stored differently.

The Distributed Feature Model (DFM) is a notable framework of a bilingual mental lexicon that takes the difference between concrete and abstract words into consideration. It was first proposed by De Groot (1992; see also Van Hell & De Groot 1998) and further developed by Kroll and De Groot (1997) into the Distributed Conceptual Feature Model (DCFM). The essence of De Groot's proposal was that the concepts that match a lexical item are never a unified, indivisible entity, but are a series of concepts represented as interconnected nodes. In earlier frameworks of semantic memory (cf. Hierarchical Network Model of Semantic Memory by Quillan 1966), it was proposed that a word can be associated with several relevant concepts, and the meaning of that word, therefore, consists of the relationship between that word and other relevant words. 'Concepts' in those frameworks are illustrated in a late-Wittgenstein style (Wittgenstein 1953); there was no clear boundary between two words or two concepts, although some 'core, stable' features that were relatively independent of contexts could be shared across speakers and languages. In some situations, a single concept may vary depending on the context in which it appears, and the meaning of a word may largely depend on the context.

Taking this as an assumption, De Groot further elaborated on the possibilities of word activation in a bilingual network. She suggested that, given that a word can be linked to several conceptual representations (hence the framework is called 'distributed conceptual'), a pair of translation equivalents may share the full set of conceptual representations, or only part of the set, as illustrated in Figure 5.1. It is also possible for a pair of translation equivalents to refer to slightly different concepts in the two languages, because some of the meaning representations are not shared between them. De Groot stated that it was very likely that some concepts may be represented by a single lexical item in a learner's L1, but not in L2; that does not indicate that the learners cannot express the equivalent of such a lexical item in general, but simply that such concepts are not representable in a single lexical item in L2. The different proficiency levels for learners, as well as learners' different understandings of the conceptual representation of lexical items, can often lead to an asymmetry in reaction time and accuracy for a pair of translation equivalents, and moreover, an imbalance in the construction of the bilingual lexicon by a L2 learner.

As shown in Figure 5.1, a pair of translation equivalents in two different languages, either cognates or non-cognates, can each connect to a series of conceptual elements. Among the conceptual elements shown, some may be experientially based (usually), relatively stable across different contexts and therefore recognized as 'core' elements. Other elements may be more context-dependent and can be constructed in an ad hoc manner. The conceptual elements are linked to either of the translation equivalents. A few of them (in grey) are shared between the two words, which means that those concepts are more language-neutral. The white elements, on the other hand, are generally more language-specific. In the situation indicated by Figure 5.1, the pair of translation equivalents has a partial meaning overlap; it is possible that, in other cases, two translation equivalents may have either a full overlap of conceptual features, or only a slight overlap.

De Groot proposes that the degree of overlap of conceptual features across a learner's L1 and L2 is a decisive factor in the learner's speed and quality of performance in translation tasks. If a pair of translation equivalents share more conceptual features, the learner is more likely to perform better in the translation task by reacting faster to the pair and providing more accurate answers. De Groot does not discuss the link between the word forms of L1 and L2; instead, she vaguely hints that the connection between L1 and L2 words is via the shared conceptual features; if the L1 and L2 words share more conceptual features, the

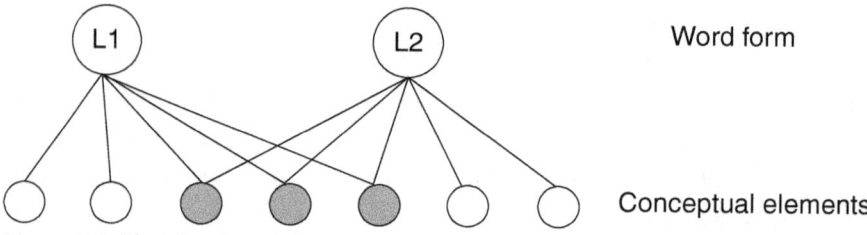

Figure 5.1 The Distributed Conceptual Feature Model (adapted from De Groot 1992)

connection between the two words is stronger. From my perspective, it should be expected that a pair of translation equivalents will be more transferable if they share more conceptual features, because there is a stronger, more stable link between the L1 and L2 words. A learner is more likely to receive cross-linguistic influence from L1 when accessing L2 words with a stronger conceptual overlap, because the L1 words are more likely to be co-activated.

In the DCFM, the degree of overlap of conceptual representations between a pair of translation equivalents can be attributed to three major factors, namely: the cognate status, the part of speech and the concreteness of a word. From a semantic perspective, the relationship between the concreteness of a word and its conceptual representation in a bilingual lexicon is of the greatest interest. Concrete words are considered to share more conceptual features than abstract words, because two concrete words are more likely to refer to one single concrete entity in the real world without any significant difference, but the concepts referred to by the abstract words would be less obvious in the real world, and it would be more difficult to evaluate the similarity of concepts cross-linguistically.

We can take the DCFM as a primary model and further extend it to a framework of a bilingual lexicon that is compatible with metaphorical meanings of lexical items. While the DCFM focuses on the differences between abstract words and concrete words in a mental lexicon, it still maintains the traditional assumption of other frameworks of bilingual lexicons as a premise; there is always a one-to-one mapping between words and meanings, even if a meaning can be decomposed to several conceptual elements. However, as discussed in Chapter 2, even a single lexical item can be linked to both concrete and abstract meanings, which is exactly the case of literal versus metaphorical expressions. Therefore, a comparison can be made between the concrete and abstract meanings of a pair of translation equivalents to see whether different meanings of a pair of lexical items are represented in different ways in a learner's mental lexicon.

Indeed, previous research has discovered that the DCFM could be an ideal model to illustrate the acquisition and processing of polysemous words in a bilingual lexicon. Finkbeiner et al. (2004; see also Xia & Andrews 2015) developed the 'Sense Model', which also utilizes distributed conceptual features and specifically focuses on polysemous words. Finkbeiner and colleagues point out that the DCFM does not reasonably explain the asymmetry between L1 and L2 and L2 and L1 priming in a translation task, and they attribute this difference to the asymmetry of polysemy status in a learner's L1 and L2. It can easily be recognized that many lexical items are polysemous; in some cases, this may result from the conventionalized use of metaphorical expressions, while other cases may be due to historical reasons. Finkbeiner and his colleagues assume that only a small number of meanings may be determinate for a pair of translation equivalents to be 'equivalent', while the rest of the meanings are not 'equivalent', and sometimes are without any counterpart in the other language. Therefore, as shown in Figure 5.2, learners may well be aware of every possible meaning of the polysemous word 'A' in their L1, but only know a couple of the most prominent meanings of the translation equivalent 'B' in their L2. Among the meanings of the translation equivalent B, it is more likely that the basic meaning(s) that makes A and B a pair of translation equivalents will be known; for example, among all the meanings of the word 'attack', a Chinese learner of English is most likely to know it as 'to try to hurt or defeat using violence', because that meaning matches the meaning of *gongji*, the translation equivalent of attack in Chinese. At the same time, the learner may not be aware of other meanings of the L2 word B; those meanings may include not only meanings that are exclusively available in L2, but also some peripheral meanings shared between L1 and L2. The above assumption of the Sense Model also explains why the priming effect from L1 to L2 is significantly stronger than the priming effect from the L2 word to L1 between a pair of translation equivalents; as indicated in Figure 5.2, the meaning(s) of the L2 word that the learner knows reflects the meaning(s) shared between the L1 and L2 words, and the presence of the L1 word can always activate all the meanings of the L2 word known by the learner. However, the presence of the L2 word can only activate part of the L1 meanings (in the graph, 20 per cent), hence a weaker priming effect. Finkbeiner and colleagues (2004) observed that, while the priming effect from L2 words to L1 semantic categories

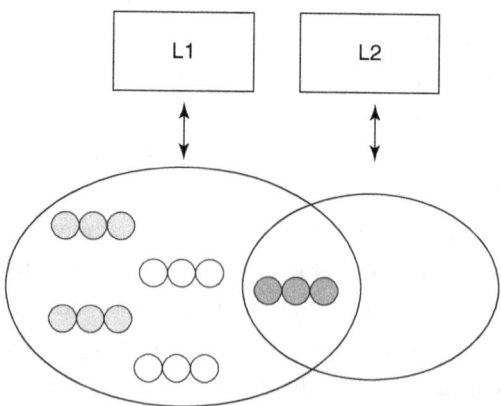

Figure 5.2 The Sense Model (adapted from Finkbeiner et al. 2004)

is robust, there is a lack of priming effect from L2 words to L1 individual words in a translation task. The Sense Model suggests that this difference is due to the lack of knowledge of polysemy in L2; learners can always activate the full L1 meaning of a semantic category if they attempt to find the semantic category of an L2 word, and thus show a robust L2 to L1 priming effect. However, they can only partly activate L1 meanings when translating individual words, and thus the priming effect is absent in a translation task.

To summarize, the concepts, features, relationships between individual words and conceptual features, and the cross-linguistic differences in conceptual representations illustrated in the DCFM (as well as in the subsequent Sense Model) perfectly fit the requirements of an investigation into the acquisition of metaphorical meanings, especially if one would like to explore the difference between metaphorical meanings and literal meanings of the same lexical item in the learner's bilingual lexicon. De Groot adopts a late-Wittgenstein view in her model, presuming that a word is not linked to a single, unified and static concept all the time, but can shift between several concepts that are largely similar, but with fine-grained, minor differences. The Sense Model also directly points out that the framework is applicable to polysemous lexical items, either monolingual or bilingual. Those views further coincide with a few works on the emergence of conventionalized metaphorical meanings from different aspects. On the one hand, a cognitive semantic approach to metaphor (cf. Sweetser 1990) would stress that there is a natural link between the literal and metaphorical concepts represented by a single word. The logic here is simple; people will use a single word to refer to two distinct concepts only if they perceive that the two concepts share much in common. On the other hand, radical contextualist approaches, such as those of Leezenberg (2001), Recanati (2004) and Stern (2000), follow the view of Wittgenstein and suggest that the metaphorical interpretation of a lexical item is triggered by the context in which it appears. Although the two branches offer distinct proposals for the actual functions of a metaphor, they do not contradict or exclude each other in terms of the relationship between the metaphorical meaning and the literal meaning of a word. They also jointly support the possibility that the metaphorical meanings and the literal meanings can be represented by several conceptual features in semantic memory, which shows congruence with the DCFM (or the Sense Model). Depending on the context, either the conceptual features related to the metaphorical meanings or those related to literal meanings can be activated.

The influence of concreteness on the distribution of conceptual features, although not the most important statement in the whole framework, leaves sufficient space for an explanation of the acquisition and real-time processing of metaphorical expressions. Due to the nature of their experiments, neither De Groot nor Finkbeiner and colleagues discussed in detail the fact that concreteness can vary according to the meaning of a single word (or 'senses' in Finkbeiner et al. 2004). In their research, words are simply divided into two categories, either concrete or abstract. This is because in a word translation task lexical items appear individually and there is no context to indicate the concrete or abstract meaning(s) of that word. In real language use, however, a polysemous word can appear with either a more concrete or a more abstract meaning, depending on the context in which it is used. This is particularly prominent in experiments wherein which the metaphorical use and the literal use of a single word are contrasted. By definition, the metaphorical use of a word is the linguistic outcome of mapping a concrete conceptual domain to an abstract one (Lakoff & Johnson 1980; Lakoff & Turner 1989) or, to take an Aristotelian view (Aristotle, *Rhetoric* III.21, 1475b1–30) the metaphorically used word is the 'transference' of a concrete word to an abstract context. Both definitions indicate that when a word involves conventional uses in both a literal and a metaphorical way, it can be linked to both concrete and abstract conceptual representations. The concrete concepts reside in their own concrete domain, associated with the literal meanings of that word, and the abstract concepts associated with the metaphorical meanings are involved in cross-domain mapping. Therefore, it may also be expected that the processing difference between concrete and abstract words indicated in the DCFM will be replicated in the concrete and abstract meanings of a single word.

De Groot, as well as Finkbeiner and colleagues, further outlines how the concreteness of words can affect the conceptual representations between a pair of translation equivalents. Although neither of them explicitly links such differences to a possible trace of cross-linguistic influence, a series of feasible connections can be made regarding the concreteness of a pair of translation equivalents, the degree of overlap in conceptual elements of that pair, and the transferability of that pair. As has been discussed above, concrete pairs share more conceptual elements than abstract pairs; if a pair of translation equivalents shares more conceptual elements, then learners are more likely to use the L2 translation equivalent in the way they use the L1 word, that is, to transfer the use of the L1 word to L2. Thus, it may be expected that a pair of concrete translation equivalents will be more transferable than a pair of abstract translation equivalents. If a further step is taken and the assumption is extended to a pair of concrete and abstract meanings of a single word, it may then be expected that the concrete, literal meaning shared by a pair of translation equivalents will be more transferable than the abstract, metaphorical meaning. Due to the influence of concreteness, it can be assumed that even if the abstract, metaphorical meaning is also shared between the pair, it will still be less transferable than the concrete, literal meaning, which may lead to an asymmetric performance when a learner is asked to judge or process the abstract, metaphorical use. Note that this seems to contradict the proposal of Jordens and Kellerman (1981), who claim that the transferability of meaning of a lexical item is not significantly influenced by the concreteness of that meaning.

While it has been well-received, problems have been identified with the DCFM in recent discussions. Although De Groot has developed a rather consistent system to describe the difference of conceptual mapping between a pair of translation equivalents, the method used in the DCFM to represent the conceptual difference, namely the feature-based approach, is a rather primitive and outdated model in cognitive psychology (Pavlenko 2009). When one perceives a concept or connects a concept to a lexical item in a language, one does not always decompose the concept into a variety of features or operate the conceptual features in a parametric way in order to formulate a concept. Instead, one may construct prototypes to represent a concept and fine-tune those prototypes to context-specific concepts according to the given context. This discrepancy can actually be reflected in the area of metaphorical expressions; the literal meaning of a lexical item is usually the prototype of a series of concepts, and the metaphorical meaning of that lexical item is modified based on the literal meaning, the context in which it appears, and the conceptual domain mentioned in the context. If a framework for the mental lexicon is intended to reflect the delicate differences in matching concepts and lexical items between languages in the human mind, it should take the form of conceptual representation into consideration. Throughout this book, I have adopted a prototype model of conceptual representation and have not decomposed a concept into several features. When I address the similarities between a literal concept and a metaphorical concept that are associated with the same lexical item, I simply use a link to show that the two concepts are interconnected.

Another point that may indicate a need for further modification is that the DCFM does not directly reflect the developmental path of L2 learners and the role of cross-linguistic influence in the developmental process. The original DFM proposal was established as a possible model for a balanced, proficient bilingual lexicon, and from Figure 5.1 it can be seen that an L2 lexical item can and should be accessed via conceptual mediation, that is, constituting a direct link from conceptual to lexical level. However, that is not usually the case, at least not for every lexical item; Dufour and Kroll (1995) report that conceptual mediation is common among more fluent bilinguals, while less fluent bilinguals may have limited direct access to the conceptual level from the lexical level. As I will show in the next section, less proficient learners are considered to rely on the lexical link between a pair of translation equivalents, from L1 and L2, in order to access the conceptual meaning of the L2 lexical item. This means the DCFM may not represent the bilingual lexicon of a less proficient learner, and the structure of the bilingual lexicon of a less proficient learner may be critically differ from the picture shown in the DCFM. The Sense Model, on the other hand, assumes that a developmental trend can be observed when a learner acquires more meanings of a polysemous word, but it does not (aim to) explain which meaning(s) are more likely to be acquired and, more specifically, how a learner decides where a meaning of a polysemous word should be placed in the mental lexicon. When a learner acquires a shared metaphorical meaning, will it be successfully placed in the area shared by L1 and L2? When a metaphorical meaning that is only available in the L1 is encountered, will it be transferred to L2? When a metaphorical meaning that is only available in L2 is encountered, will the link between that meaning and the L2 word form be successfully established? Those questions are yet to be answered.

5.3 Bilingual mental lexicon in a developmental view

While some theories of bilingual lexicon suggest that a lexical item does not always map to a solid, unified entity at the conceptual level, most of the models of the bilingual lexicon do not emphasize this feature. Instead, they pay significantly more attention to what framework can best capture the relationship between three elements: the concept (as an entire, inseparable entity), the L1 word, and the L2 word. In this way, the L1 and L2 words are usually recognized as a pair of translation equivalents without any additional need to specify their degree of 'equivalence'. This is due to the tradition of discussions on the bilingual lexicon from the era of Kolers (1963), who particularly focused on the debate over the compound or coordinate organization of bilingual lexicon. Recent discussions, including all the frameworks reviewed in this chapter, generally favour a compound organization of a bilingual lexicon, in which the L1 word and the L2 word are connected with a single concept. A sequential bilingual who acquires an L2 has already acquired an L1, and has a comprehensive structure that organizes the L1 lexicon and relevant concepts. In acquiring the L2 vocabulary, there are two major possibilities for integrating the new L2 words into the mental lexicon. Either the L2 word can be linked to the L1 translation equivalent, which is called 'word association', or the L2 word may be directly attached to the concept, without any assistance from the L1 translation equivalent, and that is called 'concept mediation'.

However, the results of experiments and even simple retrospective analysis reveal that neither of the frameworks can solely represent the structure of the bilingual lexicon of a sequential bilingual. Previous studies show that more and less proficient learners may rely on concept mediation to different extents in a single lexical decision task (e.g. Dufour & Kroll 1995). This not only shows that concept mediation is not fully available to all second language learners, but also indicates that word association is not the universal method of bilingual lexicon organization either; the presence of concept mediation among more proficient learners indicates that they may not rely on word association to make lexical judgements. Furthermore, as has been discussed, it is probable that a learner may acquire an L2 word for which the associated concept is actually not available in L1, which will lead to the absence of the link between L1 and L2 words. Therefore, a third possibility for the organization of the bilingual lexicon is a combination of the two basic assumptions, namely word association and concept mediation, depending on the learner's proficiency as well as the availability of concepts and lexical items in different languages.

At the same time it is also expected that, an increase in proficiency, learners, especially those acquiring a second language in a classroom setting, may change their way of organizing bilingual lexicon and retrieving L2 lexical items. It is common for learners to map the L2 words they have acquired to the corresponding L1 words at an early stage of acquisition; actually, it is less likely that they will display different types of lexical transfer (see Chapter 3) if the L1 and the L2 mental lexicons are separate. The effect may become more prominent if learners receive instructions in both L1 and L2, which was exactly the case with the experiments reported in this book. When learners become more proficient in their L2, they may gradually abandon the way of word association and utilize concept mediation more in L2 processing. I hope to establish a developmental model that is able to capture the whole process from non-acquisition to full mastery of a lexical item.

The Revised Hierarchical Model (RHM) of Kroll and Stewart (1994) aims to integrate the two basic assumptions, namely word association and concept mediation, and provide a comprehensive picture of the bilingual lexicon across

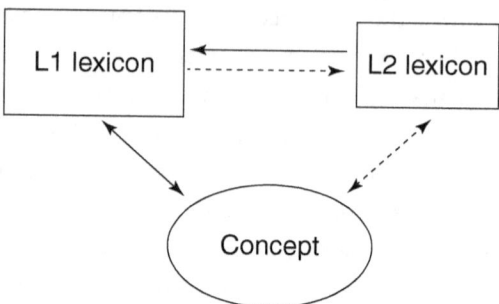

Figure 5.3 The Revised Hierarchical Model (adapted from Kroll and Stewart 1994)

L2 acquisition. The RHM is based on an old version of the Hierarchical Model, an alternative form of the shared storage system; a brief illustration is given in Figure 5.3. Three main components are usually considered to be involved in the RHM: a larger L1 vocabulary indicated by a larger rectangle; a smaller L2 vocabulary indicated by a smaller rectangle; and a group of individual concepts. One prominent feature of the RHM is that the direction and strength of the links between any two components are explicated in the framework, which leads to a possible elaboration of the developmental trend of the bilingual lexicon and more precise predictions of experimental results. The links between the L1 and L2 vocabulary stand for word association and display clear asymmetry; the link from L2 to L1 is stronger than the link the other way around. This follows the asymmetry shown in bidirectional translation tasks in which translation from L2 to L1 is usually faster than from L1 to L2. Both the L1 and L2 lexicons are linked to a group of concepts, but the strength of the links is significantly different. While the link between the L1 lexicon and concepts is solid and strong, the link between the L2 lexicon and concepts, which represents concept mediation, is relatively weaker. The weaker link indicates that concept mediation always exists, even for less proficient learners, but its function and scope may be more restricted compared with the link between the L1 lexicon and concepts. With a growth in proficiency of the L2, it is expected that the link from L1 to L2 word forms (backward translation) and the link between L2 word forms and concepts will gradually be strengthened.

The RHM provides feasible explanations for two major concerns in research on second language vocabulary acquisition that previous forms of the hierarchical model failed to cater for. The most prominent advantage of an RHM is that it illustrates the developmental order of the second language lexicon within its framework. Such an illustration can be used to explain a series of developmental changes (e.g. Dufour & Kroll 1995) in the actual learning process or among learners at different levels of proficiency, either in a classroom setting or in more naturalistic environments of vocabulary acquisition. The RHM recognizes that word association and concept mediation co-exist in the bilingual lexicon and assumes that the association between an L2 word and its L1 translation equivalent is inevitable, even if the L1 is not used as the language of instruction. While all three major components always exist in the bilingual lexicon, what changes with the progress of a learner is the strength of each link in the framework, rather than the presence or absence of each link. The differences in performance caused by different proficiency levels or different acquisition environments are, therefore, explained as a quantitative matter rather than a qualitative one.

The other strength of the RHM, which is more closely related to second language processing, is that it considers the retrieval of a lexical item in second language comprehension. From a general psycholinguistic point of view, the comprehension of a word can be seen as a real-time reactivation of the link between the word form and its corresponding concept. Only when the relevant concept is matched to the word form can the word or larger constituent be fully understood by the processer. Therefore, the reaction time to a word, no matter what language it is in, can be used to indicate the length and/or strength of the link between that word and the concept it is linked to in the framework. It is generally and naturally assumed that a learner always minimizes the temporal and cognitive cost of word comprehension; in RHMs, such minimization of costs is accomplished by taking 'the fastest route possible', which can be either the shortest link or the strongest link, depending on availability. When reading an L2 word, a more proficient learner can directly link the word and the corresponding concept together, but a less proficient learner may rely on a detour via the L1 word to establish that link because the link between the L2 word and the concept is not strong enough to minimize the temporal cost. Therefore, it can be hypothesized that a more proficient learner can react faster to a word that has been learned, while a less proficient learner may take a substantially longer time to react to a word, even if taking 'the fastest route' possible in the bilingual lexicon (cf. Athanasopoulos 2015).

The shortcomings and gaps in RHM have been discussed extensively in previous literature. Criticism comes from several points of view, such as the problem of asymmetry in terms of the lexical link between the L1 and L2 lexical items, and the over-simplified structure of the bilingual lexicon (Brysbaert & Duyck 2010). Like other models of bilingual lexicon, except DCFM, RHM assumes that a lexical item can only map onto one solid concept, and thus emphasizes the overall structure of the bilingual lexicon more, in terms of the two sets of vocabulary and a set of concepts. Without further specification, one can only assume that in RHMs each pair of translation equivalents can, and can only, connect to an individual concept, and two translation equivalents (or near-equivalents when full equivalents are not available) will always connect to the exact same concept. Such assumptions of word-concept mapping, according to Brysbaert and Duyck, largely ignore homonyms, homophones and polysemy, which are widely spread across languages, because those lexical items involve one-to-more rather than one-to-one mappings between word form and concept.

The problem with the representation of metaphorical expressions in the bilingual lexicon is in line with the over-simplification discussed by Brysbaert and Duyck. Basically, RHM cannot effectively reflect the acquisition of several meanings of a polysemous word, and one needs to duplicate the concept or create additional concepts to ensure that the learner has stored all the meanings of that polysemous word. For a metaphorical meaning of a word, the problem may be even more complicated if the relationship between the literal meaning and the metaphorical meaning of that word is considered. To clarify the current situation, I refer to a pair of translation equivalents; attack in English and *gongji* in Chinese, both of which can be used literally to describe an aggressive physical act, and metaphorically to describe an aggressive verbal argument against a theory. Thus, both the literal meaning and the metaphorical meaning are shared between the two languages. Obviously, the metaphorical meaning is related to the literal meaning, and both meanings should be connected to the word form of the lexical item in each language.

Figure 5.4 shows the structure of two-word forms and two concepts for a Chinese learner of English. The line weights indicate the length of each link.

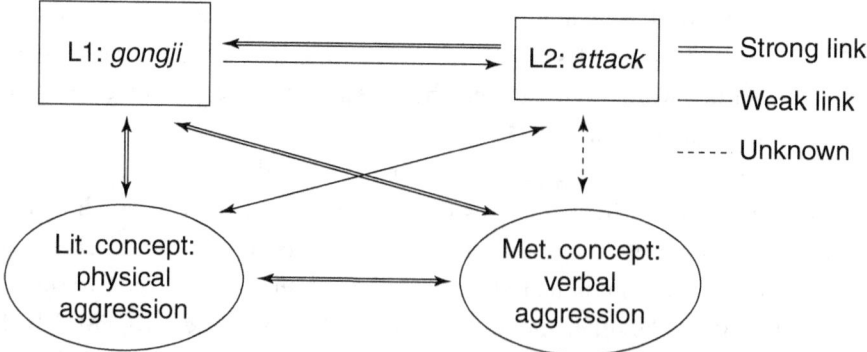

Figure 5.4 The structure of *gongji*, attack and relevant concepts in an RHM fashion presentation

The double lines indicate established strong links and the single lines indicate established weak links. The dashed lines indicate that the links are 'unknown, to be confirmed'; this means it is unknown if the learner has established those links, or how strong they are. The link between the two concepts means that they are associated with each other, while it is not clear whether a learner is aware of that. For the majority of words, the acquisition of the metaphorical meaning in L2 usually happens no earlier than the acquisition of the literal meaning of a word in L2[1]. Therefore, by the time learners experience the meaning, they will know that both the literal and metaphorical concepts are linked to the L1 word form *gongji* and will already have established the links between L2 word forms and the literal concept. They may also have subconscious knowledge that the two types of aggression are linked on a conceptual level. The RHM, however, cannot make any prediction regarding the situation above, because it does not give any explanation of how an existing concept and an existing L2 word form might be connected at the time of acquisition. In the view of the current version of the RHM, the metaphorical concept should be treated as a new concept, and the lexical items in the two languages should be treated as novel words that the learner has no knowledge of; this means that a polysemous word is seen as a homonymous word with two irrelevant meanings. In RHMs, the learner cannot make use of previous L2 word knowledge in the acquisition of a related word meaning of a known word. This view is problematic for metaphorical expressions with a polysemous nature; as is discussed in Section 2.3, a language user may be able to infer the metaphorical meaning from the literal meaning if given sufficient contextual clues and instructions. I therefore assume that it is at least possible for a learner to make use of the link between the L2 word form and the literal concept to establish the link between the L2 word form and the metaphorical concept. The mechanism of RHMs blocks the route without verifying its probability, while one target of the current research is to examine the availability of the route in different conditions.

Furthermore, in a similar way to the problem mentioned above, the RHM can neither predict how a learner will suppress a metaphorical meaning if it is only available in L1, nor how that learner will acquire a metaphorical meaning that is only available in L2. That problem leads to another shortcoming of RHMs; RHMs generally assume that all concepts are shared cross-linguistically, and thus fail to recognize the existence of language-specific concepts. Pavlenko (2009) has extensively discussed the existence of language-specific concepts and the transfer of those concepts among bilingual speakers. She then proposed the Modified Hierarchical Model (MHM) to illustrate how conceptual differences between two languages can be represented in the bilingual lexicon. The most significant difference between an MHM and an RHM is that the former demonstrates how conceptual categories can be linked to different word forms; this clearly illustrates how conceptual transfer happens in second language acquisition. The strong point of the MHM is that it proposes 'conceptual restructuring' as a special type of transfer from L1 to L2, in which a learner can transfer some L1-specific conceptual categories when establishing the link between the L2 word and the shared categories. This can explain why an English learner of Russian may transfer the conceptual category represented by cup to *chashka*. Conversely, it may also be possible to link some L2-specific categories to the L1 word form at some stages of L2 acquisition, which will lead to conceptual transfer from L2 to L1. The acquisition of L2 lexical items can thus be seen as a type of conceptual restructuring and, with progress in L2 acquisition, the learner is gradually able to categorize concepts in an L2-specific fashion. An illustration of the MHM is shown in Figure 5.5.

Considering the main emphases and the structure of an MHM, it can be seen as an integrated and updated version of both a DCFM and a RHM. It can reflect both the conceptual difference between a pair of (near) translation equivalents and the developmental trend of the bilingual lexicon. However, transfer of metaphorical meaning is a form of lemmatic transfer rather than concept transfer, and thus it

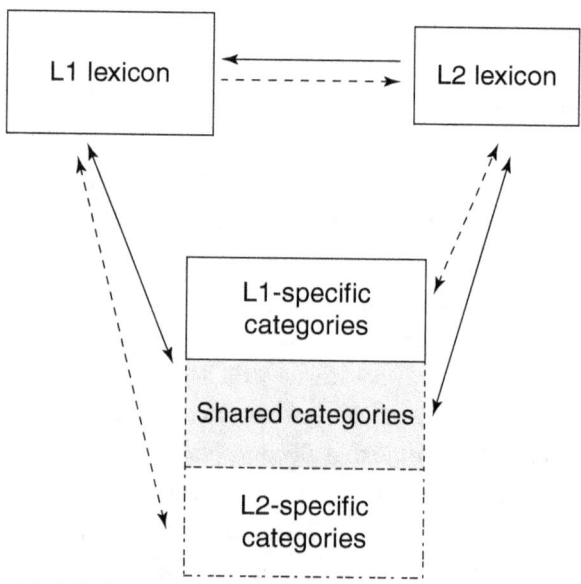

Figure 5.5 The Modified Hierarchical Model (adapted from Pavlenko 2009)

cannot be accommodated in an MHM. While Pavlenko (2009) suggests that the literal and metaphorical concepts of a single lexical item should be treated as if they were two unrelated, independent concepts, previous discussion in Section 1.2.2 has shown that these two meanings are actually relevant to each other from the perspective of both lexical and cognitive semantics. An additional proposal is still needed to elaborate the acquisition of metaphorical expressions and the relationship between the literal and metaphorical meanings (or concepts) of a lexical item.

To summarize, both RHMs and MHMs clearly illustrate how learners with different proficiencies can process words in different ways, but the acquisition of metaphorical expressions and other polysemous lexical items is left untouched. The neglect of 'one-to-many word-concept mapping' makes it impossible to explain using RHM, while MHM realizes that the problem exists, but avoids it since it is not the major topic or the main motive of Pavlenko's proposal. While other aspects of the bilingual lexicon have been discussed in detail and these two frameworks can serve as a basis for a developmental view of a bilingual lexicon framework, the interaction between the bilingual lexicon and semantic transfer is not fully explored, and this is particularly related to the acquisition of metaphorical expressions in a second language. More discussion is needed to explain how a learner can connect a pair of translation equivalents to a number of different but related concepts, and how cross-linguistic influence happens in the process of acquisition.

5.4 Acquiring different meanings in a classroom setting

While previous frameworks for the bilingual lexicon reviewed in this chapter are generally applicable to language acquisition in different environments, it is worth noting that the acquisition of metaphorical expressions may behave differently in a classroom setting. This could be Chinese learners of English, as is illustrated in the experiments in Chapter 7, English learners of Chinese or other learners of a foreign language. In these cases, the process of acquisition or learning is restricted in a classroom setting while the target language is generally not used in other environments outside the classroom. It is possible that some features of such a kind of second language classroom learning may affect the formation of a bilingual lexicon, which will make the acquisition of metaphorical expressions different from acquiring literal expressions. Therefore, the difference between classroom learning and other types of lexical acquisition should be taken into consideration in order to make better predictions for the outcome of that acquisition. This subsection is a review of the features of lexical acquisition in the classroom setting.

Ma (2009) presents in detail some advantages, as well as a larger number of constraints, in vocabulary acquisition in classroom teaching, using the English classroom in China as a prominent example. She concludes that, although highly motivated, learners usually do not receive a satisfactory outcome in the acquisition of L2 vocabulary in a classroom setting. She argues that the failure of L2 vocabulary learning is rooted in several factors, which includes a culture of learning that emphasizes only hard-work, but has no proper strategy, as well as the historical methodology of vocabulary teaching and the lack of professional teaching personnel. Observed among Chinese learners of English, the acquisition of vocabulary is consistently emphasized and students pay great attention to it, but methods are restricted simply to memorization and grammar-translation tasks, while other skills relevant to the inference of word meanings and figurative language are largely neglected due to outdated instruction methods and limited exposure to language materials. In particular, L2 formulaic expressions, such as idioms and grammatical sequences, are never the central part of vocabulary teaching, and even advanced learners are less likely to manage these expressions.

Ma does not extend her discussion to the acquisition of metaphorical uses of words in English specifically; therefore, it is not clear whether the Chinese learners of English are able to derive metaphorical meanings of lexical items, even if they are not explicitly taught such knowledge in a classroom setting. Nevertheless, it can be inferred from the current situation, especially from the lack of systematic contents related to the metaphorical uses of words and the execution of figurative thinking (see Kecskés 2000; Littlemore & Low 2006 for examples) in English textbooks and courses, that L2 learners in a classroom setting may show a gap in terms of metaphor comprehension and production, and this is a great obstacle to a higher proficiency in English.

Jiang (2000) identified two major constraints on the acquisition of lexical items in a classroom setting. He characterized classroom learning as a process that lacks a 'sufficient and highly contextualized input in the target language' (Jiang 2000: 49). The lack of natural input, in his view, creates obstacles to learners in their retrieval of semantic, syntactic and morphological information autonomously. From the perspective of lexical semantics, this constraint could indicate that, through the classroom learning process, learners may: (1) only successfully acquire some of the meanings/uses of a lexical item that have been fully mastered by the native speakers and (2) be less able to utilize the contextual information in a sentence to derive the possible meaning of a word in it.

The other constraint is the role of the L1 in the process of L2 acquisition. Although, as discussed in Chapter 3, cross-linguistic influence is inevitable in second language acquisition, the role of L1 may be even more prominent and influential in a second language classroom. When a second language is introduced as a part of curriculum, it is usually learned after learners have fully acquired their L1. By the time the learners start acquiring their L2, they have already established the connection between a series of concepts and the corresponding L1 expressions. Therefore, learners who have acquired a word in the L2 will tend to establish a lexical link between L1 and L2 translation equivalents, exactly as described in an RHM (Kroll & Stewart 1994). That may lead to a transfer of meanings from L1 to L2; the learners might connect the conceptual elements or bundles that are only available in L1 to the L2 lexical item, while at the same time not being aware of the conceptual elements that are only available in L2, since there is nothing to transfer which means there might be a failure to acquire a certain part of L2. In addition, the learner's ability to extract information from contextual cues in their L2 is also largely suppressed when they rely too much on L1. It may be more difficult to infer the meaning of a new lexical item from the given context, or to summarize the morphological or syntactic features of the lexical item. In a similar fashion, the learner may be less sensitive to the metaphorical meanings of a lexical item and may fail to derive a possible metaphorical meaning from the literal meaning of the lexical item and the contextual information, even if the literal meaning of the lexical item has already been acquired. The same problem has been identified in the teaching process; English teaching in the classroom, especially in primary and secondary education, frequently utilizes Chinese as the medium language. Teachers generally rely on translation equivalents to teach the words in L2 (Jiang 2004), especially at the initial stage when learners are relatively young (e.g. in primary education). Therefore, the connection between the L2 word and its translation equivalent in L1 is relatively strong, while the link between the L2 word and its own semantic specification is weaker, thus the transfer from L1 words to L2 words will be more obvious in that situation.

Both of these constraints, as analysed above, are likely to lead to obstacles to the successful acquisition of metaphorical expressions. A lack of sufficient input may lead to a lack of exposure to the metaphorical uses of some lexical items; as a consequence, it is highly possible that a learner will understand the literal meanings of the lexical items but fail to accept the metaphorical uses. At the same time, a weakened ability to utilize contexts and draw inferences may result in an inability to derive a valid interpretation of metaphorical expressions, and thus a learner may be unable to understand and acquire a metaphorical expression on their own. The reliance on translation equivalents in classroom teaching may also trigger some unnecessary transfer from L1 to L2, especially for those who have only limited cumulative exposure to L2 materials.

However, there is still some space left for the acquisition of certain metaphorical expressions. According to Jiang (2007), linguistic knowledge of the L2 possessed by the learners in a classroom setting comes mainly from three different sources: the learner's own knowledge of the L1 and knowledge of the L2 through cross-linguistic transfer; some internalized knowledge gained through exposure to L2 language materials and interaction; and knowledge explicitly taught by the instructors. If some metaphorical expressions appear in learning materials, a learner may be able to identify, memorize and correctly use them, even without realizing that those expressions are metaphorical. Or, in a similar fashion, if instructors point out that a direct translation of an L1-specific metaphorical expression is not acceptable in L2 (e.g. the notion of 'Chinglish' suggested by Chinese learners of English), then a learner might avoid using it. Overall, whether a learner can successfully acquire a metaphorical expression mainly depends on the classroom input, that is, the contents of textbooks and explicit teaching. That means that if a metaphorical expression has previously appeared in teaching materials, it is more likely to be acquired and accepted by a learner, compared with metaphorical expressions that are not explicitly taught in language courses. On the other hand, when a learner receives some metaphorical expressions as input in a non-guided situation, it is more difficult to take these expressions in, to make native-like judgements of them, or even to use them efficiently in production.

Two major hypotheses can be drawn from the analysis above: (1) compared to native speakers of the target language, who should accept both the literal and the metaphorical meanings of a lexical item, L2 learners will be more reluctant to accept the metaphorical meanings than the literal meanings, and this will be more obvious if the metaphorical meanings are only available in L2, and (2) L2 learners, especially those with less knowledge of L2, will demonstrate a certain degree of negative transfer when they are asked to comprehend and produce some expressions that are available in L1 but impossible in L2. These hypotheses can be tested, but only if a comparison is made between a group of learners and a group of native speakers.

5.5 Hypotheses for the status of metaphorical expressions in a bilingual lexicon

We can conclude from the previous sections that, while native speakers treat metaphorical expressions in a similar way to literal expressions, it may be more difficult for learners to treat conventionalized metaphorical meanings of a lexical item in the same way as the literal meanings of the same lexical item. The difference between literal and metaphorical meanings in a learner's bilingual lexicon is mainly due to two aspects: (1) the relative abstractness of metaphorical meanings compared with the literal meaning and (2) the learners (in)ability to infer metaphorical meanings from the literal meaning and the given contexts. While metaphorical expressions, like other figurative expressions, are not frequently included in the learning materials in a classroom setting, learners will receive less exposure to these expressions and thus are unaware of the possibility of these meanings. Also, even if some metaphorical expressions are transferable from the learners' L1 to L2, the abstractness of metaphorical meanings indicates that the links between L1 word form, L2 word form and metaphorical meanings are generally weaker than the links between the two word forms and the literal meaning.

However, despite the pessimistic prediction that metaphorical expressions are more difficult for second language learners, it is still expected that highly proficient learners, or learners with a more naturalized input, are able to acquire metaphorical expressions successfully and treat them in the same way as literal expressions. Learners might nevertheless transfer their knowledge of L1 metaphorical expressions to their L2 and, by receiving positive input, they may eventually establish the link between L2 word forms and their metaphorical meanings. It is expected that highly proficient learners can achieve native-like performance in the aspect of metaphorical expressions, particularly those shared between their L1 and L2. However, it is still unknown whether they can perform in a native-like way when they come across metaphorical expressions that are only available in their L2. Taking the available models for the bilingual lexicon and the general processing pattern of figurative language as a foundation, I can build a potential model to capture the acquisition, storage and accessing of metaphorical meanings in the bilingual lexicon. Based on that model, several possible routes of metaphorical meaning processing can be derived, depending on the availability of the metaphorical meanings in the two languages.

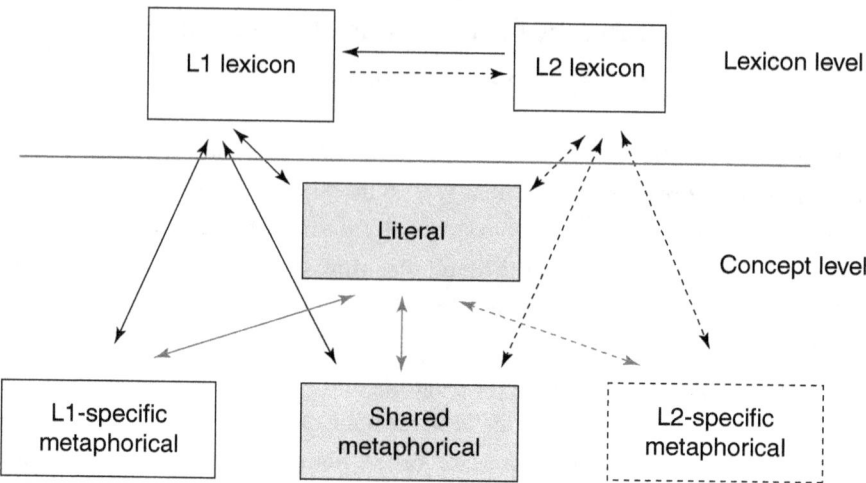

Figure 5.6 A simplified model of bilingual lexicon with literal and metaphorical distinctions

A simplified model for the storage of literal and metaphorical meanings in general can be seen in Figure 5.6, which shows a modified version of an MHM, while stressing the availability of different types of metaphorical expressions rather than the conceptual differences. Both the L1 and L2 lexicon are connected to three types of concepts: the literal concept,[2] the shared metaphorical concept and the language-specific metaphorical concept. The bold grey links show the connection between the literal and metaphorical concepts on a conceptual level; they are grey because these links are not systematically available to learners who have no prior knowledge of conceptual metaphors, but it is possible for learners to build up a connection in an ad hoc manner given sufficient contextual information. The heavier lines between the L1 lexicon and relevant concepts, as well as from the L2 lexicon to the L1 lexicon, indicate that these links are relatively strong, while the dashed links between the L2 lexicon and relevant concepts show that concept mediation may exist under limited conditions. In particular, a learner may not be fully aware of the existence of L2-specific metaphorical concepts and the links to that set of concepts; thus, both the lexicon-concept link and the between-concept link are exceptionally weak.

Since the processing of idiomatic expressions and other types of figurative language among native speakers of a variety of languages indicates that native speakers of a language can process figurative expressions in the same manner as literal expressions, I take the processing of metaphorical meanings by native speakers as a baseline. I assume that native speakers will spend the same amount

Table 5.1 Possible routes for the retrieval of the literal meaning of an L2 word

Possibilities	Route	Complexity	Proficiency
LR_1	L2 form–Literal	Low	Medium–High
LR_2	L2 form–L1 form–Literal	Medium	Low

of time processing the literal meaning and the metaphorical meaning of a lexical item; this means that native speakers will establish the link directly between the word form and the conventional metaphorical meanings of that lexical item, and they will not rely on other routes to retrieve the metaphorical meaning.

There are two ways for L2 learners to retrieve the literal meaning of an L2 word when they see the L2 word form, listed in Table 5.1. They may either directly pursue the link between the L2 word form and the literal concept, namely via concept mediation (LR_1), or they may take an additional step and establish the link via the L1 word form, namely via word association (LR_2). LR_1 is structurally less complex than LR_2, since LR_1 takes a shorter route and has fewer steps. A less complex route is generally considered faster than a more complex route, but it should be noted that speed of retrieval may vary even for the same route. Since the widespread appearance of concept mediation is largely recognized as an indicator of higher L2 proficiency (see Dufour & Kroll 1995), it can be assumed that LR_1 may be used if a learner is at medium- or high-level proficiency, while LR_2 is more likely be used by a less proficient learner. These two possibilities are taken as the fundamental assumptions for the retrieval of metaphorical meanings. Also, it is assumed that the processing of literal expressions is always consistent; if LR_2 is selected by a learner, I expect to observe word association in all cases of meaning retrieval, because that means that proficiency is not yet sufficient to allow concept mediation.

For the retrieval of the shared metaphorical meaning, a learner may have four main possibilities. The first possible route (MBR_1) is the same as the metaphorical processing of a native speaker. This means the learner can directly establish the link between the L2 word form and the shared metaphorical meaning, and thus has already integrated the metaphorical meaning as part of the mental lexicon. The second possible route (MBR_2) assumes that the learner will first adopt word association, and then directly pursue the link between the L1 word form and the shared metaphorical meaning. The third possible route (MBR_3) assumes that the learner may first arrive at the literal concept via concept mediation from the L2 word form, and then arrive at the shared metaphorical meaning via the link between the literal and metaphorical concept. The last possibility (MBR$_4$) takes the longest route; learners will first go through concept mediation to reach the literal concept and, when they find that the literal concept does not provide a valid explanation of the whole expression, they will not make any inference of the metaphorical meaning from the literal meaning. Instead, they will revert to the L1 word form, and then access the shared metaphorical expressions via the L1 word form.

When a learner tries to retrieve a metaphorical meaning that is only available in L2 from an L2 word form, it will be noted that a simple word association cannot solve the problem because the L1 word form is not directly connected to the L2-specific metaphorical concept. The first possibility (MTR$_1$) makes use of concept mediation and travels directly through the link between the L2 word form and the L2-specific metaphorical concept; that is the least complex route, but there needs to be sufficient knowledge of metaphorical expressions in L2 to establish and maintain the link. The second possibility (MTR$_2$) permits the learner to first use concept mediation to access the literal concept of that word, and then reach the L2-specific metaphorical meaning via the link between the literal and metaphorical concept. Alternatively, if it is necessary to rely on word association from the beginning of the process, it will only be possible to retrieve the literal concept after word association, and a link between the literal and metaphorical concept will still be needed (MTR$_3$).

Finally, I shall consider a condition that is only observable in experiments, that is, when a learner is forced to retrieve a metaphorical meaning that is only available in L1 from an L2 word form. For instance, when a Chinese learner of English is forced to comprehend an impossible expression such as 'eat the loss' (meaning 'suffer the loss'), such an enquiry has been designed to contrast

Table 5.2 Possible routes for the retrieval of the metaphorical meaning shared between the L1 and the L2

Possibilities	Route	Complexity	Proficiency
MBR$_1$	L2 form–Shared metaphorical	Low	Medium–High
MBR$_2$	L2 form–L1 form–Shared metaphorical	Medium	Low
MBR$_3$	L2 form–Literal–Shared metaphorical	Medium	Medium–High
MBR$_4$	L2 form–Literal–L1 form–Shared metaphorical	High	Medium–High

Table 5.3 Possible routes for the retrieval of the L2-specific metaphorical meaning of an L2 word

Possibilities	Route	Complexity	Proficiency
MTR_1	L2 form–L2-specific metaphorical	Low	High
MTR_2	L2 form–Literal–L2-specific metaphorical	Medium	Medium–High
MTR_3	L2 form–L1 form–Literal–L2-specific metaphorical	High	Low

shared metaphorical expressions, and to reflect how learners gradually give up metaphorical expressions that are only available in their L1. Ideally, when learners are exposed to the L2 they will have no channel to receive such a kind of input. In these circumstances, the learner must construct the L1-specific metaphorical meanings from the L2 input. In an offline task, such as acceptability judgement, the appearance of these meanings will lead to rejection; in an online task, however, under time pressure, a learner is given no choice and is forced to construct the intended meanings. One possibility (MSR_1) is that the learner will first access the L1 word form by word association, and then arrive at the L1-specific metaphorical concept via the link from the L1 form. The other main possibility is that the learner will first access the literal concept by concept mediation, and there will then be a second divergence – use can be made of the link at conceptual level, and the learner may reach the L1-specific metaphorical concept by referring to the literal concept (MSR_2); or, upon finding that the literal concept does not provide a feasible explanation, they may return to the L1 word form, and then use the lexical-concept link to arrive at the L1-specific metaphorical concept (MSR_3). Compared with the first two possibilities, it may take more time for the learner to construct the L1-specific metaphorical meaning from the L2 word form in these conditions in MSR_3, since there is a necessity to return to the L1 word form.

These possible routes can theoretically come in bundles, as shown in Table 5.5. The logic is that the retrieval of the metaphorical meaning does not conflict with the retrieval of the literal meaning, and a learner always takes the shortest possible route. Therefore, if a learner can make use of concept mediation consistently for one type of literal or metaphorical expression, it is assumed that word association will not be used in other types. Bundle 1 is a case where word association is extensively used, in which a learner must achieve access to the L1 word form before proceeding further. The proficiency level of a learner may

Table 5.4 Possible routes for the retrieval of the L1-specific metaphorical meaning from the L2 word form

Possibilities	Route	Complexity	Proficiency
MSR_1	L2 form–L1 form–L1-specific metaphorical	Medium	Low
MSR_2	L2 form–Literal–L1-specific metaphorical	Medium	Medium–High
MSR_3	L2 form–Literal–L1 form–L1-specific metaphorical	High	Medium–High

Table 5.5 Different bundles of possible routes of metaphorical meaning retrieval in L2

	Bundle 1	Bundle 2	Bundle 3	Bundle 4	Bundle 5
Proficiency requirement	Low	Medium	Medium to High	Medium to High	High
Literal	LR_2	LR_1	LR_1	LR_1	LR_1
Shared metaphorical	MBR_2	MBR_4	MBR_3	MBR_1	MBR_1
L2-specific metaphorical	MTR_3	MTR_2	MTR_2	MTR_2	MTR_1
L1-specific metaphorical	MSR_1	MSR_3	$MSR_{2/3}$	$MSR_{2/3}$	$MSR_{2/3}$
General complexity	High	Medium to High	Medium	Low to Medium	Low

be relatively low, while the complexity of the route is generally high. Bundles 2 to 5 are cases where concept mediation is generally used, but the destinations of concept mediation vary depending on the availability of links in the model as shown in Figure 5.6. A learner using the Bundle 2 strategy is considered not to be able to infer the shared metaphorical meaning directly from the literal meaning of the word and the given context, so it is necessary to revert to the L1 word form. The improvement in the Bundle 3 strategy permits the learner to infer the shared metaphorical meaning from the literal meaning and the given context, which is more like the 'literal-first' assumption of figurative language processing. In Bundle 4 and 5 strategies, a learner can bypass the literal meaning and directly link the shared metaphorical meaning to the L2 word form. Bundle 5 is the strategy that resembles the word-processing of native speakers of the target language because, in such cases, the learner can establish links directly to the metaphorical meanings that are available in the L2, just as with the links to the literal meaning of that word. No 'literal-first' effect will be observed in the Bundle 5 strategy in cases of shared metaphorical meanings or L2-specific metaphorical meanings.

In terms of the general complexity of processing each bundle, the reading times of different metaphorical expressions, as well as literal expressions, can be utilized to speculate which strategy a learner is using in the processing of different metaphorical expressions. If a learner does not show a significant difference in reading time when processing a literal expression and a metaphorical expression, it can be inferred that there is no need to refer to the literal concept to obtain access to the metaphorical concept. Similarly, if a learner spends significantly longer processing a metaphorical expression than processing a literal expression, it can be inferred that an additional path has been taken to reach the metaphorical meaning.

5.6 Summary

This chapter, as the third aspect in the literature review, has extensively focused on the 'position' of metaphorical expressions in the bilingual lexicon of L2 learners; at a later stage, I shall further restrict the discussion to sequential L2 learners in a classroom setting. This review provides some insights into possible processing patterns for metaphorical expressions. Specifically, the feasibility of the 'literal-first' hypothesis in figurative language processing among L2 learners remains a core question in terms of the acquisition and processing of metaphorical expressions, especially because the teaching of the learners will have promoted literal usage before metaphorical meanings.

Although none of the currently available models of bilingual lexicon is fully applicable to the acquisition of metaphorical expressions, I have constructed a hybrid model that can reflect: (1) the difference between concrete, literal meanings and abstract, metaphorical meanings and (2) the difference between learners at different levels of proficiency. Based on the hybrid model, I can then generate a series of possibilities regarding the storage and access of metaphorical meanings of a lexical item and make further predictions regarding the reading and comprehension of metaphorical expressions by L2 learners. Some of the hypotheses generated by the hybrid model contradict the predictions based on the literature on cross-linguistic influence in Chapter 3; I will look into these contradictions in the experiments and discussions.

6

Methodologies in second language metaphor research

6.1 Introduction

This chapter aims to provide a partial list of research methodologies that can be used to investigate the acquisition of metaphorical expressions in a second language. Due to the scarcity of established studies in this area, it is relatively difficult to find well-tested methodologies that have previously been used in studies examining the acquisition of metaphorical expressions; therefore, it is difficult to present a full list of instruments with detailed references to previous studies, and I do not aim to do so. Under such circumstances, this chapter looks more like an exploration of possibilities. While it mainly focuses on ecological-friendly research methods, that is, with a lower cost and the possibility of being executed in a classroom setting, it includes not only the experimental tools that have been used in prior research, but also some possible tools that can be further utilized.

Apart from the main experimental tasks that can tackle the question of the acquisition of metaphorical expressions, this chapter will, from the beginning, include actual research questions that have been discussed in previous studies as well as potential research questions. Furthermore, considerations on the selection of participants, guidance on the selection of test materials (such as the choice of lexical items under investigation), the construction of metaphorical expressions as well as the test sentences will be provided. Finally, at the end of this chapter, some suggestions of possible supplementary tasks for well-established experiments will also be provided – after the introduction of the main experimental methodologies.

6.2 Formulating specific research questions on the acquisition of metaphorical expressions

Designing research questions on the acquisition of metaphorical expressions is a very personal issue. By the word 'personal', I mean that research questions can vary depending on the purposes of the project; it could be an experiment of a new second language teaching strategy, a simple test of learners' knowledge of L2 metaphorical expressions at a particular stage of acquisition, a comparison between native speakers and learners on the processing patterns of metaphorical expressions or, as is described in Chapter 7 of this book, a more comprehensive investigation on cross-linguistic influence in the acquisition of metaphorical expressions. While it depends on individual researchers to decide the research questions, it is important to formulate specific questions prior to the selection of experimental methodologies.

Extant studies on the acquisition of L2 conventionalized metaphorical expressions, such as Türker (2016b) and Xia (2017), primarily focus on the cross-linguistic influence in the process; this topic is also a major focus of the book, and the reason for this focus will be demonstrated, mainly, in the rest of this subsection. It is very natural to think of the acquisition of metaphorical expressions in terms of cross-linguistic influence; as seen in the previous chapters, there seems to be a conflict regarding the acquisition of metaphorical expressions if this issue is investigated from different perspectives. To start with, I take the premise of CMT and assume that the metaphorical meaning of a lexical item is more abstract than the literal meaning of that lexical item. If the assumption stands, the acquisition of metaphorical meaning will result in a comparison between the acquisition of a more concrete meaning and a more abstract meaning of a polysemous word. On the one hand, Jordens and Kellerman (1981) suggest that markedness of an element would be a major influential factor of cross-linguistic transferability, while the presence of metaphoricalness in the meanings of a lexical item *may not* play an important role; on the other hand, from the viewpoint of the construction of bilingual lexicon, particularly the DCFM by De Groot (1992), whether the meaning of a lexical item is abstract or metaphorical may be a crucial factor that influences the transferability of that meaning.

The seemingly conflicting theories lead one to think about the possible cross-linguistic transferability of metaphorical expressions in the process of the acquisition, that is, whether a metaphorical expression is perceived by learners as transferable from L1 to L2, which can be reflected by the degree of acceptability of metaphorical expressions across different conditions. The logic here follows Odlin's (1989) observation on the lexical acquisition of L2; a learner may directly transfer the usage of an L1 lexical item to L2 by using the L2 translation equivalent of that lexical item, even if there is a possibility of semantic mismatch. It is likely that the same situation applies to the acquisition of different meanings of a lexical item; if a learner assumes that the literal meaning of an L1 lexical item is transferable to L2, they might suggest that the metaphorical meaning(s) of the same lexical item is transferable to L2 as well; or, if they believe that the metaphorical meaning(s) and the literal meaning of a lexical item should be treated differently, they may reject the transfer of the metaphorical meaning.

The observation on the transferability of lexical items from L1 to L2 (as described in Chapter 3), together with the current frameworks of bilingual lexicon (as described in Chapter 5) and the possible influential factors of transferability, could lead to a paradigm which can be used to examine the transferability of metaphorical expressions in L2 acquisition. When I take a pair of translation equivalents between L1 and L2, I assume that some, if not all, literal meaning(s) of that lexical item are transferable from L1 to L2, because it is shared between the two languages in order to qualify as a pair of translation equivalents. At the same time, I can compare the difference between that shared literal meaning and the metaphorical meaning(s) of the same lexical item to examine whether they are transferable to the same extent. Moreover, it can also be observed whether the learners treat the metaphorical meanings and the literal meaning of a same lexical item in the same manner in the construction of the bilingual lexicon. The transferability of the different meanings of a single lexical item can then be reflected by the following two factors: the degree of acceptability of an expression as perceived by the language learners and the reaction time to that given expression.

Other research topics, though not investigated to the same degree, are still possible and are valuable in the area of acquisition of L2 metaphorical expressions. While a number of instruction methods have been proposed to boost the acquisition of different figurative expressions (see Boers & Lindstromberg 2008; Danesi 1986; Holme 2004; Littlemore & Low 2006; among others), one can combine pedagogy and experiments together to evaluate the efficiency of the instruction on metaphorical expressions. Also, as part of vocabulary acquisition, acquisition of metaphorical expressions should also be examined by reference to the framework of vocabulary learning and vocabulary size estimation. Since metaphorical expressions are closely connected to pragmatic ability, acquisition of metaphorical expressions can also be examined together with the learners' pragmatic ability in a second language. As I have stressed repeatedly in this book, this area has been largely neglected in previous research, but it deserves attention and should be studied from different perspectives.

6.3 Possible experimental instruments to test the acquisition of metaphorical expressions

6.3.1 Productive experiments

The most direct outcome of an acquisition of a metaphorical expression is to successfully reproduce that expression in an appropriate context; productive experiments are designed to demonstrate learners' ability in this aspect. Productive experiments require learners to produce metaphorical expressions, either in spoken or written form, with or without specific instruction, such as hints, translations, and so on in either a natural way or structured manner.

One of advantages of a productive experiment is the opportunity to monitor which metaphorical expressions learners can manage in their active vocabulary. If learners use a metaphorical expression, especially in an appropriate way, it then indicates not only that they can identify the expression, but also that they probably understand what the expression means and where it should appear. In case of errors, it is easier to specify why such errors appear, and whether there is a strong influence from learners' L1.

However, it might be difficult to track the use of metaphorical expressions in an ideal, natural way, especially if one intends to observe the systematic use of linguistic realization of certain conceptual metaphors, such as ARGUMENT IS WAR or LIFE IS JOURNEY. Even if learners are instructed to write freely about their ideas on topics like arguments or life, metaphorical expressions may only appear infrequently. In such way, a productive method with more guidance, for example, discourse completion or translation, might work better than simply collecting raw spoken or written materials from learners, because such a method can lead to a more focused elicitation.

6.3.1.1 Corpus analysis from free speaking/writing tasks

Corpus-based analysis is applicable when a large mass of written or spoken data from learners is available by collecting writing samples or records of interviews. Under such circumstances, a concordancer, like 'WordSmith', could easily list the most frequent collocations in the corpus, together with their frequencies and contexts. It can clearly show if learners favour collocations with a literal bias or a metaphorical bias in the given writing or speaking tasks. This method is quite direct, especially if a range of target lexical items are to be investigated; one can check the lexical items one by one to see if the learners show different frequencies of use of metaphorical expressions when they use different lexical items. It is also possible to compare the frequency of metaphorical expressions used by learners to that of native speakers.

Apart from the quantitative data generated from a corpus analysis, as mentioned above, some qualitative analyses can also be used to provide additional information. A combination of large-scale quantitative data and a smaller scale of individual case analysis using MIP can connect the learners' use of more frequent, widely accepted metaphorical expression, and some evidence of their creativity when producing metaphorical expressions. One can also observe traces of cross-linguistic influence where individual learners have used metaphorical expressions that are available in their L1 but not L2.

It is also possible to use a well-established learner corpus, but this is riskier because it may lead to some bias in the analysis. The crucial problem is being unable to control the content of an established learner corpus, and it is unknown whether learners are able to use metaphorical expressions when they discuss the content. It is possible that learners who contribute to the corpus have a good knowledge of metaphorical expressions generally, but cannot show it due to the task instructions when the corpus data is collected. Although it could present a very general picture of the frequency of the metaphorical use of certain lexical items, it is also highly likely that at the end of the analysis there are no, or few, metaphorical expressions suitable for a research topic, especially if the focus is on the metaphorical use of content words. Well-established corpora may be more useful if one wishes to examine the difference of use of metaphorical expressions between native speakers and learners in a specific area, such as academic language or business language. In this kind of analysis, a corpus-driven study is more applicable; instead of constructing a list of possible metaphorically used lexical items, one could calculate the frequency of each lexical item using a concordancer. The next step, then, is to look at how often metaphorical collocations appear for each lexical item.

Compared with other methodologies, be it productive or receptive, the whole process of corpus construction and analysis is relatively more time-consuming and less focused, because: (1) it takes time to collect desirable corpus data, and the tasks used for data collection should be well-designed in order to reflect the learners' knowledge of L2 metaphorical expressions; (2) even with carefully designed data collection tasks only part of the information can be collected, rather than a broader picture of learners' metaphorical knowledge; and (3) more importantly, anyone who analyses the metaphorical collocations should have experience in the use of a metaphor identification paradigm (such as MIP) in order to identify metaphorical expressions consistently. Nevertheless, corpus analysis is a useful and straightforward task to research metaphorical expressions in second language writing or speaking since it demonstrates which expressions are more likely to be produced by learners in actual communication. The use of learner-initiated language materials in corpus analysis, that is, all of the materials are provided by the learners, also skip the procedure of construction and selection of metaphorical expressions.

6.3.1.2 Sentence or discourse completion

A sentence or discourse completion task is a classic productive task used to investigate learners' usage of expressions in a given context. It can appear in various forms, including multiple choices, filling the blank freely, or filling the blank with phrases including given words. The use of a sentence/discourse completion task is well established in the research on other figurative expressions, particularly idioms; dating back to Irujo (1986b), sentence or discourse completion tasks have already been utilized to elicit the production of L2 idioms. Türker (2016b) also makes use of sentence completion tasks to examine whether English learners of Korean are able to produce metaphorical expressions involving the concept of anger and heat.

The various forms of sentence or discourse completion task can be altered to fit particular research questions. A free completion task, without any hints or given words, is closer to a free writing task; as described in the corpus analysis, learners will show their own preferred word or phrase selections when they fill the blanks, and one can investigate whether they prefer literal expression or conventional metaphorical expressions or, as in some cases, even the creation of unconventional metaphorical expressions. A completion task with given words, especially words that can be used metaphorically, can encourage learners to produce the exact metaphorical expressions one would like to investigate. Alternatively, the given information in a sentence or discourse completion task can also be found in a learner's L1, which forms a translation task. Learners then look for the best expressions in their L2 that can match the L1 translation. A completion task in the form of multiple choices can be seen as a combination of the examination of both productive and receptive knowledge. Learners should be able identify the metaphorical expressions prior to expressing their choice, and they also need to know the productive knowledge in order to fit the appropriate metaphorical expressions in the sentences or discourses.

It can easily be seen from the descriptions above that the restrictions attached to sentence or discourse completion tasks somehow correlate to how accurately the task reflects the learner's knowledge of metaphorical expressions. The version with fewest restrictions, namely the free completion task, faces the same problem as other free writing tasks. Learners may well have knowledge of metaphorical expressions, but for certain reasons they do not use these expressions in the task. While the task can clearly indicate that in this situation learners have a strong preference of literal expressions over metaphorical ones, it is still unknown what expressions are actually acquired (or probably transferred if the focus is on cross-linguistic influence) by learners. Completion tasks with given words, or tasks in the form of multiple choices, present researchers with more detailed information about what learners are able to produce when they are fully encouraged to 'speak metaphorically'. Nevertheless, encouraging learners to 'speak metaphorically' already implies that learners may rely on mere guessing to complete the task; the more details there are, the greater the likelihood that learners rely on guessing in the 'production' of metaphorical expressions, and the more likely one is to overestimate learners' knowledge of metaphorical expressions in L2. Thus, it is necessary for researchers to choose an appropriate form of sentence or discourse completion task in their studies, to both maximize the results of production of metaphorical expressions and to reduce overestimation.

An additional issue with a completion task with an L1 translation is the possibility of a more significant cross-linguistic influence. Although cross-linguistic influence may affect learners throughout the process of acquisition, it is more likely to appear when the two languages are present at the same time. The two languages in the learners' bilingual mental lexicon are co-activated, which may lead to a stronger effect of cross-linguistic influence. Therefore, if a sentence or discourse completion task is used to investigate how their L1 metaphorical expressions learners transfer into their L2, L1 translation or even L1 instructions, the results should be considered carefully because any L1 materials might bias the learners' production.

6.3.2 Receptive experiments

While productive experiments focus on learners' ability to produce metaphorical expressions, receptive experiments mainly reflect whether learners are able to identify, interpret and accept metaphorical expressions in the given contexts, which means that learners have the receptive knowledge of metaphorical expressions. It would be efficient and accurate to examine learners' receptive knowledge if a large corpora of learners' writing texts were not available for a particular group of learners, or if the researchers were not involved in teaching the target participants.

Compared with productive experiments, receptive experiments have both advantages and disadvantages. As discussed before, productive tasks should be designed with care to keep a balance between 'encouraging learners to speak up and to speak metaphorically' and 'preventing learners from guessing at an answer'. The balance issue is no longer a problem in receptive tasks, since (in most cases) learners need not produce any expressions, and there is no need to worry about the outcome and motivation of their production. Also, for learners with a lower proficiency or less experience in L2, they may be less likely to voluntary produce expressions; receptive tasks can, however, ease their anxiety of 'being tested'.

One issue concerning the potential problems with receptive experiments is that they only test the learner's knowledge of passive vocabulary, and it is known to everyone that knowing a meaning of a word is far from using it actively in a learner's production. However, this should not be considered as a real disadvantage; primarily, experimental methodologies are selected based on the research questions while a receptive task is selected only if the intention is to examine the learner's passive knowledge of metaphorical expressions. Moreover, as I will show later, a hybrid of receptive and (partially) productive tasks can be used in an experiment to test both active and passive knowledge of metaphorical expressions.

The major disadvantage of receptive experiments comes from the issue of 'false positivity', and it is more likely to happen when only receptive linguistic data (e.g. judgements, reading time and reaction time of individual linguistic elements) are collected and analysed. Similar to the problems emerging in a sentence or discourse completion task with multiple choices, in some receptive tasks it is relatively more difficult to distinguish whether learners manage to understand the metaphorical expressions successfully, or whether they merely guess when reading the expressions. This is particularly prominent if cross-linguistic influence is targeted in a study; as discussed in Chapter 3, it is necessary to distinguish between native-like performance and positive transfer before measuring the impact of cross-linguistic influence. Therefore, when necessary, additional questionnaires or interviews should be provided to reflect the learner's possible metalinguistic knowledge of metaphorical expressions.

In this section, all the receptive tasks are placed into two main categories: offline tasks with no restriction of time and online tasks in which the reaction time of the learners is usually measured. All the offline tasks can be conducted as either a pen-and-paper test, an electronic document or an online questionnaire, while all the online tasks require, as a minimum, a computer and the relevant software in order to complete the task. Note that if receptive tasks are used with an aim to discover the differences between native speakers and L2 learners when they receive metaphorical expressions, it is strongly recommended that the experiment on native speakers is conducted first to set up a better baseline for comparison.

6.3.2.1 Offline experiment

6.3.2.1.1 Acceptability judgement task

Acceptability judgement tasks have been widely used in second language acquisition studies to track learners' preference of linguistic elements. Untimed acceptability judgement tasks are regarded as typical offline tasks, and timed acceptability judgement tasks are typically online tasks. The core idea of acceptability judgement tasks is that both native speakers and learners are able to use their intuition to make judgements about metaphorical expressions, although their intuition may be differ. The purpose of acceptability judgement tasks, therefore, is to analyse what differs between the intuition of native speakers and that of learners when they perceive metaphorical expressions and, further, what differs between learners' intuition when they perceive different metaphorical expressions.

Usually the test items used in an acceptability judgement task are sentences containing metaphorical expressions. Theoretically, it is also possible to use individual phrasal metaphorical expressions as test items, but these cases are relatively rare. Sentences and individual expressions both have advantages and disadvantages. Full sentences, on the one hand, can provide more contextual information alongside the metaphorical expressions and help the participant to understand the intended meanings of the expressions, especially for those who are not familiar with the metaphorical expressions. On the other hand, full sentences might also disguise the designated target of the experiment, namely the acceptability of metaphorical expressions. It is possible that a participant might accept the metaphorical expression in the test sentence, but, thereafter, rated the whole sentence as unacceptable due to the suspicion that some other element in the sentence is unacceptable, such as the tense/aspect or the use of articles. The advantages and disadvantages of using individual metaphorical expressions are simply the reverse; using metaphorical expressions can largely eliminate misjudgements caused by other linguistic elements in the sentences, but participants may get lost in the middle of the task because they may fail to understand the metaphorical expressions, or do not know whether they have been used appropriately.

The restrictions mentioned above identify several ways to improve an acceptability judgement task for metaphorical expressions, but one needs to ensure that the participants are judging the metaphorical expressions when reading the sentences. It is important to get feedback from the participants when/after they perform the task; the feedback can be spoken or written. If their feedback shows that their judgements are irrelevant to the metaphorical expression, then it is better to exclude such judgements from the final dataset. This method is not fully accurate though; if only written feedback is collected from the acceptability judgement task, there may be occasions when some participants choose not to provide any feedback. That means, whatever they base their judgement on and regardless of their relevance to the metaphorical expressions, all of their judgements will be preserved in the analysis. In sum, such adjustments to the result of an acceptability judgement task, based on the participant's feedback, serves to maximize the reliability of the data, while accepting that the noise from the judgement of other non-critical constituents in the sentence could not be fully eliminated due to the nature of the task. Figure 6.1 shows an excerpt of an acceptability judgement task with feedback space and confidence rating.

As a well-used research methodology, acceptability judgement tasks have been developed into different forms, particularly in measuring the degree of acceptability. The 'acceptable/unacceptable' dichotomy is no longer widely used in more recent paradigms, and the scales of acceptability that could reflect more fine-grained differences between individual test sentences have become mainstream – gradually. Popular designs of acceptability judgement tasks include the use of Likert scale and the use of Magnitude Estimation (see Bard, Robertson & Sorace 1996). In an acceptability test using the Likert scale, each sentence is presented with a numeral or text which can vary from 0 points to 11 points, and participants are asked to select the choice that best indicates their 'score', 'preference' or 'feeling' towards that sentence. Generally, a large Likert scale can better capture the subtle difference of acceptability in individual

40. My mother said that these books would be food for thought.

0	1	2	3	4	5	6	7	8	9	10
Not at all confident		Not very confident		Neutral		Confident		Very confident	

41. The mother held a belly of gas because her son failed in the exam.

0	1	2	3	4	5	6	7	8	9	10
Not at all confident		Not very confident		Neutral		Confident		Very confident	

Figure 6.1 An excerpt of an acceptability judgement task for research on acquisition of metaphorical expressions

participant's judgements, but it is also more likely to lead to participants forming their own interpretations of the scale. Thus, it is crucial to unify the form of data prior to the data analysis, for example, by using z-score standardization or using statistical tools that can help to minimize individual variability, such as adding random effects in a linear model.

In an acceptability judgement task with Magnitude Estimation, participants are required to create and use their own numerical scales to evaluate the degree of acceptability of a sentence. Magnitude estimation is a psychological paradigm that is widely used in psychology studies on sense, perception and grammatical judgement in syntax. Its mechanism is to guide participants to estimate the perceived degree of one feature of a target object (e.g. the loudness of sound, the brightness of a shade, the grammaticality of a sentence, the appropriateness of a sentence in a context, etc.), using a given example as reference. A typical procedure of magnitude estimation starts with a briefing session, in which the participants try to convert the length of given lines to numbers with reference to a standard, reference line. After the line length task, participants are introduced to the mechanism of magnitude estimation and start the trial session, but they need to convert the degree of acceptability of a sentence to a positive integer by allusion to a reference sentence. After the trial session, the main session continues in the same format as the trial session. In the experiment, it is advised to use a way of presentation that prevents the participants from backtracking their answers (i.e. they cannot check and modify their previous answers). The standard treatment of data collected from Magnitude Estimation is z-score standardization; usually, a z-score above 0 indicates that a test sentence or test expression is accepted by a participant, and a z-score below 0 means that the test item is rejected.

The form of acceptability judgement task is highly flexible. It can be conducted as pen-and-paper test, an online questionnaire survey (which is better for magnitude estimation), or even short face-to-face interviews sessions in which participants can give spoken feedback. In actual implementation, acceptability judgement tasks can be combined with other tasks, such as sentence correction, interpretation or elicited production. If a study aims to investigate the impact of cross-linguistic influence, a measurement of confidence is also a possible component in the task. In Chapter 7, the results of an acceptability judgement task will be presented to show the information it can provide about the result of the acquisition of metaphorical expressions in a second language.

6.3.2.1.2 Interpretation task

An interpretation task, or a paraphrasing task, aims to discover how individual participants understand the meanings of metaphorical expressions. The aim is to determine: (1) whether there is a difference of understanding or interpretation between native speakers and learners, (2) whether the learners know the meanings of conventional metaphorical expressions and (3) whether learners are able to deduce the meanings of conventional metaphorical expressions, especially those not available in their L1. Interpretation tasks, although requiring the participants to produce some interpretations (possibly in their L2 if paraphrasing is used), do not necessarily involve the production of metaphorical expressions and thus are viewed as receptive tasks. It also focuses on the receptive knowledge of metaphorical expressions; learners are required to explain what the metaphorical expressions mean, in either their L1 or L2.

The design of an interpretation task can be very simple; it can be an open-ended task in which participants give their own interpretations of each given sentence or expression, or, in some cases, a close-ended task in the form of multiple choices. While the latter is easy to implement and analyse, the former is more accurate if one intends to investigate the learners' ability to explain metaphorical expressions. An open-ended design allows the participants to freely express their ideas or even guess at the meaning of a metaphorical expressions, and it is possible that some participants may reveal some clues about their contextual inferences.

Much like a sentence/discourse completion task, an interpretation task can provide a rich context, from an individual sentence to an excerpt from a monolog or from a conversation. When more context is provided in a task, the participants will provide more accurate answers; the answers thus represent a better reflection of their lexical knowledge, their pragmatic ability and even their linguistic creativity. Different from other offline receptive tasks, all the test sentences given in an interpretation task are assumed to be fully correct, and participants should try their best to 'make sense' of these sentences, particularly the metaphorical expressions in the sentences. This, then, provides an excellent opportunity to observe how learner participants can interpret metaphorical expressions that are not available in their L1, and even some expressions that they have rarely, if ever, seen.

While it is optional to recruit native speakers of the target language in an interpretation task, the recruitment of native speakers can present valuable data for the comprehension of metaphorical expressions, particularly if some metaphorical expressions that are not available in the target language are involved in the task. For example, if the expression 'eat the loss', which is a Chinese metaphorical expression that is not available in English, is given in the task together with some contexts, then one can observe how native speakers of English, who have never seen such a collocation before, can explain the expressions. It is easy to assume that, without the relevant knowledge of metaphorical expressions in Chinese, native speakers of English are less likely to give an accurate interpretation of such an expression when compared to Chinese learners of English. Not only can this result show how native speakers of the target language try to 'make sense' of these expressions, but also how learners' knowledge of L1 is forced to be activated in an interpretation task in the target language.

6.3.2.1.3 Sentence correction task

It is somewhat difficult to classify sentence correction tasks as being part of a receptive/productive dichotomy, because this involves both aspects of knowledge of metaphorical expressions. For the completion of a sentence correction task, learners should be able to detect whether there are any errors or misuse of expressions in a sentence, which requires them to possess receptive knowledge of metaphorical expressions. Meanwhile, they should also be able to produce new expressions, either literal or metaphorical, to convey the intended meaning, which is an opportunity to examine their productive knowledge, although it does not aim to elicit metaphorical expressions. In the experiments reported in Chapter 7, a combination of an acceptability judgement task and a sentence correction task was used, where the sentence correction task can be seen as a natural continuation of acceptability judgement. When the participants feel that a sentence is not acceptable, they can provide a correction sentence, and information can be gathered from the sentence they provide to determine whether they favour literal or metaphorical expressions or whether they demonstrate any transfer from their L1, and so on.

A sentence correction task has an important advantage compared with other receptive tasks; it can be used to better monitor the effect of cross-linguistic influence on learners. Occasionally, it can be observed that learner participants translate metaphorical expressions from their L1 in a sentence correction task, and even use the translated L1-specific metaphorical expressions to replace the given L2 metaphorical expressions. Due to the nature of sentence correction tasks, when learner participants make such a decision they tend to 'correct' the L2 metaphorical expressions as 'incorrect expressions', which shows that they already have difficulty acquiring the given L2 expressions. The use of L1-specific expressions, on the other hand, can be seen as evidence that learner participants actively transfer their L1 knowledge into L2 production.

Compared with other productive tasks that are able to disclose cross-linguistic influence from L1, sentence correction tasks, due to the nature of 'correction', can demonstrate an inhibition of transfer if carefully designed. Most of the productive tasks listed above aim to guide learner-participants to produce the metaphorical expressions that are available in their L2, but they do not necessarily reflect learners' treatment of metaphorical expressions that are only available in their L1. Considering the effect of cross-linguistic influence, the learners' knowledge of metaphorical expressions in L2 should also include how to avoid negative transfer and not to use metaphorical expressions that are not available in their L2. This knowledge can be tested in a sentence correction task; if a task includes test sentences containing word-to-word translations of metaphorical expressions that are only available in the learner's L1, it allows the researchers to observe whether learners are able to identify these L1-specific expressions, treat them as an 'incorrect use' of L2, and provide correction.

Finally, just the same as interpretation tasks, if native speakers of the target language are also recruited for a sentence correction task, the test can then be used to provide additional information about the native speakers' preference for metaphorical expression and, in certain designs, demonstrate their ability to interpret or paraphrase those expressions that are not available in their native language. Sentence correction tasks provide an excellent opportunity for further research and even second language pedagogy; they can also be used to elicit metaphorical expressions produced by native speakers, and these expressions can be used either in subsequent research on learners or in the teaching materials on second language metaphorical expressions.

6.3.2.2 *Online experiment*

6.3.2.2.1 Lexical decision task using metaphorical expressions as priming items

Lexical decision task research has been widely used in studies research on monolingual word processing and bilingual lexicon examination, and it has been gradually applied in studies on figurative language processing, although in limited usage. The mechanism of a lexical decision task is relatively indirect compared with other online tasks; while the primary task for participants is to judge whether a string on the screen is a valid word or not, the object of the task is to observe whether there is a semantic priming effect. Semantic priming effect is a phenomenon in which participants are more likely to react faster to a semantically related word than an irrelevant word after seeing the prime. For example, after the display of a prime stimulus 'argument', participants, regardless of whether they are native speakers or second language learners, are more prone to decide that 'debate' is a valid word when compared with the semantically irrelevant 'chair'. Lexical decision task research is based on the premise that participants are more likely to co-activate the words that are in the same semantic domain. This task can be used to examine whether a metaphorical meaning is successfully triggered after participants have read the metaphorical expression as the priming item.

Lexical decision task research is generally not self-paced. Participants cannot control the length of display of the priming words; instead, the priming words are displayed on the screen for a limited time (usually less than 50 ms), and then the target words will show up for around 200 ms. Such a design allows a minimum time for both native speakers and learners to activate the literal or metaphorical meaning as well as the relevant semantic domains. If priming effect is shown by native speakers but not learners, then it could be argued that native speakers can directly access the metaphorical meanings, but learners are not sensitive enough to them, at least in the given period (like 50 ms). Learners might still be able to access the metaphorical meanings in an offline task or in a self-paced task (see self-paced reading as an example), but the process is not instant, and may involve some semantic inferences.

The prototypical form of lexical decision tasks always utilizes single words as the priming item, because single words are visually more salient and can be easily recognized in a very short period. Recently, studies using this methodology on figurative expressions have also started to use multi-word expressions and phrases. Blais and Gonnerman (2013) used a masked priming paradigm (i.e. a mask appeared before the priming item) to examine whether second language learners were able to react to phrasal verbs in the same way as native speakers. Heredia et al. (2007) applied lexical decision task research to the processing of idioms by Spanish learners of English and discovered that the priming effect was robust when learners processed idioms in their second language, particularly when the idiom had identical forms in Spanish and English (see Irujo 1986b for the definition of 'identical'). These successful examples suggest that metaphorical expressions are also a possible choice as priming items. Comparisons can be made between literal and metaphorical meanings to see whether learners can: (1) instantly access the metaphorical meaning after seeing the priming items, (2) activate the literal and metaphorical meanings at the same time and (3) whether learners have the similar processing matter to native speakers.

Since the priming words are only displayed for an extremely short time, more attention should be paid to the selection of the metaphorical expressions used as the primer, especially the length of them. If a metaphorical expression is too long, learners may not react to it fast enough before it disappears, and thus the priming effect may not be clear enough. Such a restriction also means that the metaphorical meaning of a lexical item must be activated using minimal context, for example, to activate the meaning 'strong criticism' of the word 'attack', only the phrase 'attack the idea' should be used, and not the full sentence 'John attacked Mary's idea in the meeting'. In the analysis of the result, conclusions should be drawn cautiously, especially if there is no priming effect. It may be the case that learners are able to understand metaphorical expressions, even instantly access the metaphorical meanings, but only with more supportive context.

6.3.2.2.2 *Self-paced reading*

A self-paced reading task is a well-established experiment that can monitor learners' reading patterns of metaphorical expressions when more advanced methodologies (e.g. eye-tracking) are not available. While eye-tracking monitors the movement of pupils when the participants read a sentence or a passage, a self-paced reading task monitors the length of reading time of each segment when participants read from a screen. The most common paradigm of a self-paced reading task is a non-cumulative moving window; at each moment in time, only one segment is shown on the screen, at the exact position it should be in the sentence or passage. When participants proceed to the next segment, the previous segment will disappear, and the next segment will appear in place of the previous segment (see Figure 6.2 for an illustration). Therefore, participants cannot backtrack to what they have read, and they will spend more time than usual when reading a segment when processing difficulties occur. Such hesitation in the self-paced reading task can be seen as a method of compensation when back-tracking of reading text is not possible.

The stimuli for self-paced reading tasks are usually in the form of sentences, which is ideal for research on the acquisition of metaphorical expressions; the activation of metaphorical meanings of a lexical item always requires a well-constructed context. Even though presenting a metaphorically used word together with its collocation is somehow effective, which is the case of a lexical decision task, a sentential stimulus can provide more contextual information and allow the participant to understand the metaphorical meaning more accurately. Also, by comparing the reading time of the metaphorical expression and the rest of the sentence, one can get a better picture of whether participants slow down significantly when they read the metaphorical expressions. When using sentences containing metaphorical expressions as stimuli, the hesitation in a self-paced reading task can be seen as a process by which the participants do not directly access the metaphorical meanings of the expressions, but, instead, derive the meanings from the literal meaning and the context.

In some cases, each sentential stimulus used in a self-paced reading task can be accompanied by a comprehension question, which is shown in Figure 6.2 (in the last slide). The use of a comprehension question kills two birds with one stone; on the one hand, it can maintain the participants attention to the contents

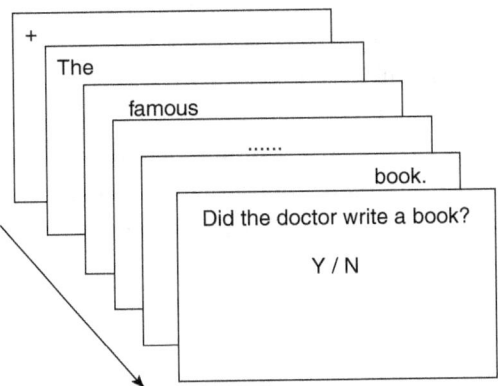

Figure 6.2 A simplified illustration of a self-paced reading task (the comprehension question is shown on the last slide)

of the stimuli so that they do not press the key randomly; on the other hand, it can also test whether the participants, especially second language learners, are able to understand the metaphorical expressions successfully.

When creating a self-paced reading task for a study on metaphorical expressions, one should carefully consider all the possible side effects of a self-paced reading paradigm in data analysis. The first issue is to ensure that all the sentential stimuli should be structurally simple and straightforward. Historically, self-paced reading tasks were first used to research the processing of long dependencies and other syntactically complex structures, and the efficacy of those studies proved that a self-paced reading paradigm was highly sensitive when monitoring the processing of complex structures. When this paradigm is used for the processing of metaphorical expressions, it is better to avoid any possible delay or processing difficulty caused by morphological or syntactic factors other than the metaphorical expressions themselves. Simple sentence structures and the avoidance of complicated case matching and reflexive, long-distance binding can help in the design of the sentential stimuli.

Further, a self-paced reading paradigm is renowned for the presence of the so-called 'spill-over effect'. Different from eye-tracking, self-paced reading, especially in a non-cumulative format, does not allow any backtracking to previous words when participants proceed to the next word. This means that if participants come across an unexpected word, they can be aware of that word when they find out that the next word cannot support the previous string. For instance, if participants read 'the rich manager ate some loss when he started his business', in which 'ate some loss' meant 'suffered some loss', which is a direct translation from Chinese, they can only realize that 'loss' does not fully match 'ate' when they read 'when'. In order to figure out what the interpretation of 'ate some loss' is, they will show hesitation when reading 'when' instead of 'loss'; that means the delay is 'spilt over' the critical region, and it is named 'spill-over effect' for that reason. Therefore, in the design of the sentences, the position of metaphorical expressions in the sentences should be consistent, and usually in the middle. This is to allow spill-over effect after reading metaphorical expressions, and sometimes not overlapping with the wrapping-up effect at the end of the sentences.

6.3.2.2.3 Maze task

The major problem with self-paced reading tasks, namely spill-over effect, has been clearly demonstrated in the last subsection; if the participants have difficulty understanding a metaphorical expression, the difficulty is mostly reflected in the spill-over area rather than the exact position of the metaphorical expressions. Maze tasks, as an alternative computerized online experimental tool, can effectively avoid the influence of spill-over effect; meanwhile, when compared with a moving window reading task, a maze task is less natural and the participants may feel that they are reading in an uncomfortable way.

The mechanism of maze task is to force participants to choose between two words as they proceed with reading. After a couple of words at the beginning of a test sentence, two words (or a word and a non-word) are shown on the screen at two fixed positions, and the sentence will proceed only when the participants choose the correct word, which is similar to walking through a maze with a number of divergences. After participants choose the correct word, the next pair of words then appear, and the task will continue until a full, grammatical or meaningful sentence is constructed.

Similar to a self-paced reading task, maze tasks make use of sentences as stimuli. The sentences are presented in a word-by-word way, and some words are presented together with the maze distractors side-by-side, as shown in Figure 6.3. Maze distractors can either be legal words of the target language, which should be different from the target words in part of speech, or non-words. A maze task using real word distractors is called a 'G-maze', short for 'grammatical maze', since participants must select grammatically correct words in order to proceed with the task. A maze task using non-word distractors is called L-maze, short for 'lexical maze'. No matter which form is utilized, there should be a clear mismatch between the maze distractors and the target words/sentential stimuli. Participants are forced to choose and parse the target words, no matter how 'strange' the full sentence sounds to them.

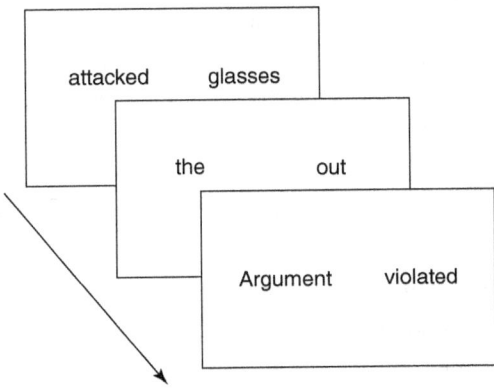

Figure 6.3 A simplified illustration of a maze task

The benefits of maze tasks include the fact that there is no spill-over effect, and participants are less likely to develop a specific pattern of pressing keys. Since participants are required to actively make decisions in the maze task, they need to think of the meaning of established constituents before they make that decision. This means that when the participants reach the last word of a metaphorical expression, say 'ate the loss' – they have already read 'ate' and 'the', and are forced to choose between 'loss' and 'of' (or 'sols' if using a word/non-word paradigm) – they must actively process the string 'ate the loss' before they make a final decision, which may lead to some hesitation. Therefore, the delay caused by the processing of metaphorical expressions will not appear as a spill-over effect, but a delay within an area of that metaphorical expression. Also, because participants need to make decisions during the process of the task, they cannot simply remember all the words that have appeared on the screen and comprehend the full sentences at the very end, which prevents them from pressing keys rhythmically and developing a key-pressing strategy, which reflects the real time they spend on reading the words more accurately.

The most prominent disadvantage of maze task reading can be attributed to the mechanism. When a reader processes a sentence, either in a free eye-movement setting (like eye-tracking) or a self-paced setting, they do not spend the same amount of time reading each word; they sometimes skip functional words, like articles and prepositions, because they only play definite roles in sentence construction and carry limited semantic information. Maze task reading obviates such problems by letting participants pay equal attention to every word in the sentence, which clearly violates the normal reading habit, and makes the whole reading process more artificial. One criticism is that that maze task reading does not clearly reflect how participants process metaphorical expressions in real life; the outcome is worse than a self-paced reading task. In fact, maze task reading is one of the least utilized experimental paradigms in the research of figurative language processing in a second language. The implementation of a maze task should be subject to extra care.

6.4 Selection of research participants

When compared with other aspects of research design, fewer restrictions apply to the selection of research participants, but some issues must be addressed before recruiting experiment participants. This section will briefly introduce some issues that impact on participants, which may influence experiment design or data collection. This is to ensure that the researchers get optimal results from their experiments.

Since the investigation of metaphorical expressions is closely related to identifying and understanding a large number of lexical items, there may be more obstacles to surmount, such as further research on learners with a restricted vocabulary size, that is, beginners. If one intends to look into the impact of cross-linguistic influence in the acquisition of metaphorical expressions, or a comparison between: (1) native speakers and learners, (2) learners at different levels or (3) learners with different L1s, beginner learners are not an ideal choice because they may have difficulty recognizing some of the words used in the experiments, and sometimes these words may have been used metaphorically. Learners who have a greater vocabulary, on the contrary, can ease the burden of researchers in the design of the experiment and the selection of metaphorical expressions.

However, that does not mean that people are unable to carry out research on how metaphorical expressions are acquired among L2 beginner learners. One can still examine the beginners' performance through finely-designed productive experiments and probably a combination of teaching and receptive experiments. Depending on the research questions to be investigated, sometimes beginners can provide a better picture of the acquisition of metaphorical expressions. For example, beginners may perform differently from more advanced learners when they try to produce a meaning that can be metaphorically expressed in their L1 but not in their L2. It is possible to observe a more significant negative transfer by beginners in both production and reception, while such a transfer might quickly disappear when learners become more proficient. In a word, the restrictions in the selection of learner participants is essentially determined by the object of the experiment. It is always important, not only in the investigation of metaphorical expressions but also in other areas of second language acquisition, to match the research questions with the potential participants.

Finally, it is crucial for most, if not all, receptive tasks to include a group of native speakers of the target L2. Although a native group is almost a necessity for many experiments on second language acquisition, in the case of metaphorical expressions, a native group can provide more valuable information than merely serving as a baseline. A decent number of native participants can provide a more balanced, collective view of the availability of metaphorical expressions. Given a random sampling, the native group can help to ensure when a metaphorical expression is *generally* acceptable and when it is not. Even native speakers display variability when they use metaphorical expressions, and it seems that there may always be a couple of speakers who, when compared with other native speakers, have a different understanding of the availability of metaphorical expression. For instance, in the experiment in Chapter 7, the researcher observed that some native speakers of English accepted metaphorical expressions that were confirmed as not being available in English, while other native speakers rejected some expressions that have appeared in extant literature as 'authentic metaphorical expressions in English'. If one investigates the judgements of these native speakers, this may lead to different baseline that cannot faithfully reflect the general picture of the use of metaphorical expressions. By including a native group with a similar sample size to a learner group, the impact of variability can be minimized.

The benefit of including native speakers in an experiment extends beyond that particular experiment, it can also benefit further studies and even language instruction. Native participants could become a more important source in sentence correction tasks or interpretation tasks. When they are asked to provide a 'correction' or 'interpretation' of a metaphorical expression, their results can be treated as paraphrases, alternatives, or other types of valid use of metaphorical expressions. This can also be observed in Chapter 7, wherein native participants were required to correct some Chinese-specific metaphorical expressions in their task. The interpretation and correction made by native speakers can reveal: (1) how native speakers attempt to interpret expressions that are not available in their native language; and (2) what metaphorical expressions can be used by native speakers when they intend to express such meanings. Native speakers' interpretation of metaphorical expressions in other languages has been observed in Carrol et al. (2018), in which English native speakers were required to infer the meanings of idioms and metaphorical expressions translated in other languages. Native speakers' production of metaphorical expressions can be used by teachers when they teach metaphorical expressions, particularly in answer to questions from students such as, 'what native speakers will say if they do not want to sound too literally'.

6.5 Selection, construction and classification of metaphorical expressions for an experiment

In most of the experimental instruments discussed in Section 6.2, the reaction of the participants to metaphorical expressions were recorded. Therefore, it is essential to prepare a collection of metaphorical expressions, or sentences containing metaphorical expressions, for the said experiments. Although the semantic fields of metaphorical expressions may vary according to the research backgrounds of individual studies, for instance, metaphorical expressions in academic English or English for business purposes, the paradigm of the construction of metaphorical expressions stays the same across the research context. This subsection aims to introduce a feasible paradigm to prepare L2 metaphorical expressions, with an illustration of a study on the cross-linguistic influence on the acquisition of metaphorical expressions.

The preparation of metaphorical expressions starts with the selection of the lexical items involved in the expressions. As discussed in Chapter 2, the meanings of conventional metaphorical expressions are highly conventionalized, so a learner can easily get access to the metaphorical meaning when they look up a lexical item in a dictionary. Thus, with respect to several issues, it is important to ensure that: (1) participants do not refer to a dictionary when they participate in the experiment and (2) if the study aims to compare learners' reactions to the literal and metaphorical meanings of a single lexical item, it is necessary to guarantee that participants can, at least, recognize the literal meaning of that lexical item.

Depending on the target participants of the study, there are several ways to select the words to be used in the experiments. In a classroom setting, using the vocabulary list in the participants' textbook is effective. For offline studies that do not involve reaction time, the word list can contain words from different parts of speech, orthographic length, general frequency or number of syllables, although it is recommended that all the words in the list should be as unified as possible. For online studies reaction time, more restricted criteria may apply, especially for: (1) parts of speech, because even for native speakers there is a difference in reaction time between nouns and verbs, and (2) orthographic length and number of syllables – the length of the words used generally correlates to the processing time needed.

After the selection of critical lexical items to be used in the experiment, the next step is to construct the metaphorical expressions that are to be tested in the experiment. The most secure way to construct metaphorical expressions is to research established literature and databases on metaphors in the designated languages, and to find out if any of the metaphorical expressions recorded in these languages contain the critical lexical items selected. 'Secure' means that all the expressions collected are guaranteed to be metaphorical in cognitive semantics. However, this procedure may be highly time-consuming, especially if there is a dearth of literature with metaphorical expressions in one of the designated languages. Alternatively, one can construct one's own metaphorical expressions following the criteria of MIP or other frameworks by selecting the phrases that contain the metaphorical meanings of the target words. Deignan (2005) suggests that a corpus research prior to the construction of metaphorical expressions can ensure that the metaphorical expressions under investigation are actually authentic and natural. It should be noted that, when selecting the metaphorical meanings to be tested, it is important to draw a delicate line between semantically more transparent, productive metaphorical meanings and semantically less transparent, more idiomatic meanings. That is because, as I have proposed, learners may have the opportunity and/or ability to deduce the metaphorical meaning of a lexical item from the context and its literal meaning, and this route should be allowed to be accessible by default. Therefore, a meaning that is not closely related to the literal meaning of that lexical item is less favoured. For instance, if one aims to test the metaphorical meaning of 'kick', it is better to select the meaning of 'someone behaving unfairly because they are attacking you when you are in a weak position', which is realized in the use of 'kick someone when they are down', while using a semantically opaque expression like 'kick the bucket' is less appropriate.

For some receptive tasks, such as all of the online tasks and acceptability judgement tasks, it is sometimes necessary to provide a baseline from the results of the acquisition and the patterns of processing. Researchers should ensure that when learners do not show evidence of acquisition of a metaphorical expression, it results from their lack of knowledge of that expression rather than their lack of knowledge of the lexical items in the expression. Literal expressions that use the same critical lexical items are a good choice for a baseline.

After the construction of metaphorical expressions and baseline literal expressions, the next step is to create the test sentences or sentential stimuli, which is the context of the metaphorical expressions. Test sentences or sentential stimuli are utilized in acceptability judgement tasks, interpretation tasks, sentence correction tasks, self-paced reading tasks and maze tasks. For the offline tasks, including acceptability judgement, interpretation and sentence correction, there is no strict restriction on the construction of test sentences; a couple of sentences with contextual information to fully support the metaphorical meaning of an expression is sufficient. As introduced in the description of acceptability judgement tasks, other parts of the test sentence are used as distractors to hide the actual intention of the experiment; a longer test sentence is more likely to distract participants, and is also more likely to evoke a 'false rejection' that does not target the metaphorical expression.

The restrictions of sentences used in self-paced reading and maze tasks are stricter. It is advised that all the sentences adopt the same, simple structure, with similar openings and limited variations in the middle. Sentential stimuli for the online receptive tasks should be unpredictive; there is no pattern for participants, either learners or native speakers, to predict whether a sentence contains a literal expression or a metaphorical expression, or whether it is simply a filler. It is best to match the position of metaphorical expressions in different sentential stimuli, which means matching part of the speech of the critical lexical items; expression structures may also be necessary in such experiments.

The final step in the construction of experimental material is to create fillers. The primary function of fillers is to cover the aim of the experiment and prevent participants from deducing the purpose of the study and thereby providing 'altered' results. When applicable, filler sentences can be the target items of a different, irrelevant study, which forms a nested design; two studies are conducted in one experiment, and the test items of each study become one another's filler items.

The number of filler sentences varies according to the nature of the experimental task. For an offline task, such as an acceptability judgement task or a discourse completion task, the filler sentences should take no less than one-third of the total number of the test sentences. For an online task, such as a self-paced reading task, filler sentences should take no less than two-thirds of the total number of the test sentences. Filler sentences used in an online task should be constructed with the same length and structure of the test sentence so as to avoid easy identification by the participants. While the repeated appearance of critical lexical items should be maximally avoided in filler sentences, it is possible to utilize the same non-critical lexical items that appear in test sentences when constructing filler sentences.

6.6 Possible supplementary experiment instruments

6.6.1 Lexical evaluation survey

Although, and as shown in the last subsection, the selection and construction of metaphorical expressions follows a series of strict rules, individual differences between metaphorical expressions are somewhat inevitable. This is particularly prominent if: (1) one assumes that the degree of metaphoricalness is continuous rather than binary – that said, some metaphorical expressions may sound more metaphorical than others; (2) following Jordens and Kellerman's research, one would like to provide a solid definition and a reliable quantification of 'markedness' (see Section 3.2.1); and (3) one would like to investigate the acquisition of metaphorical expressions under a usage-based framework, which means that the frequency of metaphorical expressions may affect the outcome of acquisition. Under such circumstances, gathering opinions and judgements from a range of native speakers of the language(s) under investigation is crucial, since it could avoid the difference of perception between the experimenters and novice language users.

A lexical evaluation survey can be conducted to collect native speakers' attitudes toward literal and metaphorical expressions. Such a survey could be backtracked to Jordens and Kellerman's (1981) sorting of the meanings of 'breken' prior to the investigation into the transferability of meaning. In the original experiment, the experimenters made use of a card-sorting task (Miller 1969) to categorize the different meanings of a polysemous word and, based on the results, they reduced all the meanings of that word into two dimensions, concreteness vs abstractness (namely literalness vs metaphoricalness) and coreness vs peripheral-ness (which was later selected as their definition of markedness). While a card-sorting task provides an easy way of categorization for a number of meanings of a single word, it may not be applicable to the evaluation and categorization of meanings of different words. Thus, a lexical evaluation test was introduced as a simplified version of a card-sorting task.

Several 'dimensions', or several properties of word meanings, can be included in a lexical evaluation survey, depending on the purpose of experiment. In the version used in Chapter 7, three dimensions were included: (1) degree of concreteness, which can be transformed as the degree of metaphoricalness of a meaning, if it is assumed that metaphorical meanings are more abstract than literal meanings; (2) degree of markedness, following the definition of Jordens and Kellerman (1981), as evaluated by the 'coreness' or not of a given meaning; and (3) frequency in daily language use as perceived by novice language users, that is, whether a meaning appears more frequently in everyday language use as observed by a participant. Other dimensions can be added if the properties of a word's meaning needs quantification in an experiment, but it should be noted that some of the properties or dimensions may be correlated. Although Jordens and Kellerman argue that markedness and metaphoricalness are independent from each other, as discussed in Chapter 3, there may be possible correlations between the two properties. Such a correlation does not influence the result of a lexical evaluation survey,

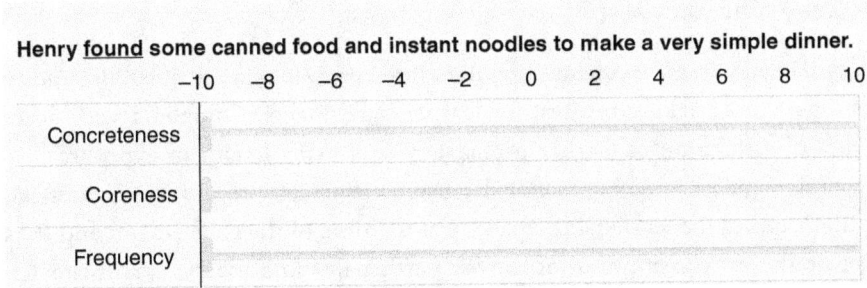

Figure 6.4 An excerpt from an online lexical evaluation survey

but it may impact any analysis in which quantified lexical properties are included. Thus, statistical tools should be used to separate the correlation before analysing the lexical properties that can influence the outcome of the acquisition of metaphorical expressions.

The presentation of a lexical evaluation survey, shown in Figure 6.4, can be very similar to that of an acceptability judgement task; instead of giving individual literal and metaphorical expressions, presenting literal and metaphorical expressions within a sentence or within a small paragraph, it is better for the participants if they understand the intended meanings of these expressions. After the presentation of the target sentences, Likert scales or magnitude estimation can be used for the evaluation. If several properties of a meaning are being evaluated, several scales can be presented at the same time; different to an acceptability judgement task, the words to be evaluated in a lexical evaluation survey must be explicitly marked out and participants should be assured that they are evaluating the intended words and/or expressions. A lexical evaluation survey can be created online, or in pen-and-paper form and, when necessary, it can be conducted in both the L1 and L2 under investigation.

It is advised to conduct a lexical evaluation survey among the native speakers of a language after the selection and construction of metaphorical expressions, but before the main experiment; this further rules out the possibility of outliers of metaphorical expressions, such as very rare or controversial metaphorical expressions, before learners participate in the experiment. This also means that the participants in the main experiment should not participate in the lexical evaluation survey; for learner participants, they should not participate in the lexical evaluation survey in either their L1 or L2. That is to avoid any possible revelation of the intention of the main experiment.

6.6.2 Proficiency test

A proficiency test is frequently required in second language acquisition studies as a part of a background test for learner participants. Compared with other types of estimation of learner proficiency (e.g. using length of exposure in a second language, language vs non-language majors, etc.), a proficiency test can better capture the learners' proficiency at the time of the experiment, and thus negate the misclassification of learner participants and thereto any mismatch in the results. However, conducting a proficiency test takes time. That may be especially prominent if participants with lower proficiency levels are included in the study; more time in second language testing usually creates greater anxiety for the participants. If a proficiency test takes too long to accomplish, then the learner participants may be less willing to complete the main tasks of the experiment, which will impact on the accuracy of the experiment results. Since the target of experiments related to the acquisition of metaphorical expressions is not an assessment of proficiency, but an evaluation of learners' knowledge of metaphorical expressions, one should attempt to focus on the target by reducing the time that is spent on other supplementary tasks.

Considering the above factors, the criteria of selection for a proficiency test is generally clear: (1) the proficiency test should cover different aspects of general proficiency of a second language, among which vocabulary, morphology and syntax are relatively more important, and (2) the proficiency test should not be too long, preferably around half-an-hour for intermediate learners. Therefore, instead of a fully-fledged proficiency test that measures the learners' ability to listen, speak, read and write, a brief proficiency test that: (1) tests one or two aspects of language proficiency and (2) widely covers the use of grammar and vocabulary may be more suitable as a supplementary task. A quick placement test, or a cloze test, with around thirty blanks, either in pen-and-paper or computerized form, are considered to be appropriate for a proficiency test. Proficiency tests should be given to the participants prior to the experiment, so that the proficiency of participant groups can be better controlled.

In certain settings, learner participants may have attended a standardized proficiency test in their second language; this is common when the target participants are overseas students and employees. If a participant can provide the results of a recently taken standardized proficiency test, and the result can be fully integrated into an established paradigm of second language proficiency (e.g. CEFR), then it is possible to omit a separate proficiency test and ask the participants to directly participate in the main experiment.

6.6.3 Vocabulary size test

Apart from a learner's general proficiency in a second language, which includes vocabulary and morphosyntax, an additional supplementary task can be conducted to estimate the learners' size of vocabulary. This task is crucial if one links the acquisition of metaphorical expressions to general vocabulary acquisition, and conducts experiments to discover the potential correlation between vocabulary size and the acquisition of metaphorical expressions. As proposed by Schmitt, vocabulary size should be measured from two main perspectives simultaneously, namely the width of vocabulary (how many words are mastered by a learner, and whether they can establish the connection between words) and the depth of vocabulary (how many meanings of a word are acquired by a learner, and whether they can establish the connection between meanings). The depth of vocabulary is closely associated with the acquisition of metaphorical expressions, and it is expected that learners with a deep vocabulary master metaphorical expressions better than other learners.

A vocabulary size test is usually conducted in a 'passive' way, in which the participants are asked to recognize words from a given list. Meanwhile, it is possible to test the participants' active vocabulary using a collocation or semantic category test; in the former, participants are given a lexical item and are asked to produce as many valid collocations as they can in a limited period of time; in the latter, participants are given a semantic category and are required to name words belonging to the semantic category. For beginners, a picture-naming task may be more participant-friendly than a collocation or semantic category task.

While most vocabulary size tests focus on a measurement of the width of a vocabulary, a timed collocation test can also be used to test the learners' depth of vocabulary. It is possible to calculate the number of meanings listed in a learners' production of different collocations and, in some cases, to calculate the percentage of metaphorical meanings in the production. That will facilitate the main experiment when comparing a learner's uncontrolled production of word meanings against their comprehension of metaphorical meanings. When this paradigm is used, it is important to ensure that the lexical items used in the collocation task do not overlap with the critical lexical items used in the main experiment.

6.6.4 Working memory capacity test

A working memory capacity test is required when conducting an online experiment, particularly self-paced reading or maze tasks. Since only one word appears on the screen at any point in time in each of these two paradigms, the participants need to store the words they have read in their working memory in order to understand the full sentence. The size of working memory capacity may influence the participants' reading speed and reading pattern regardless of their level of proficiency; therefore, when analysing the data collected from these online tasks, the impact of different working memory capacities should be reduced or eliminated before drawing any conclusion. In this way, working memory capacity is treated as a random factor that only influences individual performance, not unlike that of the participants' background information.

The most commonly used working memory capacity test is the digit span test. The digit span test measures how many digits a person can remember in a very short period, either following the exact sequence of the presentation of digits (i.e. forward digit span), or in the reversed sequence of the presentation (i.e. backward digit span). When a participant completes a string correctly, the next string will be longer – until the participant fails to complete a new, longer string. The participant's working memory capacity is then equal to the number of digits of the longest string they have completed correctly. Alongside the traditional test which involved writing down the digits, this task has been computerized and is also available on mobile devices. It can be flexibly added prior to the computerized reading experiment. The computerized version of a digit span test gives a presentation of the digits visually, which avoids the problem of presenting the task in the participants' second language, as well as avoiding the possible influence of a cross-linguistic difference in the pronunciation of numbers.

Other common working memory capacity tests include 'N-back', a complex, memory updating task; most of these tasks have been computerized. It is advised to use the computerized version and to conduct the test before the main experiment; this serves as an introduction to the main experiment and, at the same time, provides the participants' information to the experimenters, so that the experimenters are able to observe any anomaly when the main experiment is ongoing.

6.7 Summary

Instead of showing a summary of all the experimental tools used in previous studies, what this chapter does is to open several possibilities for future research on the acquisition of metaphorical expressions. On the one hand, a number of main experiment instruments are, in fact, not utilized in the area of acquisition of metaphorical expressions, although they are very mature tools and may have been applied to studies on other types of figurative language. On the other hand, the instruments presented in this chapter are limited. Only ecological-friendly methods are discussed, while more advanced technologies, such as eye-tracking and EEG, are excluded. Also, due to the limited available examples and the limited knowledge of the author, it is likely that some other powerful instruments have not been included in this chapter; however, the list of experimental tools will expand and will definitely enrich research in this area.

Other aspects discussed in this chapter, including the construction of test items and the selection of participants, however, are applicable to all research on the acquisition of metaphorical expressions. With a clear research target, all the test items should be carefully constructed in order to best capture the learners' reaction to, and production of, metaphorical expressions. One should be cautious before testing a metaphorical expression on learners, and before recruiting a learner for the experiment. Is the lexical item involved in the expression recognizable to learners? Is the meaning subject to the test a real 'metaphorical' meaning? Is the metaphorical meaning conventional enough so that even native speakers do not need to construct it? Is a learners' slow reaction due to the appearance of metaphorical expression, other (morphosyntactic) processing difficulties, or low working memory capacity? All these questions should be fully answered, even during the design of the experiment, so as to ensure that the results faithfully reflect the learners' behaviours.

7

Two experiments on the acquisition of metaphorical expressions

7.1 Introduction

This chapter presents two experimental studies in the acquisition of metaphorical expressions by Chinese learners of English at different proficiency levels. To compensate for the lack of systematic experimental works on the acquisition of L2 metaphorical expressions, this chapter aims to provide some first-hand data in this area.

This chapter consists of two major parts: the first part is an untimed, offline study in which learners and native speakers were both asked to judge the acceptability of a series of metaphorical expressions in different sentences; the second part is a timed online reading task, in which learners and native speakers read and processed metaphorical expressions in a self-paced manner. Both studies aim to reveal how Chinese learners of English perceive metaphorical expressions in their second language, and how they react to metaphorical expressions with different availability. The results of these two studies can be considered to be the baseline of the outcome of acquisition of metaphorical expressions; the learner participants in the two experiments did not receive any systematic instruction on metaphorical expressions, and their performance of reading and judging metaphorical expressions should be regarded as the result of an untutored acquisition of these expressions. The results of the two studies can help second language instructors to understand what strengths and weaknesses L2 learners have in terms of metaphorical expressions, and thus design course contents and tasks to improve their performance. They can also be used by researchers to compare whether the learners' performance can be improved in different learning environments, or between different L1–L2 pairs.

7.2 Judging metaphorical expressions

7.2.1 Participants

Eighty-six Chinese learners of English and twenty-four native speakers of British-English were recruited for an acceptability judgement task. The learners were divided into four groups, namely 'Int' (intermediate), 'Low-adv' (low-advanced), 'High-adv' (high-advanced) and 'Overseas' (high-advanced overseas) based on their proficiency of English as estimated by their performance in the Oxford Quick Placement Test (UCLES 2001) as well as their linguistic backgrounds. The English proficiency levels of High-adv and Overseas groups were matched, and the only difference between the two groups was that the participants in the overseas group had received long-term exposure to a native English-speaking environment prior to the experiment. The basic information of learner participants is listed in Table 7.1.

7.2.2 Materials

All the test materials used in the acceptability judgement task took the format of individual sentences (henceforth 'test sentences'), and each sentence contained a critical lexical item to be tested. Each critical lexical item appeared in a pair

Table 7.1 Linguistic backgrounds of the learner participants in the acceptability judgement task

		Int	Low-adv	High-adv	Overseas
Group size		21	26	21	18
Average OQPT score (SD)		36.81 (3.44)	44.5 (1.79)	52 (2.74)	53.18 (4.52)
Average age (years;months) (SD)		18;5 (3.16)	20;2 (3.70)	22;7 (2.31)	24;2 (2.96)
Gender	Male	10	9	7	6
	Female	11	17	14	12
Number of participants with overseas experience		0	1*	4†	18‡

*The participant (twenty-eight years old) stated that she had been in the US for thirty-six months, two years before the experiment (when she was twenty-three). Considering that she had been living in China ever since and had not received any exposure to a native English environment since her return, she was categorized in the low advanced group according to her performance in the OQPT.

†All overseas experiences recorded had taken place at least one year before the experiment. The average length of stay was 3.5 months (SD=3.79). The average age of first overseas experience was 16;3 (SD=8.10).

‡The average length of stay was 32.11 months (SD=30.62). The average age of first overseas experience was 20;1 (SD=3.7).

of test sentences in an experimental task; in one sentence the intended meaning of the lexical item was metaphorical while in the other it was literal (in both cases). All the critical lexical items were selected from the established literature on metaphors in Chinese and English (particularly from Lakoff & Johnson 1980; Link 2013; Liu 2002; Yu 1998).

Three categories of metaphorical expression were designed: (1) the Metaphorical-Both (MB) category, including metaphorical expressions that were available in both Chinese and English with the same meaning; (2) the Metaphorical-Source (MS) category, which included metaphorical expressions only available in the source language Chinese, but incomprehensible after translation into an English word-for-word manner; and (3) the Metaphorical-Target (MT) category, which included metaphorical expressions that were only available in the target language of English, but became incomprehensible after translation into Chinese in a word-for-word manner. This classification corresponded to the different possible levels of transferability in the acquisition of metaphorical expressions; the expressions in the MB category were generally transferable while those in the MS category were not transferable because there was no word-for-word corresponding expression in the target language. The expressions in the MT category were not transferable either, since the learners did not have any equivalents for the expressions in their L1. To provide a baseline for the results of acquisition and the patterns of processing, three categories of literal expression were also designed and examined in these experiments: (1) the Literal-Both (LB) category – the literal, baseline counterpart of the MB category; (2) the Literal-Source (LS) category – the literal, baseline counterpart of the MS category; and (3) the Literal-Target (LT) category – the literal, baseline counterpart of the MT category. The LB and MB, LS and MS, and LT and MT categories made use of the same group of critical lexical items. The availability of the different types of expression in Chinese and English is shown in Table 7.2.

In the acceptability judgement task, each category consisted of eight different critical lexical items, including four nouns and four verbs. The twenty-four critical lexical items were either one-syllable or two-syllable words (M=1.208, SD=0.415) and their orthographic lengths were between three and seven letters (M=4.458, SD=1.503). The lexical items were extracted from an English course syllabus used in secondary schools in China so as to ensure that all the learner participants, who were secondary school and college students in China, were able to recognize the lexical items without dictionary assistance.

The test sentences that included literal MB or MT expressions were extracted from established literature on metaphors, the British National Corpus

Table 7.2 Availability of different types of expression in Chinese and English

	Availability in Chinese	Availability in English
MB (Metaphorical-Both)	Yes	Yes
MS (Metaphorical-Source)	Yes	No
MT (Metaphorical-Target)	No	Yes
LB (Literal-Both)	Yes	Yes
LS (Literal-Source)	Yes	Yes
LT (Literal-Target)	Yes	Yes

and selected works of English literature. Small modifications were made to ensure that: (1) the sentences were of similar length and (2) intermediate learners could understand each word without referring to a dictionary. The sentences that included MS expressions were selected from literature on Chinese metaphors and then translated by the experimenter. Additionally, twenty-six fillers were included in the task, half of which were grammatical, half ungrammatical. After modification and translation, all the sentences were examined and verified by three native English consultants to confirm that: (1) all the sentences in the MB and MT categories, literal counterparts and grammatical fillers were acceptable to native English speakers; (2) all the ungrammatical fillers were indeed unacceptable; and (3) all the sentences in the MS category were unacceptable. Three Chinese native speakers, with a high proficiency English, also examined and verified the sentences to confirm that: (1) all the sentences containing MB expressions had exact word-for-word translation equivalents in Chinese, (2) none of the sentences containing MT expressions could be understood after a word-for-word literal translation into Chinese and (3) all the sentences containing the literal uses of the critical lexical items could be understood after a word-for-word literal translation into Chinese. All literal and metaphorical expressions in corresponding test sentences in both Chinese and English versions were surveyed in a lexical evaluation task, in which Chinese and English native speakers assessed their degree of concreteness (metaphoricalness), coreness (markedness) and perceived frequency in everyday language.

7.2.3 Method

All the test sentences in the acceptability judgement task were presented with an 11-point Likert scale of acceptability (henceforth 'the score scale'), a blank for sentence correction and a 5-point Likert scale of confidence (henceforth 'the confidence scale'). For each sentence, participants were asked to give a 'score for the sentence' on the score scale, to indicate how confident they were when they gave the score on the confidence scale and, when appropriate, to provide a sentence showing corrections in the blank space provided. The range of the score scale varied from 0 to 10, which resembled the typical scoring system in Chinese secondary schools, so naïve participants could easily understand the concept of acceptability judgement by converting 'the degree of acceptability' to 'the score that the sentence should receive'.

This experiment was conducted as a pen-and-paper test. Two versions of the acceptability judgement questionnaire, with two different sequences of test sentences, were provided to avoid any sequencing effect. Each participant was assigned a version randomly. A brief instruction with examples was provided in the introductory part; participants were asked to imagine that they were marking the compositions for their classmates, and asked to give a score for each sentence. It was also explicitly stated in the instructions that the participants were not allowed to refer to any sort of dictionary; rather, they should follow their intuition for the entire task. The instruction aimed to help secondary school students who participated in the experiment to understand their task, as well as easing any anxiety or fear of authority when they received the materials from the experimenter. Although this setting might guide some participants to judge the sentences in a prescriptive way, they were encouraged to utilize their intuition in their judgements.

7.2.4 Procedure

All participants were told to send an email to the experimenter to express their interest at the stage of recruitment. When the experimenter replied to the emails from the prospective participants, each was assigned a participant number together with a consent form and information about the experiment. After they had confirmed that they would like to participate in the experiment and signed the consent form, they were sent the proficiency test (learners only), the language background and linguistic experience survey (learners only), and the acceptability judgement task (learners and native speakers), all in the Microsoft Word Document (.docx) format. In each part of the experiment they were asked to enter their participant number and complete the task, and they were required to complete the tasks entirely on their own. After completion, all the questionnaires were sent back to the experimenter via email, and a small remuneration was sent to the participants after the experimenter had confirmed that all parts of the experiment had been fully completed.

7.2.5 Data adjustment

The adjustment of data obtained from this experiment involved the adjustment of acceptability scores, the selection of feedback sentences and the coding of confidence levels. The procedure of data adjustment was not extensively discussed in Chapter 6, since dependence on the distribution of data can sometimes be excluded from a standard data analysis procedure. However, in this experiment, the raw result of acceptability judgement task was adjusted to: (1) obtain the most relevant data for analysis and (2) to maximize the reliability of the data at current stage. The data, after data adjustment, would be used for further analysis.

As discussed in Chapter 6, judging the acceptability of a metaphorical expression in the context of a sentence brings both advantages and disadvantages. It was observed in this experiment that participants, both native speakers and learners, were sometimes 'distracted' from the acceptability of metaphorical expressions and, instead, pointed out 'errors' in the test sentences. This required data adjustment based on the participants' feedback sentences to ensure that the degree of acceptability being measured in the test was the acceptability of metaphorical expressions. The first step of data adjustment was based exactly on this criterion; if a feedback sentence showed irrelevance to the metaphorical expression or the designed grammatical error included in the sentence, for instance, the participant focused on the tense of the sentence, or 'corrected' an acceptable literal counterpart or a grammatical filler, then the score for the sentence given by that participants was excluded from the data set.

A second problem with the acceptability judgement task was that participants' preference varied when they evaluated the acceptability of sentences on the 11-point Likert scale. For instance, it was observed that some participants only used the second half of the 11-point scale, despite the demonstration in the instruction. To deal with such divergences (in the second step of data adjustment) mixed-effect linear models were adopted as the main statistical tool in analysing the results of the acceptability judgement experiment by individual participants, with individual test items being considered random factors (i.e. noise factors). At the same time, a data adjustment based on linear mixed-effect modelling was also conducted to reduce 'between-group' differences. The output of that model, namely 'the acceptability score' of each judgement, would assume that every participant in each group treated the scale in the same way, and thus made the results between proficiency groups more comparable. After data adjustment, a positive acceptability score indicated that a participant had accepted the given test sentence when compared with: (1) other participants judging the same test sentence and (2) the same participants judging other test sentences. Similarly, a negative acceptability score indicated that the participant had rejected a given test sentence when a comparison was made across participants or across test sentences.

For the feedback sentences, only sentences that targeted the use of metaphorical expressions were included in the analysis. Meanwhile, some participants, for certain reasons, pointed out the possible problems of a test sentence without giving their correction. This type of response was also included in the study and categorized as 'error indicated without correction'.

Finally, the level of confidence of each judgement, which was recorded on a 5-point Likert scale, was converted into numerical confidence scores from 1 to 5, with 'not at all confident' being assigned 1 and 'very confident' being assigned 5. Based on feedback from participants, I used the boundary between points 3 and 4 to classify whether a participant was confident about a judgement; if a participant gave a confidence score of 4 or 5 points, that data point was coded as 'confident', otherwise, the data point was coded as 'not confident'.

After data adjustment, unless further specified in the results, all of the data was analysed using linear mixed models, with the maximal random factors including: **individual diversity** of learners (e.g. age, average exposure to English and working memory capacity as measured by backward digit span), **individual differences** of critical words (e.g. orthographic length, general frequency) and confidence level of learners' judgement.

7.2.6 Results

7.2.6.1 Degree of acceptability of literal and metaphorical expressions

A general picture of the acceptability scores of literal and metaphorical expressions is given in Figure 7.1. Overall, native speakers and learners accepted all literal expressions. Less proficient learners gave lower acceptability scores to the literal expressions compared with more proficient learners and native speakers ($\chi^2(4)=9.56$, $p=0.048$). Other than that, no significant differences were observed, particularly in the case of differences in the degree of acceptability of literal expressions as between more proficient learners and native speakers.

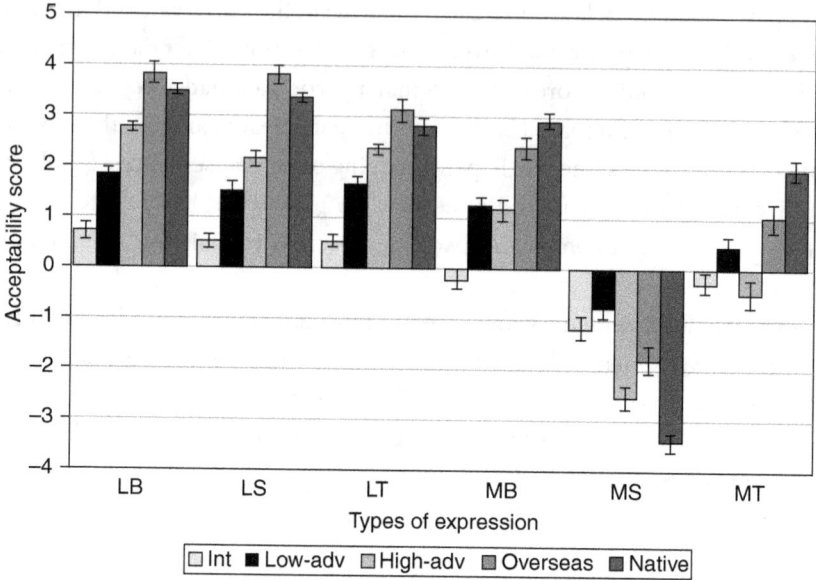

Figure 7.1 Acceptability scores for literal and metaphorical expressions by group

Turning to the comparison between metaphorical and literal expressions, all learner groups gave significantly lower acceptability scores to MB expressions than to the LB expressions: ($\chi^2(1)=5.06$, p=0.025 for intermediate; $\chi^2(1)=3.86$, p=0.0496 for low-advanced; $\chi^2(1)=11.78$, p<0.001 for high-advanced; $\chi^2(1)=5.35$, p=0.021 for overseas); such differences, however, were not observed in the native group. Compared with the native group, the intermediate, low-advanced and high-advanced learner groups gave significantly lower acceptability scores to the MB expressions: ($\chi^2(1)=9.19$, p=0.002 for intermediate; $\chi^2(1)=8.24$, p=0.004 for low-advanced; $\chi^2(1)=11.87$, p<0.001 for high-advanced), while the difference between native group and overseas learner groups was marginal ($\chi^2(1)=3.80$, p=0.051). Although it seemed that more proficient learners generally gave higher acceptability scores to the MB expressions than less proficient groups, this difference was not significant.

The acceptability score for the LS and MS expressions clearly showed a contrast between 'acceptable' meanings and 'unacceptable' meanings, since the LS expressions were available in English, but the MS expressions were not. All learner groups and native speakers gave significantly lower scores to MS expressions than to the LS expressions: ($\chi^2(1)=7.67$, p=0.005 for intermediate; $\chi^2(1)=10.69$, p=0.001 for low-advanced; $\chi^2(1)=19.30$, p<0.001 for high-advanced; $\chi^2(1)=21.56$, p<0.001 for overseas. Compared to the native group, the intermediate and low-advanced groups gave significantly higher scores to the MS expressions – ($\chi^2(1)$=13.94, p<0.001 for intermediate; $\chi^2(1)$=10.28, p=0.001 for low-advanced) – however, the high-advanced and overseas groups did not show such a significant difference when compared with native speakers. In the case of the MS expressions, proficiency was a significant influence on the acceptability scores ($\chi^2(3)$=8.95, p=0.030); more proficient learners, such as the high-advanced and overseas groups, gave significantly lower scores to the MS expressions than less proficient learners. In particular, a distinct shift could be observed between the low-advanced group and the high-advanced group; learners classified as 'highly advanced' in the experiment were able to make judgements about the MS expressions, which were similar to the native group. Such a division suggests that there might be a threshold of 'native-likeness' for learners, with learners not reaching the threshold, which demonstrates a significant difference in their judgement when compared to native speakers of English.

The result of the comparison between the LT and MT expressions was similar to that between the LB and MB expressions; all learner groups gave significantly lower acceptability scores to the MT expressions than to the LT expressions – ($\chi^2(1)$=5.70, p=0.017 for intermediate; $\chi^2(1)$=5.93, p=0.015 for low-advanced; $\chi^2(1)$=9.37, p=0.002 for high-advanced; $\chi^2(1)$=8.50, p=0.004 for overseas) – again, such differences were not present in the native group. Compared with the native group, the high-advanced and overseas learner groups gave significantly lower acceptability scores to the MT expressions – ($\chi^2(1)$=7.63, p=0.006 for high-advanced; $\chi^2(1)$=5.94, p=0.015 for overseas) – but there was no significant difference between the intermediate group and the native group, and the difference between the low-advanced group and the native group was marginal ($\chi^2(1)$=3.83, p=0.050). Even though there were minor differences when each learner group was compared with a native group, no significant difference was observed between all the learner groups, indicating that the proficiency of the learners did not significantly influence the acceptability scores of the LT or MT expressions.

The acceptability scores of different expressions showed that native speakers and Chinese learners of English gave distinct judgements depending on the type of expression. The native speaker group accepted all the expressions that were available in English, including all the literal expressions and the MB and MT expressions; at the same time, they clearly rejected the MS expressions that were not available in English. However, all the learner groups still showed a strong preference for literal expressions when comparing acceptability scores for literal and metaphorical expressions available in English (i.e. MB and MT expressions); this was the case even for highly proficient participants with

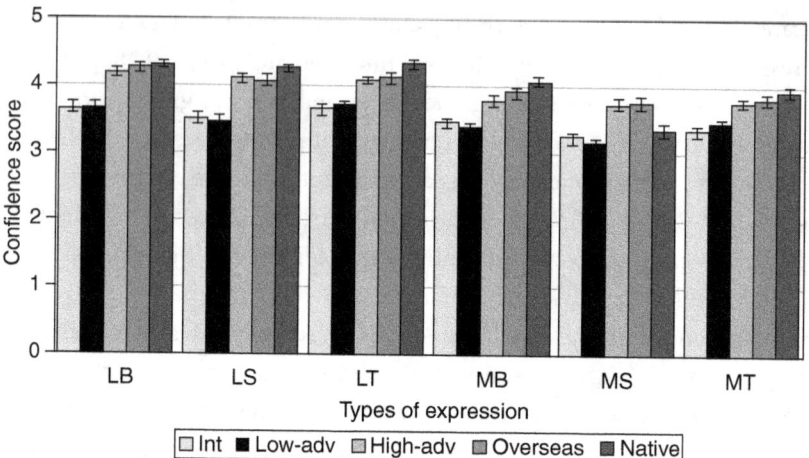

Figure 7.2 Confidence scores for the six target types for each group

overseas experience. For the three types of metaphorical expression, learners showed a general acceptance of MB expressions and a general rejection of MS expressions, but it seems that learners with a relatively high proficiency level did not accept MT expressions, yet.

7.2.6.2 *Confidence levels when making acceptability judgements*

The confidence scores given by all the participants is shown in Figure 7.2. In general, the native group was the most confident when allocating scores to the given expressions, save for MS expressions. However, the native group was also more confident when judging the literal expressions than the metaphorical expressions – ($\chi^2(1)=3.16$, p=0.076 for the LB/MB pairs; $\chi^2(1)=8.53$, p=0.003 for the LS/MS pairs; $\chi^2(1)=10.40$, p=0.001 for the LT/MT pairs). The relatively low confidence score for MS expressions from the native group should be attributed to the unfamiliarity of these expressions; none of the MS expressions were available in English and the native participants would not have encountered them. As a result, they may have difficulty inferring the meaning of the MS expressions in the task, and may not be confident about their judgement.

The learner participants, as with the native group, were more confident when judging the literal expressions than the metaphorical expressions – ($\chi^2(1)=10.06$, p=0.002 for the LB/MB pairs; $\chi^2(1)=12.21$, p<0.001 for the LS/MS pairs; $\chi^2(1)=7.47$, p=0.006 for the LT/MT pairs). The intermediate and low-advanced groups were less confident than other learner participants with all metaphorical expressions; in particular, the two groups were significantly less confident than other participants when scoring the MB and MT expressions ($\chi^2(2)=10.98$, p=0.004 for MB; $\chi^2(2)$=9.06, p=0.011 for MT). The confidence scores for both MB and MT expressions for high-advanced and overseas groups, on the other hand, did not significantly differ from those of the native group. As proficiency levels increased, learners were significantly more confident when rating all metaphorical expressions ($\chi^2(3)$=9.56, p=0.026 for MB; $\chi^2(3)$=10.14, p=0.017 for MS; $\chi^2(3)$=7.95, p=0.047 for MT).

A picture of the confidence scores can help to determine whether a learner showed indeterminacy in the judgement task by investigating whether their confidence was low when they made a judgement. It can be deduced from the discussion above that less proficient learners gave low acceptability scores for the MB and MT expressions, mainly because of indeterminacy. A point worth noting is that the high-advanced and overseas groups were no less confident than the native participants when they provided judgements for the MB and MT expressions; however, the scores given by the two learner groups, compared to those given by the native speakers, were significantly different. Just as the native group generally accepted the MT expressions, the high-advanced and overseas participants tended to reject the MT expressions. I argue, therefore, that, in contrast to the indeterminacy of the less proficient learners (mentioned above), more proficient learners seemed to assertively reject the metaphorical expressions that they had seldom experienced in their L1, even though their intuition was entirely different from the native participants' judgements. The negative attitude shown by more proficient learners toward the MT expressions, especially in comparison to the relatively positive attitude towards MB expressions, might be largely due to the lack of availability of these metaphorical expressions in their source language. Remember, native speakers had similar confidence problems with expressions not known in their language. In the current study, the MT expressions were specific to English, while the MB expressions were shared between the language pair. The fact that none of the learner groups genuinely seemed to accept the MT expressions indicates that some language-specific use of lexical items is more difficult to acquire than the shared use of lexical items; this may be because learners can only encounter the former in their L2, but the latter in both languages.

7.2.6.3 Cross-linguistic influences on the judgement of metaphorical expressions and possible influencing factors

7.2.6.3.1 Identification of traces of transfer in the acceptability judgement task

One of the focuses of this study is on the possible cross-linguistic influence in the acquisition of metaphorical expressions; therefore, it is crucial to provide a quantification of cross-linguistic influence and to examine how it is distributed when learners acquire different metaphorical expressions. Prior to an analysis of how different factors can influence a learner's 'strategy of transfer', I will first identify the point at which learners transfer their knowledge from L1 to L2 in the acceptability judgement task.

Theoretically, traces of transfer should be identified by judgements that are similar to those that would be made in the learners' L1. The cases that are most clearly identifiable as transfer are those in which their judgement does not correspond to the judgement made by most native speakers, such as accepting MS expressions and rejecting MT expressions. When the cases of possible transfer are not readily distinguishable from cases of possible acquisition, such as accepting MB expressions, I refer to the confidence scores to see if the learners were confident about the judgements they had made. I categorize all the individual judgements made by learners into three main groups: judgements that (possibly) show traces of transfer; judgements that (possibly) show traces of native-like performance; and judgements that do not belong to either of the groups mentioned above, termed 'transfer not shown'. The criteria for the categorization for the three types of metaphorical expression are listed in Tables 7.3 to 7.5. It should be noted that the identification of traces of transfer is a rough, statistical estimation rather than a case-by-case analysis, and there may be misidentification in the process. Considering that all the judgement data is analysed in groups, the accuracy of a statistical estimation is sufficient for meaningful analysis.

By adopting this criteria for identification, I can estimate how pervasive the traces of transfer can be when learners judge different types of metaphorical expression, or a type of expression is judged by different groups of learners. Table 7.6 shows the estimated percentage of traces of transfer among all the judgements given by the learner groups. A higher percentage in Table 7.6 indicates that: (1) a group of learners was more likely to transfer knowledge when making a judgement or (2) learners were more likely to transfer knowledge when judging that type of metaphorical expression.

Table 7.3 Identification of traces of transfer in the judgements of MB expressions

	Confident (>3)	Not confident (≤3)
Acceptance (≥0)	Native-like performance	Possible positive transfer
Rejection (<0)	Transfer not shown	

Table 7.4 Identification of traces of transfer in the judgements of MS expressions

	Confident (>3)	Not confident (≤3)
Acceptance (≥0)	Possible negative transfer	Transfer not shown
Rejection (<0)	Native-like performance	

Table 7.5 Identification of traces of transfer in the judgements of MT expressions

	Confident (>3)	Not confident (≤3)
Acceptance (≥0)	Native-like performance	Transfer not shown
Rejection (<0)	Possible negative transfer	

Table 7.6 Estimated percentage of traces of transfer of different metaphorical expressions in the learner groups

	Intermediate (%)	Low-advanced (%)	High-advanced (%)	Overseas (%)	Average (%)
MB	27.15	30.73	16.44	17.86	23.69
MS	58.13	43.56	20.37	20.14	36.50
MT	35.10	40.70	51.55	46.76	43.38
Total	40.48	38.45	29.85	28.23	34.66

On average, learners were most likely to transfer their knowledge when they judged the MT expressions, while they were least likely to transfer their knowledge when they judged the MB expressions. There was a clear declining trend in traces of transfer for MS expressions; traces of transfer were identified among more than half of the judgements provided by the intermediate group, while the percentage declined to only 20 per cent when it came to both the high-advanced and overseas groups.

Following Jordens and Kellerman, once traces of transfer have been identified it should be established, when traces of transfer and traces of non-transfer are compared, which aspect of 'non-transfer' is of greater interest. As shown in Table 7.3, non-transfer cases included both native-like judgements and 'transfer being blocked'. Although it seems, at first glance, unreasonable to compare traces of transfer and traces of native-like judgement, for transfer always implies the absence of native-like judgement, it is theoretically feasible to simply compare cases of 'transfer' and 'non-transfer' instead of dividing 'non-transfer' cases into more fine-grained categories. The reason for this is that at least one factor, namely general knowledge, suggests that non-transfer includes both native-like judgements (which makes use of existent knowledge) and transfer being blocked, rather than the latter exclusively. The comparison between 'transfer' and 'non-transfer', including native-like judgement and transfer being blocked, was adopted throughout the following analysis.

7.2.6.3.2 *The influence of the degree of markedness and metaphoricalness on transfer in the acquisition of metaphorical expressions*

In previous subsections, when I analysed the scores of metaphorical expressions, I defined 'metaphorical' in a binary way; an expression is either metaphorical or literal, and there is no finer distinction between metaphorical expressions. However, as in Jordens and Kellerman's discussion, metaphoricalness may not be as important as one might consider it to be in terms of its influence on transfer; rather, markedness may have a more prominent influence. By Kellerman's definition, the degree of markedness is perceived as a continuum, and it is possible that metaphorical expressions with different degrees of markedness would show different degrees of cross-linguistic influence. In this subsection, I will focus on a continuous factor, a binary factor and their influence on transfer, namely the degree of markedness (in Chinese) and binary metaphoricalness. The degree of markedness was measured in a lexical evaluation task in which markedness was represented as a coreness score. A positive coreness score meant that the expression is less marked, and a negative coreness score meant that the expression is marked. By this comparison, I will investigate which factor plays the more important role in transfer; markedness or metaphoricalness.

For the analysis of the relationship between the degree of markedness and the possibility of transfer, I examine the distribution of coreness scores within traces of transfer, that is, whether a frequently transferred expression has a higher or lower coreness score. If more traces of transfer are associated with a higher coreness score, then it might be inferred that core meanings are more likely to be transferred; if more traces of transfer are associated with a lower coreness score, then this would show that peripheral meanings are more likely to be transferred. Therefore, I examined the correlation between the extent of traces of transfer and the coreness scores. Only the MB and MS expressions were included in the analysis because they may be transferred from Chinese; within each proficiency level, the MB and MS expressions were compared as one, since together they formed a longer continuum of degree of markedness, and the influence of markedness would be more significant on a larger scale.

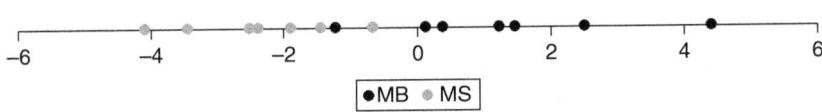

Figure 7.3 Distribution of coreness scores for the MB and MS expressions in the AJT, as perceived by Chinese native speakers

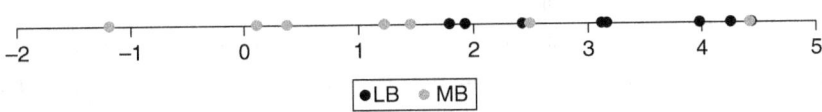

Figure 7.4 Distribution of the coreness scores of the LB and MB expressions in the AJT, as perceived by Chinese native speakers

The distribution of the coreness scores for the MB and MS expressions in the judgement task is shown in Figure 7.3.

Using Spearman's rank correlation coefficient test, a significant negative correlation was found in the intermediate group between the number of judgements showing traces of transfer and the coreness score for each critical item (rho=−0.70, p=0.003). However, after the influence from the type of metaphorical expression used was excluded, the influence of the coreness score was no longer significant. No other significant correlation was found in other groups of participants. It seems that, when compared with the influence of types of metaphorical expressions, the influence of the degree of markedness of metaphorical expressions was not significant.

Similarly, I can also compare LB and MB expressions with different degrees of markedness. The LB and MB expressions were all shared between the learners' L1 and L2, and the major differences between the two types were metaphoricalness and degree of markedness; the distribution of the coreness scores is demonstrated in Figure 7.4. In general the coreness scores of LB expressions were rated higher than those of MB expressions ($\chi^2(1)=8.13$, p=0.004), as revealed by a linear mixed-effect model.

The same statistical tool, as used in the previous analysis, was used for this analysis. No significant correlation was found between the numbers of instances of transfer and the coreness scores for each test expression in any learner group. The reason for this lack of difference may come from the distribution of the coreness scores of these two types of expression, as illustrated in Figure 7.5. Compared with Figure 7.4, the coreness scores of most LB and MB expressions were uniformly high, with only one expression below 0. It is possible that the difference in the coreness scores was not significant enough to demonstrate their impact on the subjective transferability of a meaning.

While the degree of markedness of an expression only had a limited influence on the transferability of metaphorical expressions, one (main) question emerged from the results of the experiment; if markedness does not influence traces of transfer when learners judge metaphorical expressions, what is the main reason for differences in acceptability scores between LB and MB expressions? Then it is time to look back and explore the possible influence of binary metaphoricalness on the subjective transferability of an expression. In order to control other influential factors, the comparison between LB and MB expressions will be demonstrated.

Table 7.7 shows the distribution of traces of transfer in LB and MB expressions across learner groups. Clear quantitative differences were shown in the distribution; compared with LB expressions, MB expressions generally showed fewer traces of transfer among learners in each group, and the transfer of MB expressions was also less likely to surface than that of LB expressions when both types of expression are objectively transferable. In general, learners seemed to be less likely to transfer MB expressions than LB expressions. On this basis, it is possible to conclude that it was more difficult for them to acquire the MB expressions via transfer than the LB expressions.

A follow-up analysis showed that the degree of markedness of an expression did not significantly influence the extent of traces of transfer being blocked. Therefore, markedness did not significantly contribute to the low subjective transferability of the MB expressions; the major possible reason for the differences shown in Table 7.7, between LB and MB expressions, may be metaphoricalness. Being metaphorical or, to be more precise, being 'non-literal' does not simply indicate that an such an expression will receive a lower acceptability score from learners compared to a literal expression, it may also indicate that a metaphorical

Table 7.7 Distribution of traces of transfer on LB and MB expressions across learners' proficiency

	Types of expression	IN (%)	LA (%)	HA (%)	HO (%)
Possible positive transfer	LB	26.49	24.61	11.11	9.70
	MB	27.15	30.73	16.44	17.86
Native-like performance	LB	52.98	50.79	84.03	80.60
	MB	37.09	39.06	52.05	55.00
Transfer not shown	LB	20.53	24.61	4.86	9.70
	MB	35.76	30.21	31.51	27.14

expression is less transferable and, more importantly, learners are generally less likely to benefit from the potential for positive transfer.

7.2.6.3.3 The influence of general proficiency on transfer in the acquisition of metaphorical expressions

To examine whether the general proficiency of learners may have affected the transfer strategies they used, the Mann-Whitney test was used to compare the OQPT score for all participants who showed traces of transfer, and those who did not. If a participant provided two judgements that were identified as showing traces of cross-linguistic influence, the OQPT score was counted twice in the test, since cross-linguistic influence weighed more in the overall data set. Similarly, if, at the same time, a participant provided one score showing traces of possible transfer and another showing traces of possible non-transfer, the OQPT score would appear both in the 'transfer' and the 'transfer not shown' lists. This method of calculation allows one to account for the variability of learners; a learner may present a certain degree of cross-linguistic influence on some critical items, but not on others. Including a data point according to its weight in the whole data set could help to capture the delicate differences between participants, and thus provide a better picture of the factors that are influential on transferability. The OQPT scores were compared within each type of expression.

A comparison of the OQPT scores reveals that the participants who presented traces of transfer when judging the MB expressions had significantly lower OQPT scores than those who did not present traces of transfer (U=41764, p=0.002). The mean OQPT score achieved by the participants showing traces of transfer was 44.59 (SD=7.11), while the mean OQPT score for the participants who did not show traces of transfer was 46.79 (SD=6.98). It seems that the less proficient learners were more likely to rely on a transfer of their L1 knowledge to score the MB expressions in the task.

As for the MS expressions, the participants who showed traces of transfer had a significantly lower OQPT result than those who did not show traces of transfer (U=31786, p<0.001). The mean OQPT score achieved by the participants showing trace of transfer was 43.43 (SD=6.40), while the mean OQPT score for the participants who did not show traces of transfer was 47.89 (SD=6.86). Again, general proficiency seems to have influenced the transfer strategies; less proficient learners were more likely to show negative transfer when they scored the MS expressions.

However, the influence of general proficiency was not prominent on the subjective transferability of the MT expressions. Only marginal significance from the OQPT scores was observed between the participants who showed traces of transfer and those who did not (U=56192, p=0.069). The mean OQPT score achieved by the participants showing traces of transfer was 46.89 (SD=7.20) and the mean OQPT score for the participants who did not was 46.04 (SD=6.75). There was no clear difference between the two groups; the participants presenting traces of transfer achieved a slightly higher average OQPT score than those who did not show any traces of transfer. Furthermore, from the estimated percentage of instances of transfer listed in Table 7.6, it can also be seen that the percentage did not change drastically between different proficiency groups. Compared with the MB and MS expressions, the influence of proficiency on traces of transfer with the MT expressions was less clear. Considering that even highly proficient learners still rejected the MT expressions in general, it could be inferred that the cross-linguistic influence on MT expressions was more persistent. That is possibly because there were no correspondences to the MT expressions in the learners' L1, and the learners failed to perceive the possibility of those MT expressions.

Overall, as proficiency rose, participants gradually presented fewer traces of transfer from their L1 to their L2 in judging metaphorical expressions. While that decrease in influence was prominent among the MB and MS expressions, the MT expressions seem to be the exception, with the level of proficiency in English not influencing the transferability. This provides some evidence that the acquisition of the MT expressions may be different from that of the MB and MS expressions. The learners gradually mastered the knowledge of metaphorical expressions if there were corresponding expressions in their L1; in such cases, they were able to accept the MB expressions available in L2 and reject the MS expressions that were not available in their L2. However, since the MT expressions were not available in their L1, they did not have any knowledge to transfer and remained suspicious of those expressions, which eventually led to their rejection.

7.2.6.4 Distribution of feedback sentences and learners' strategies

After analysing the acceptability scores and possible traces of transfer in the judgement task, I will now focus on the production part of this experiment, namely feedback sentences. Only relevant feedback sentences that are aimed at the use of metaphorical expressions are included in the discussion below. Also, when a participant explicitly pointed out a problematic constituent (e.g. a misused L1-specific metaphorical expression, but did not provide any sentences) the response was counted, but categorized as an 'error indicated

Table 7.8 Distribution of relevant feedback sentences provided by each group of participants across different metaphorical conditions

	IN	LA	HA	HO	NS	Total
MB feedback sentences	6	6	15	7	6	40
MS feedback sentences	20	40	86	56	118	320
MT feedback sentences	17	28	44	29	43	161
Total relevant feedback sentences	43	74	145	92	167	521
Relevant feedback sentences per person	2.05	3.19	6.90	5.11	6.96	4.74

without correction'. The distribution of these relevant sentences is listed in Table 7.8.

The relevant feedback sentences obtained from this study can be categorized in two different ways: (1) whether the participants provided feedback sentences as an alternative, a rejection, or a correction to the given expressions and (2) what types of expression the participants used to produce the feedback sentences, that is, literal or metaphorical, shared or language-specific. The first method reveals how the participants react to metaphorical expressions in a more detailed manner, while the second method reveals what strategies the participants can use when they encounter a metaphorical expression, especially a metaphorical expression that they do not find appropriate. This subsection is devoted to these two aspects of the analysis respectively.

The categorization of the reaction types involved a joint analysis of the acceptability scores of metaphorical expressions and the feedback sentences provided, resulting in one possible reaction type per item. On the one hand, a participant who accepted a given correct expression (i.e. gave a positive score to an available expression) and provided a feedback sentence at the same time is likely to have provided an alternative expression to a given item, which was thought to be better in the context. On the other hand, if a participant gave a negative score to an available expression then any feedback sentence was more likely to have been a replacement for the test item. If a test item was designed not to be available, but the participant accepted it and presented a feedback sentence, this can be understood as a kind of tolerance to the incorrect expression, because the learner is indicating a belief that the expression was acceptable, although there could be a better way to phrase it. Rejecting an expression that was not available with a feedback sentence may be seen as a typical case of correction, especially when the instructions for the judgement task are taken into consideration. These four possible types of reaction were further categorized into two groups: The reaction types 'alternative' and 'rejection' were applied to the MB and MT expressions, while 'tolerance' and 'correction' were applied to the MS expressions.

Table 7.9 provides a summary of the percentages of different reaction types for all participants at different proficiency levels. It can be argued that the native group clearly and exclusively concentrated on the unacceptable use of MS expressions; over 70 per cent of the relevant feedback sentences produced by the native participants focused on the MS expressions. However, the native group occasionally produced replacement sentences for the MB and MT expressions; this provided a good indication of the use of individual differences for metaphorical expressions. Even though the test items had been verified by native English informants prior to the experiment, some participants still did not accept those expressions; they preferred to provide their own versions to express the same meanings.

The distribution of feedback sentences for the learner groups was qualitatively similar to that for the native group. As proficiency rose, there was a general trend for participants to correct the MS expressions rather than replace the MB and MT expressions with their own expressions. However, when compared with the native group, the learner groups showed a more diverse focus in the sentence correction section. Learner participants produced fewer sentences that targeted the incorrect use of MS expressions; they still devoted a high percentage of feedback sentences to expressions that were available in English as seen, for example, in the higher proportion of sentences targeting the MB expressions used by high-advanced learners (over 10 per cent) and around one-third of the sentences targeting the MT expressions among all the learner groups.

Although both native speakers and learners made corrections to the MB and MT expressions that were available in English, there was a quantitative difference in the results for both the acceptability judgement task and the

Table 7.9 Distribution of the types of reaction across different proficiency groups

	MB (%)		MS (%)		MT (%)	
	Alternative	Replacement	Tolerance	Correction	Alternative	Replacement
IN	9.30	4.65	9.30	37.21	6.98	32.56
LA	5.41	2.70	8.11	45.95	12.16	25.68
HA	2.07	8.38	1.38	57.93	0.69	29.66
HO	1.09	6.52	3.26	57.61	2.17	29.35
NS	0.60	2.99	2.99	67.66	4.19	21.56

sentence correction section. This indicates that native participants accepted the MB and MT expressions more than any other group of learners. Such differences should be attributed to the learners' (lack of) knowledge of L2 metaphorical expressions, rather than to the participants' individual preference for metaphorical expressions.

After analysing the strategies that participants used to provide the feedback sentences, four categories can be created to cover all the sentences: full paraphrase; near- or mis-paraphrase; alternative metaphorical expression; and error indicated without correction. Examples of the four types are given in Table 7.10, all extracted from the feedback sentences provided by the native participants. *Full paraphrase* means that a participant chose to rephrase the given metaphorical expression in a literal way, while the intended meaning of the sentence was fully preserved in the feedback sentence. *Near- or mis-paraphrase* is similar to full paraphrase, but the feedback sentence failed to preserve the intended meaning of the test sentence due to a misunderstanding by the participant. The third strategy, namely *alternative metaphorical expression*, indicates that the participant used another metaphorical expression or an idiom that was available in English, which was equivalent in meaning to the given expression. Finally, when participants were sometimes not sure how to express the intended meaning accurately, or failed to understand the test sentence, they may have decided not to leave any feedback sentence. In that case they would usually point out that 'this part is Chinglish'; 'the sentence is not comprehensible' or is 'awkward to me' with an indication of the problematic words or phrases (e.g. by underlining, colouring and question marks). These cases are categorized as *error indicated without correction*.

Three of the four strategies shown in Table 7.10, that is, full paraphrase, near paraphrase and error indicated without correction, are 'language-neutral'; that is, they do not involve the appearance of a language-specific expression. Both the full paraphrase and the near/mis-paraphrase strategies are closely related to paraphrasing and the use of literal language; since literal expressions are generally shared between languages, these strategies are fully language neutral. The last strategy, namely *error indicated without correction*, does not lead to the production of any expressions, so it should be seen as language-neutral as well. The production of an alternative metaphorical expression can be either language-neutral or language-specific, depending on the resulting expression.

Table 7.11 shows the levels of production for the four types of strategy commonly used in the sentence correction component by different groups of participants. The use of full paraphrase and near paraphrase, both of which are

Table 7.10 Examples of types of strategies adopted by participants in the sentence correction section

Strategy	Test sentence*	Relevant feedback sentence
Full paraphrase	Brian <u>*ate* some loss</u> when he started his own business.	Brian <u>suffered some loss</u> when he started his own business.
Near/Mis-paraphrase	Sally always <u>*bites* the words and phrases</u> whenever she writes an article.†	Sally always <u>cuts words and phrases</u> whenever she writes an article.
Alternative metaphorical expression	The mother <u>held a belly of *gas*</u> because her son failed in the exam.	The mother <u>blew a fuse</u> because her son failed in the exam.
Error indicated without correction	Sophie <u>lost her golden *bowl*</u> after her boss decided to shut down the company.	Sophie <u>lost her golden *bowl*</u> (?) after her boss decided to shut down the company.

*The words in italics are the critical lexical items that are used metaphorically in the sentences. The underlined constituents are the constituents that include the critical lexical items, and they were usually changed or rephrased in the relevant feedback sentences.
†Intended meaning: Sally always cares too much about wording whenever she writes an article.

Table 7.11 Average number of relevant feedback sentences with different strategies provided by individual participants at different proficiency levels

	Full paraphrase	Near-/ Mis-paraphrase	Alternative metaphorical expressions	Error indicated without correction
IN	1.00	0.19	0.71	0.14
LA	1.15	0.19	0.92	0.58
HA	5.10	0.10	1.33	0.38
HO	3.44	0.44	1.11	0.11
NS	3.50	0.79	2.13	0.54

language-neutral, is pervasive among all groups. Near-paraphrase is particularly prominent in the native group, and most instances appear when participants attempt to correct the MS expressions; that is, because the native participants lack the relevant knowledge and fail to understand the meanings of those expressions. The result reveals that both learners and native speakers prefer changing a metaphorical expression to a corresponding literal expression to other strategies, and paraphrasing is used to 'correct' all three types of metaphorical expressions, particularly L1-specific expressions. It should be noted that the choice of strategy may be biased due to the description in the instructions; in the experiment, participants were told that they were correcting sentences for their peers, and the 'recipients' of the feedback sentences were English learners, so they might prefer choosing more literal and direct expressions to make the feedback sentences more accessible. Still, a preference for literal paraphrasing may indicate that literal expressions are indeed considered 'less marked' and metaphorical expressions 'more marked and more difficult to comprehend'.

At the same time, all learner groups displayed a degree of creativity in language use in the sentence correction component, particularly in proposing other metaphorical expressions to replace the given metaphors. For example, the relevant feedback sentences for one test sentence provided by learner participants are recorded and categorized in Table 7.12; learners were able to select lexical items that they believed could accurately present the intended meaning when paraphrasing the test sentence, or derive metaphorical expressions based on the literal meanings of the lexical items. All feedback sentences, except for (9), were classified as 'replacement' sentences; this means the participants rejected the use of the given metaphorical expressions and replaced them with their own expressions.

It may also be noted in the feedback sentences listed in Table 7.12 that some learner participants transferred their knowledge from L1 into their production of an L2 sentence. Expressions like 'nutrition', 'nourishment' (both corresponding to *yingyang* in Chinese), 'fountainhead' and, possibly, 'source' (both corresponding to *yuanquan* in Chinese) are common metaphorical expressions in Chinese to describe the importance of books for studying and thinking. When learners chose these expressions to replace 'food for thought', they seemed to assume that these expressions were shared by Chinese and English speakers. It may also have been the case that they directly translated these expressions into English, even if they were actually less favoured in English compared to 'food for thought'. No matter what kind of belief learners hold, the use of these alternative expressions should be identified as transfer from their L1 to the L2.

To conclude, when the participants encountered a metaphorical expression that they believed questionable, the most widely-used method was to paraphrase it using a literal sentence that conveyed the same meaning. This strategy was pervasive among learners at all proficiency levels as well as native speakers. While less proficient learners produced feedback sentences mainly by paraphrasing them literally, even the more proficient learners chose to paraphrase the shared metaphorical expressions to literal expressions. On the other hand, the fact that learner participants at all proficiency levels felt the need to paraphrase some shared metaphorical expressions indicates that the metaphorical meaning of a lexical item is more difficult to acquire, even if a learner has already reached a high

Table 7.12 All 16 relevant feedback sentences for 'My mother said that these books would be _food_ for thought' given by different groups of participants

Group	Strategy	Relevant feedback sentences*
Int	Full paraphrase	(1) … would be useful.
	Alternative metaphorical expression	(2) … would be *supply* for thought.
		(3) … would be *nutrition* for thought.
		(4) … would be *sources* of thought.
Low-adv	Full paraphrase	(5) … would be good for thinking.
	Alternative metaphorical expression	(6) … would be good *materials* to develop thinking.
		(7) … would *feed* our thought.
		(8) … would be the *fountainhead* of thoughts.
	Error indicated without correction	(9) … would be food for thought (?)
High-adv	Full paraphrase	(10) … would be a resource for thought.
		(11) These books are to human thought what food is to people.
		(12) … would be helpful for thinking.
	Alternative metaphorical expression	(13) … would be mental *nourishment*.
		(14) … would be a *necessity* to thought.
Overseas	Full paraphrase	(15) … would be resource of thought.
	Alternative metaphorical expression	(16) … would be spiritual *nourishment*.

*All italicized words are lexical items used in a metaphorical sense under the MIP framework (Pragglejaz Group 2007). No native participant provided relevant feedback sentences for this item; they generally accepted the metaphorical meaning of 'food'.

level of L2 proficiency. All learner participants demonstrated lexical creativity both in paraphrasing and in the construction of alternative metaphorical expressions; at the same time, a trace of transfer from their L1 could still be detected in the feedback sentences provided by the learner participants.

7.3 Processing metaphorical expressions

7.3.1 Participants

Eighty-one Chinese learners of English and twenty-one native speakers of British English were recruited for the self-paced reading task. The same as the judgement task, the learners were divided into four groups, namely: Int (intermediate); Low-adv (low-advanced); High-adv (high-advanced); and Overseas (high-advanced overseas) based on their proficiency of English as estimated by their performance in the Oxford Quick Placement Test (UCLES 2001) as well as their linguistic backgrounds. English proficiency level of the HA and HO groups were matched, and the only difference between the two groups was that the participants in the HO group had received long-term exposure to a native English-speaking environment prior to the experiment. The basic information relevant to the learner participants is listed in Table 7.13. The average age of the native speaker participants was 21;1 (years;months) (SD=2.23), and the average backward digit span was 5.48 digits (SD=1.17), slightly lower than learners.

7.3.2 Materials

Twenty-four monosyllabic verbs were selected as the critical lexical items, and their average orthographic length was five letters (SD=1.38). All the critical lexical

Table 7.13 Linguistic backgrounds of the learner participants

		Int	Low-adv	High-adv	Overseas
Group size		21	22	20	18
Average OQPT score (SD)		35.47 (3.59)	44.27 (1.80)	51.45 (3.0)	51.44 (2.36)
Average age (years;months) (SD)		22;2 (2.85)	21;3 (2.62)	23;2 (2.28)	23;5 (2.18)
Gender	Male	6	4	2	5
	Female	15	18	18	13
Number of participants with overseas experience		1*	1†	4‡	18§
Average backward digit span (SD)		6.71 (1.89)	6.89 (1.53)	6.7 (1.67)	7.47 (1.58)

*The participant (twenty-seven years old) stated that he went to the UK for one month when he was twenty-two.
†The participant (twenty-three years old) stated that she had been in the UK for twelve months, four years before the experiment (when she was nineteen). Considering that she had been living in China ever since and had not received any exposure to a native English environment since her return, she was categorized in the low-advanced group according to her performance in the OQPT.
‡All overseas experiences recorded had taken place at least one year before the experiment. Average length of stay was 4.75 months (SD=5.68). The average age of first overseas experience was 20;9 (SD=3.77).
§The average length of stay was 37.78 months (SD=29.3). The average age of first overseas experience was 19;3 (SD=3.04).

items appeared in the literal or metaphorical expressions and test sentences in the past tense form. The procedure for the selection of critical lexical items, as well as the categorization of metaphorical expressions, was the same as the procedure in the acceptability judgement task. The twenty-four metaphorical expressions were divided into three categories: (1) the Metaphorical-Both (MB) category, containing twelve expressions; (2) the Metaphorical-Source (MS) category, containing six expressions; and (3) the Metaphorical-Target (MT) category, containing six expressions. To provide a baseline for the results of acquisition and the patterns of processing, three categories of literal expressions were also constructed and examined in the experiments: (1) the Literal-Both (LB) category, as the literal, baseline counterpart of the MB category; (2) the Literal-Source (LS) category, as the literal, baseline counterpart of the MS category; and (3) the Literal-Target (LT) category, as the literal, baseline counterpart of the MT category.

To ensure that the reading time for literal and metaphorical expressions were comparable, all the metaphorical expressions in the self-paced reading task, regardless of availability, were constructed in the form of Verb-Article-Noun, led by the critical lexical item. A pair of examples are provided below to demonstrate the structure.

a) Literal: <u>built</u> a balcony

Metaphorical: <u>built</u> an argument

In example (a), the underlined verb was the critical lexical item, which was followed by the noun phrase that included an article. The noun served as the direct object of the verb. When a participant read the noun, she was expected to know whether the verb was used literally or metaphorically.

After the construction of metaphorical and literal expressions, each expression was assigned a test sentence, which provided sufficient contextual information for participants to deduce the meaning of the target expression in case they were not familiar with the expression. In total 144 sentences were constructed for the self-paced reading task. That included: (1) twenty-four sentences each containing metaphorical expressions, among which every metaphorical expression only appeared once; (2) twenty-four sentences each containing a literal expression constructed from the critical lexical items; and (3) ninety-six filler sentences. Each sentence consisted of twelve words. In both metaphorical and literal sentences, the first three words formed the subject of the sentence in the form of 'The-Adjective-Noun', the fourth to sixth words included

Table 7.14 A pair of sample test sentences and their structure

The	famous	doctor	built	a	balcony	for	his	home	near	the	city
The	famous	doctor	built	an	argument	in	his	article	in	the	book
W01	W02	W03	W04*	W05	W06†	W07	W08	W09	W10	W11	W12
Segment 01			Segment 02			Segment 03			Segment 04		
Subject			Literal/metaphorical expression			Spill-over area			Wrapping-up area		

*W04 was the position of the main verb in all the sentences. In a metaphorical or literal sentence, W04 was the position where a critical lexical item appeared, either metaphorically or literally.

†W06 was the disambiguation position. When reading that part, the participant would know whether W04 was metaphorical or literal.

the metaphorical or literal use of the target lexical item, and the final six words provided the contextual information and enough space for a spill-over effect. The filler sentences were in the same format, the only difference was that they did not contain any critical lexical items. Except for the different noun phrase and necessary contextual information to support the literal or metaphorical meanings, the rest of the sentences shared a highly similar structure. For example, the words immediately following the metaphorical expressions were the same, and the same words were utilized where context was allowed; when different words were needed to fit different contexts, the length of the words was controlled. An example of a pair of test sentences with the illustration of their structure is shown in Table 7.14. All literal and metaphorical expressions in corresponding test sentences, in both the Chinese and English versions, were surveyed in a lexical evaluation task in which Chinese and English native speakers assessed their degree of concreteness (as metaphoricalness), coreness (as markedness) and perceived frequency in everyday language.

7.3.3 Method

All the test sentences in the self-paced reading task were divided evenly into two counterbalanced lists and presented to the participants randomly. The sentences were presented in a word-by-word fashion in a moving window paradigm (cf. Section 6.3). At the beginning of each sentence, the participant would see a fixation marker '+' on the left of the computer screen, which indicated the position of the first word. After pressing the spacebar, the fixation marker would disappear and the first word 'The' (in every sentence) would appear at the position of the fixation marker. As the participant pressed the spacebar, the next word would appear spatially following the previous word, and the previous word would disappear. The participant could not go back to read the previous words, but could only proceed to the next word. After each sentence, a comprehension question would appear, which required the participant to press the F key (with the 'Y' sticker, for a 'yes' answer) or the J key (with the 'N' sticker, for a 'no' answer) to give their answer. However, prior to the main reading task the participant was given a trial session with eight sentences to familiarize themselves with the operation and the flow of the reading programme. In the middle of the experiment, a short break was assigned for the participant.

7.3.4 Procedure

Prior to the reading experiment, all the learner participants were required to fill in a language background survey and complete the OQPT, as well as an online survey of psychotypology. They were invited to attend a lab session after they had completed all the sections mentioned above. At the beginning of the lab sessions, participants, both native speakers and learners, were instructed to complete a visual backward digit span task using an iOS app named 'Digit Span' (Fu 2012), which allowed them to complete a customized digit span test on the touchscreen. The average backward digit span was calculated by the app automatically after the participant had completed all the cycles. Then the experimenter briefly introduced the task to the participants, and they began the self-paced reading task. In the trial session, the experimenter supervised the participants and answered any questions regarding the operation of the programme, after which the participants were left alone to accomplish the main session; the experimenter observed silently in the lab. The experiment was completed when the participant had finished the self-paced reading task. After completion, all the participants received a small remuneration or a small souvenir from the experimenter.

7.3.5 Data adjustment and analysis

Reading time data is treated by a two-step trimming method, which is the conventional method of reaction time data normalization. The first trim removed the outliers below 100 ms, reduced the outliers above 200 ms for native speakers to 2000 ms, and above 4000 ms for learners to 4000 ms (see Papadopoulou, Tsimpli & Amvrazis 2013 for a summary of trimming criteria). In the second trim, an upper bound for individual participants was set as the average of residual reading time plus two standard deviations (mean+2SD); any reading time above the upper bound was trimmed to fit within the upper bound. After the trimming modification, the residual reading time for each word and each three-word segment for each participant was calculated; the three-word segments are shown in Table 7.14. In this way, two large three-word segments were the focus of the data: the second segment of the whole sentence, which included the fourth to sixth words and reflected the reading time for the whole metaphorical expression; and the third segment, that is, the seventh to the ninth words, which showed a potential spill-over effect that may continuously affect more than one word after the critical region (Jegerski 2013).

The reaction time for the comprehension questions was treated in a similar way to the reading time for individual words. However, only the second trim in the two-step trimming method was applied to the reaction time for the questions, because there is no conventional threshold for the trimming of comprehension questions (cf. Papadopoulou et al. 2013). The upper bound of the reaction time to the questions was set to the average reading time plus two standard deviations for each participant (mean+2SD). Then the residual reaction time was calculated in a similar way to the residual reading time for individual words.

After the data adjustment, all data was analysed using linear mixed models, with the maximal random factors including individual diversity (e.g. age, average exposure to English, working memory capacity as measured by backward digit span) of learners and individual differences (e.g. orthographic length, general frequency) of critical words and presentation orders of sentential stimuli. Two fixed factors were focused in the analysis, metaphoricalness (literal or metaphorical) and language specificity (shared, L1-specific or L2-specific). An analysis was conducted within each proficiency group.

7.3.6 Results

7.3.6.1 The reading time pattern

In the analyses below, I will concentrate on the reading times for Segments 3 and 4, that is, the segments following the target metaphorical (or literal) expression which are likely to show spill-over from the processing of such expressions. I first compare the reading times of literal versus metaphorical expressions of the same type (for example MS and LS), and then compare the reading times for metaphorical expressions of different types (MB, MT, MS). The segment-by-segment reading time pattern for the native group, used here as baseline information, is shown in Figure 7.5.

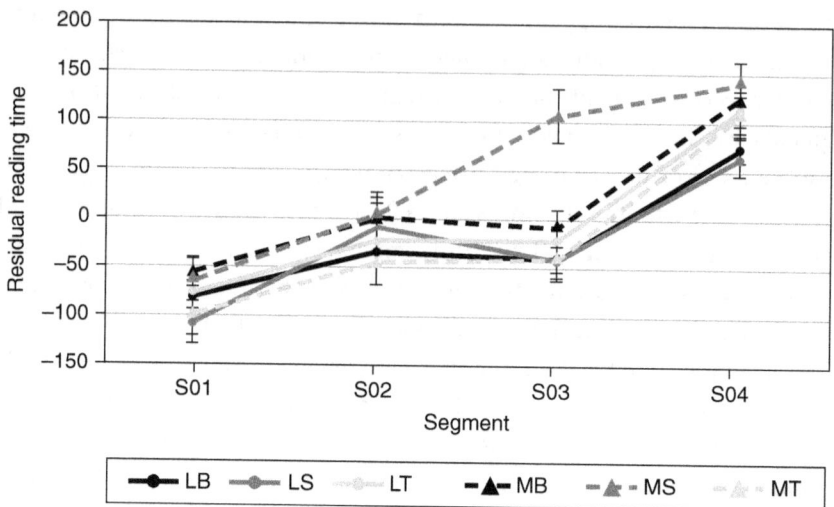

Figure 7.5 Segment-by-segment reading time pattern for the native group

It can be observed that only the MS sentences caused a major delay; native participants spent significantly more time reading Segment 3 in all the MS sentences compared with the LS sentences ($\chi^2(1)=5.52$, $p=0.019$), the delay continued into the fourth segment ($\chi^2(1)=4.40$, $p=0.036$). Other than that, all other parts of the sentence, all acceptable in English, entailed a similar reading pattern for metaphorical and literal expressions. In general, the native group spent similar amounts of time reading and processing a metaphorical expression that is available in English, and its corresponding literal expressions. This indicates that, if a metaphorical expression is available in English, native speakers are able to connect the metaphorical meanings directly to the word form; the 'literal-first' hypothesis did not come into effect. The significant delay after reading the MS expressions showed that the native group spent additional time 'making sense' of these expressions and that the effort to 'make sense' continued until the end of each sentence.

It was further expected that, when two metaphorical expressions were both available in English (i.e. an expression in the MB and MT class), a native speaker would spend the same amount of time reading them; however, if two metaphorical expressions were both available in Chinese (i.e. an expression in the MB and MS class), there would be a difference in reading time, since the availability of those expressions in English should also be taken into consideration. Therefore, comparisons can be made between: (1) the MB and MT sentences and (2) the MB and MS sentences. In accordance with the prediction above, native participants spent a similar amount of time reading Segment 3 of the MB and MT sentences, but they spent significantly more time reading Segment 3 in all MS sentences compared with MB sentences ($\chi^2(1)=6.83$, $p=0.009$).

The segment-by-segment reading time patterns for the four learner groups are shown altogether in Figure 7.6. It can be clearly observed that learners displayed a more diverse reading pattern compared with native speakers, and significant differences in reading times can be observed between the literal and metaphorical sentences in the Segment 3 position, regardless of the type of metaphorical expression.

Among intermediate learners, significant differences in reading times between the literal and metaphorical sentences were observed in the Segment 3 position; the participants spent significantly more time reading the segment after reading all types of metaphorical expressions compared to reading the corresponding literal expressions ($\chi^2(1)=5.26$, $p=0.022$ for MB; $\chi^2(1)=10.48$, $p=0.001$ for MS; $\chi^2(1)=4.11$, $p=0.043$ for MT). Furthermore, the delay in processing the MS sentences also continued into the fourth segment ($\chi^2(1)=4.02$, $p=0.045$). This suggests that the processing cost for the retrieval of all types of metaphorical meanings continues to exist and that learners showed a 'literal-first' preference, but only after they had read the metaphorical expression. Interestingly, although it seems that the intermediate learners showed more of a difference between LS and MS expressions than between MB and LB, and MT and LT expressions, there was no significant difference between the reading times for Segment 3 of the MS and MB sentences. Also, there was no significant difference between the reading times for Segment 3 of the MB and the MT sentences. It seems that intermediate learners produced quantitatively similar patterns both during and after reading different metaphorical expressions, which might indicate a global hesitation after reading metaphorical expressions.

The low-advanced learners again showed differences in reading times between literal and metaphorical expressions at the Segment 3 position, indicating that the retrieval of metaphorical meanings might happen after the entire expression is read. The low-advanced participants spent significantly more time reading the segment after the MS expressions rather than after the LS expressions ($\chi^2(1)=5.02$, $p=0.025$), but such differences were marginal in the fourth segment ($\chi^2(1)=2.71$, $p=0.0997$). The participants also spent marginally more time reading the segment after the MT expressions rather than the segment after the LT expressions ($\chi^2(1)=3.54$, $p=0.060$), and in this case the difference became more significant in the fourth segment ($\chi^2(1)=3.97$, $p=0.046$). There was no clear difference between the reading patterns for the LB and MB

164 *Acquiring Metaphorical Expressions in a Second Language*

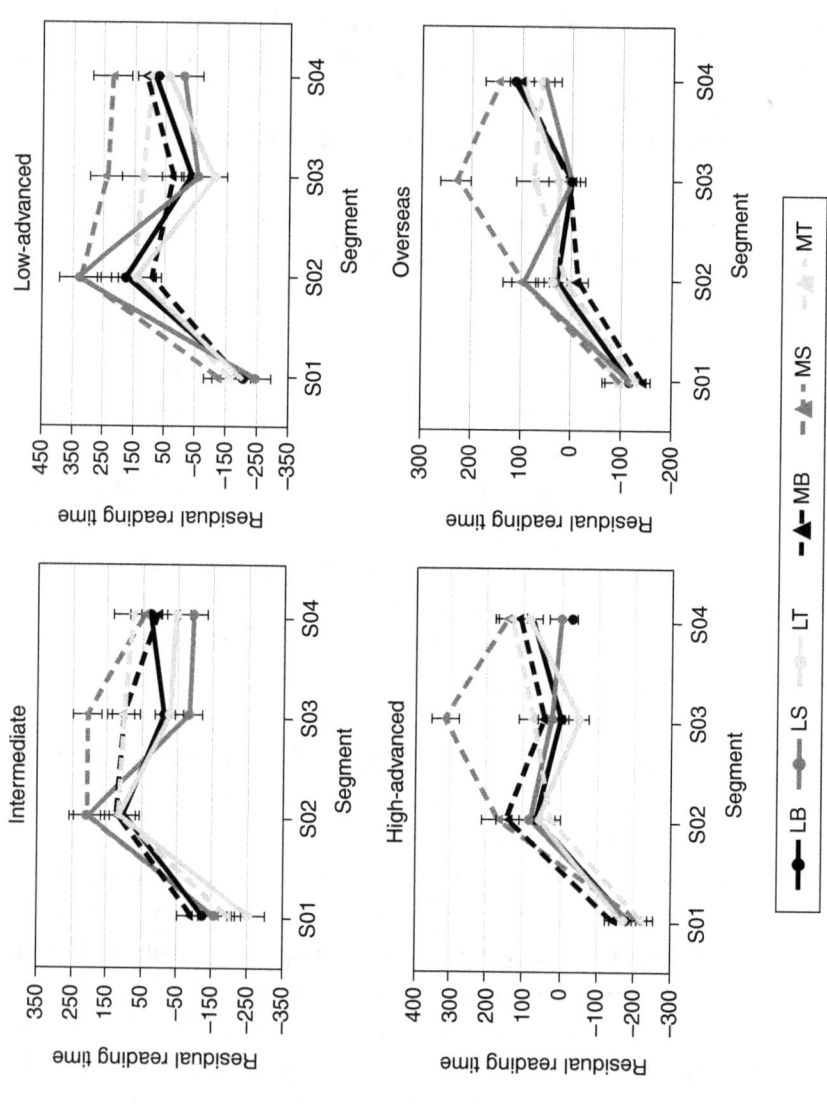

Figure 7.6 Segment-by-segment reading time pattern for the learner groups

sentences. It seems that for the low-advanced learners, both the MS and MT expressions entailed more processing effort, but this was not the case with the MB expressions. Considering the availability of the three types of metaphorical expression, it could be argued that shared metaphorical expressions were easier for learners to process than other metaphorical expressions. However, there was no significant difference between the reading time for the segment after the MB and MT expressions; significant differences were only observed between the MB and MS expressions ($\chi^2(1)=4.42$, p=0.035). Another conclusion one might draw, based on this data, is that the low-advanced learners realized the specific problem with MS sentences.

In general, the high-advanced learners showed similar reading time patterns as the low-advanced learners, but their hesitation with sentences containing MT expressions was less evident. High advanced learner participants spent significantly more time reading these two segments after an MS expression than after an LS expression ($\chi^2(1)=8.02$, p=0.005 for Segment 3; $\chi^2(1)=4.26$, p=0.039 for Segment 4), and also spent marginally more time reading Segment 3 after an MT expression than after an LT expression ($\chi^2(1)=3.53$, p=0.060). Also, in much the same way as low-advanced learners, high-advanced learners only showed a significant difference in the segment after MB and MS expressions ($\chi^2(1)=15.41$, p<0.001), and not in segments after MB and MT expressions ($\chi^2(1)=0.001$, p=0.97).

Finally, there seems to have been a slight improvement among overseas learners, who behaved like native speakers. The only difference between the reading time for literal sentences and metaphorical sentences appeared between the LS and MS sentences. The participants showed a significant hesitation after reading the MS expressions compared to the LS expressions ($\chi^2(1)=4.44$, p=0.035), while such differences disappeared in Segment 4. There was no significant difference in reading time between LB and MB, or LT and MT, sentences; thus the same reading pattern was presented for the native speaker group. Interestingly, it was recorded that the overseas learners spent significantly less time reading the segment after MB expressions than after MT expressions ($\chi^2(1)=5.28$, p=0.021) and MS expressions ($\chi^2(1)=16.11$, p<0.001).

A native-like processing pattern, as discussed by Sanders and Neville (2003), means that non-native speakers of a language demonstrate a processing pattern (e.g. reading time, ERP pattern) that is qualitatively similar to that of native speakers of that language. In the current experiment, the most prominent properties of a native-like processing pattern included the following: (1) there was no significant difference between LB and MB sentences, (2) there was no significant difference between LT and MT sentences and (3) there *was* a significant difference at Segment 3 between LS and MS sentences, with participants showing significant hesitation toward MS sentences at Segment 3.

In terms of the reproduction of the properties of such a native-like processing pattern, there seems to be a hierarchy of difficulty. While the third property, namely a significant difference between the LS and MS sentences, was demonstrated in every learner group, the first two, especially the second property, were only found at higher proficiency levels. The intermediate group hesitated after reading the MB expressions, while the advanced learners could process the MB expressions without obvious hesitation. However, even the high-advanced participants were not able to process the MT expressions in the same way as native speakers, indicating that the MT expressions were generally more difficult for learners to process than the MB expressions. Such a hierarchy was similar to the hierarchy of difficulty displayed in the acceptability judgement task; it seemed easiest to detect a lack of acceptability in MS expressions, followed by the acceptability of MB expressions and, finally, by the acceptability of MT expressions.

The results also show that some learners could achieve a native-like processing pattern, although extensive native L2 input was still required. As stated earlier, the high-advanced group and the overseas group were at the same level of proficiency, and the most prominent difference between the two groups was that the overseas participants had been residing in an English-speaking environment for an average of three years at the time they were tested, which means that they had received extensive exposure to the discourse produced by native speakers of English. Neither group hesitated significantly when processing the MB sentences and both showed a delay after reading the MS expressions; however, the high-advanced group showed a minor delay after reading the MT expressions, but such a delay was not present in the overseas group. It can be argued that, as well as being highly proficient, a learner also needs to have received sufficient exposure to the native discourse in order to process all the metaphorical expressions in a native-like way.

7.3.6.2 Reaction time to the comprehension questions and scores for responses

The residual reaction time for the comprehension questions, as well as the scores for responses, were analysed in the comparisons. Comparisons were made between: (1) questions targeting the meaning of metaphorical expressions and those targeting the meaning of literal uses and (2) questions targeting different types of metaphorical expressions. A shorter residual reaction time indicates that participants reacted faster to questions related to that type of expression, and a higher mean score indicates that participants answered the comprehension questions more accurately.

The native group, as shown in Figure 7.7, did not show any difference when answering the LB and MB questions. However, significantly more time was spent answering questions related to MS sentences than those related to LS sentences ($\chi^2(1)=4.21$, p=0.040). There was also a clear difference in the mean score for MS and LS questions ($\chi^2(1)=4.05$, p=0.044). The native group reacted significantly faster to questions related to MT expressions than those related to the LT questions ($\chi^2(1)=11.96$, p<0.001), but there was no difference in the mean score for the two types of questions.

Compared with questions related to metaphorical expressions available in the target language (the MB and MT expressions), participants spent significantly more time answering MS questions ($\chi^2(1)=5.38$, p=0.020). However, when the mean scores for MS questions were analysed, it was found that they were significantly lower ($\chi^2(1)=10.75$, p=0.001). Although the mean score for MS questions (M=0.65, SD=0.48) was above chance, meaning the native participants could deduce the meaning of the MS expressions from the word form and the given sentence, it was still difficult for them to answer these questions accurately. Among the three types of metaphorical expression, the questions related to MT expressions were answered the fastest; however, the reaction time for MT questions was significantly lower than that for MB questions ($\chi^2(1)=4.52$,

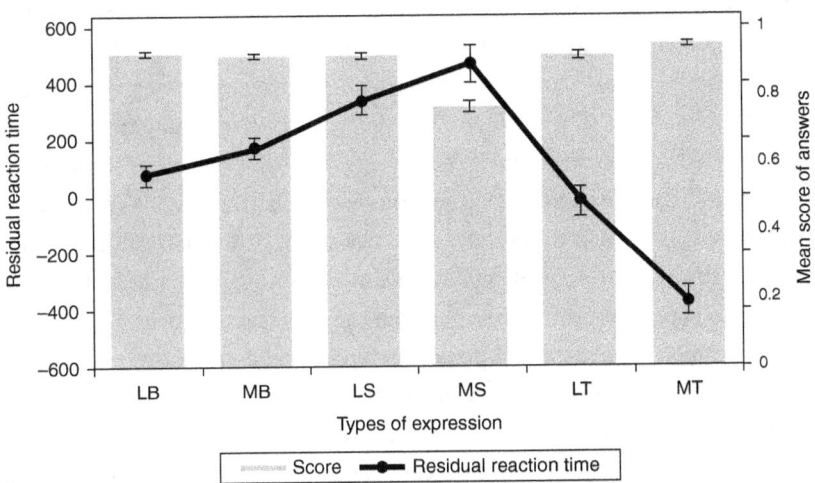

Figure 7.7 Reaction times (left axis) and mean scores for answers for the native group

p=0.033). There was no difference in the mean score for MB and MT questions. It seems that native participants were best at identifying and processing the MT expressions, followed by the MB expressions.

The learner groups' reaction to the comprehension questions, including reaction time and scores for answers, formed a different pattern from the reaction time for the native group, which is displayed in Figure 7.8. The reactions of the intermediate group, as shown in the top-left of Figure 7.8, will be discussed first. These learners did not take more time to answer questions related to metaphorical expressions than questions related to literal expressions. In particular, there was no difference in reaction time between the LS and the MS questions, and a trend was observed of slightly less time being spent reacting to MS questions, although no significant differences were found. While it seems that the scores for the MS questions were lower than those for the LS questions, there was no significant difference between the two scores. No difference was observed, either, when the intermediate learners answered the LB/MB questions or the LT/MT questions.

Compared with the questions related to the metaphorical expressions available in English (the MB and MT expressions), the intermediate learners spent significantly more time answering the MS questions ($\chi^2(1)=5.38$, p=0.020). Also, the scores for the MS questions were significantly lower than those for other metaphorical expressions available in English ($\chi^2(1)=10.75$, p=0.001). It could be inferred that, even in the case of the intermediate learners whose English proficiency is relatively low, there is some awareness that the MS expressions are not readily available in English when they read them.

The low-advanced group, the high-advanced group and the overseas group displayed qualitative and quantitative similarities in terms of their reaction to the comprehension questions. No difference was observed in terms of reaction time and the answers to the LB and MB questions. Participants from all three groups spent slightly more time answering the MS questions than the LS questions, and the scores for MS questions were slightly lower than for the LS questions; however, such differences were not significant. Also, all three groups spent slightly less time answering MT questions than LT questions, but, again, there was no significant difference between the two reaction times.

When comparing different types of metaphorical expressions, it was found that, among the low-advanced learners and the overseas learners, the scores for MS questions were significantly lower than that for MB and MT questions ($\chi^2(1)=3.91$, p=0.048 for low-advanced; $\chi^2(1)=4.11$, p=0.043 for overseas). Conversely, the high-advanced learners spent marginally more time answering

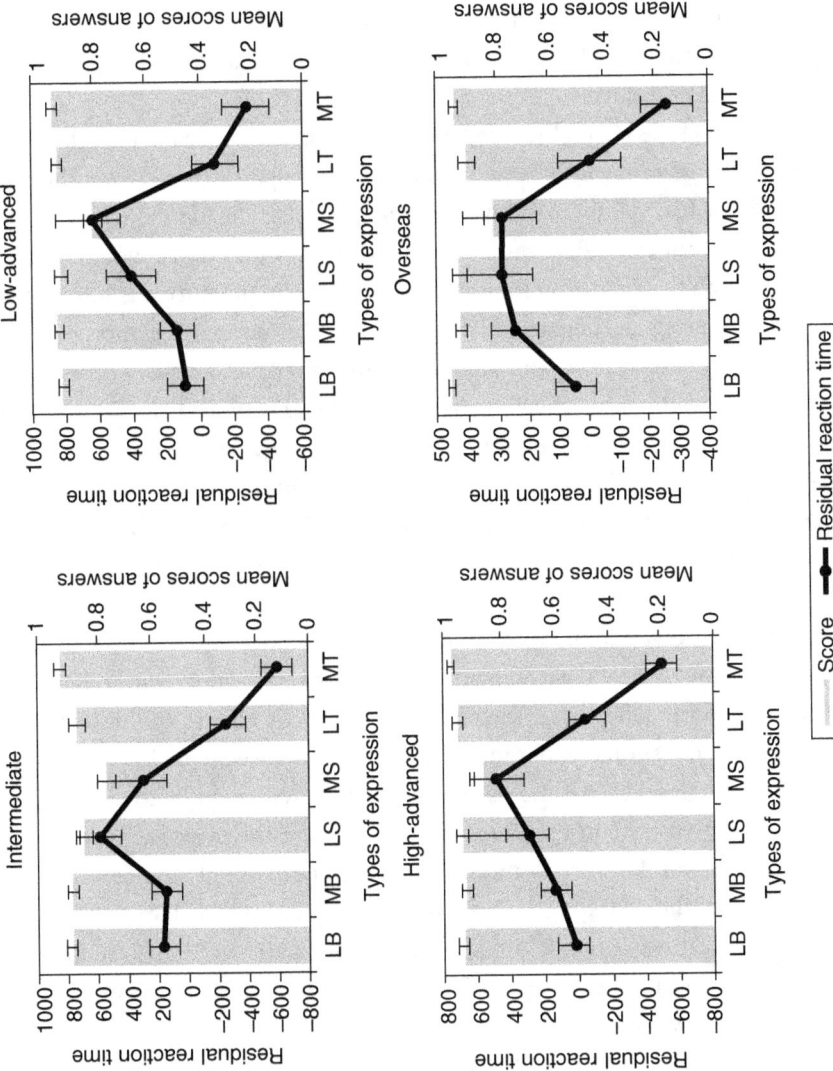

Figure 7.8 Reaction times (left axis) and mean scores for answers for the learner groups

MS questions than MB and MT questions ($\chi^2(1)=2.86$, p=0.091), but the score for the MS questions was not significantly lower than that for the other two types of question. The high-advanced group spent marginally less time answering MT questions compared with MB questions ($\chi^2(1)=3.34$, p=0.067), and the difference became more significant in the overseas group ($\chi^2(1)=7.23$, p=0.007). There seems to be a trend which shows that more proficient learners are more likely to react faster to MT questions, which is similar to the reaction pattern of the native speaker group.

It can be concluded from these results that the learner participants performed in a markedly different way when compared to native participants, even though some of them had achieved high proficiency levels. The native participants showed significant difficulty when answering the MS questions, which can be reflected in both their reaction time and accuracy. Such difficulty was not shown among the learner participants. Although the learner participants showed clear hesitation after reading the MS expressions, they had already successfully resolved the meanings of the MS expressions by the time of answering the comprehension questions. This indicated that the learners were able to build up a connection from the unacceptable L2 translation of the expressions to the L1-specific metaphorical meanings (cf. Section 5.5), even though more time was required and the learners occasionally failed to establish the connection accurately.

There was, however, a close-to native-like performance that could be achieved by the learner participants when answering the comprehension questions. As proficiency rose, learners were gradually able to spend less time answering MT questions, while the accuracy of the answers to MT questions was also at a high level. All the learner groups showed a qualitatively similar pattern of reaction time to the LT/MT questions, and the overseas group even performed in a similar way to the native group; both spent significantly less time answering the MT questions than the LT questions. This phenomenon made an interesting contrast with the reading patterns for MT sentences; while most of the learners hesitated after reading the MT expressions, they did not hesitate when answering questions related to those expressions. The processing difficulty shown in the reading pattern did not necessarily lead to comprehension difficulties. This might suggest that the learners could actively and effectively infer the meanings of the MT expressions, and this process of inference may largely happen in the hesitation period. A further contrast can then be made between the results of the self-paced reading task and those of the acceptability judgement task (referenced earlier in this chapter); even though learners could infer the meanings of the MT expressions, it was still difficult for them to accept this type of expression. It should be noted that the difference in the results for the acceptability judgement task and the self-paced reading task should be seen as a demonstration of a general discrepancy between online and offline results, rather than as a phenomenon specific to metaphorical expressions.

7.4 Summary and loose ends

The two experiments, as part of this author's PhD project, provide some preliminary information about how an experiment on the acquisition of metaphorical expressions can be conducted, and what reactions can be observed from the learners. Learners differ from native speakers in a variety of aspects when they come across metaphorical expressions; they give different judgements, they spend different times reading and comprehending these expressions, and they also provide different alternatives when asked to 'correct' these expressions. More importantly, metaphorical expressions, in the context of second language acquisition, are far from a single, unified identity; from the two experiments, it can be observed that second language learners show a different reaction to metaphorical expressions with a different cross-linguistic availability and, sometimes, even with different tasks (online reading vs. offline reading). The results show that metaphorical expressions, although not perceived as being different to other figurative expressions, still diverge from literal word meanings in an acquisition context; perhaps a more fine-grained distinction between different types of metaphorical expressions should be drawn in order to provide a better picture of acquisition.

Moreover, I report the two experiments here, not only as a simple summary of results, but to give some actual realization of the methodologies discussed in the previous chapter. These experiments can be developed into possible paradigms for further studies, on other language pairs, on different learners (such as longitudinal classroom learners, or learners in a naturalistic setting), and, possibly, with other experiments on vocabulary acquisition in general. With more research on learners with different linguistic backgrounds, as well as the utilization of various experimental instruments, one will have a better understanding of the acquisition of metaphorical expressions in general, which will help to build a clearer framework of vocabulary acquisition and mental lexicon.

8

Acquiring and teaching metaphorical expressions in a second language

8.1 Introduction

This chapter serves as both a conclusion and an exploration of some aspects of acquiring and teaching metaphorical expressions in a second language. After experimental investigations, it is possible and essential to: (1) get a general picture of the acquisition of metaphorical expressions and (2) think about how this can help to improve the outcome for learners. This chapter, therefore, is an attempt to integrate current research on the acquisition of metaphorical expressions into second language pedagogy in order to boost learners' awareness and usage of native-like metaphorical expressions.

I will base the discussion in this chapter primarily on the results of the experiments reported in Chapter 7; at the same time, other experiments may also be included in the discussion. I will start with the learners' performance in the experiments to see how their reaction to metaphorical expressions differs from their reaction to literal expressions, which is presented in Section 8.2. I will then analyse those factors that may influence the acquisition of metaphorical expressions in Section 8.3; here, I will exclusively focus on the language-internal factors and learner-internal factors, such as the degree of metaphoricalness and markedness of a metaphorical expression, and learners' proficiency levels. Finally, in Section 8.4, I will explore other possible methodologies to help learners acquire metaphorical expressions based on their observations. There is a crossroad at this stage; second language researchers and instructors can either treat the metaphorical meanings of a lexical item as 'a new lexical item', or they may try, more explicitly, to show the relationship between the metaphorical meanings and the literal meanings of the same word, and even teach students the basic theories of metaphors. While it seems that both methods could achieve the same outcome, an emphasis on the connection between literal and metaphorical meanings can help learners establish a structurally complicated mental lexicon and even boost their acquisition of other figurative expressions.

8.2 The acquisition of metaphorical expressions with different availability in a second language: What can be achieved and what cannot

As shown in the experiments in Chapter 7, there is a divergence between English native speakers and Chinese learners of English when they make judgements to process conventional metaphorical expressions. In the judgement task, English native speakers accepted all of the expressions available in English, but rejected the metaphorical expressions available only in Chinese. In the reading task, the native speakers read the metaphorical expressions available in English without any processing difficulties, showing a processing pattern similar to the literal expressions using the same critical lexical items, but they did experience processing difficulties when reading the metaphorical expressions available only in Chinese. They also showed difficulty answering questions related to the meaning of the metaphorical expressions available only in Chinese.

To focus on the topic of this book, Chinese learners of English performed both qualitatively and quantitatively differently from the native speakers. In the judgement task the learners accepted the shared metaphorical expressions, but to a lesser extent when compared with the native speakers, and to a lesser extent still when compared with the learners' own judgements of the literal expressions. When they read the metaphorical expressions in a sentence, less proficient learners tended to spend more time processing it. The learners generally rejected the metaphorical expressions available only in Chinese, showing a great difference between the literal meanings and the metaphorical meanings of lexical items. While less proficient learners rejected them, to a lesser extent compared with the native speakers, more proficient learners were able to perform in a native-like way. Interestingly, although all learners showed processing difficulties when reading the expressions exclusively available in Chinese, they had no difficulty answering the questions related to the meaning of these metaphorical expressions after reading the entire sentences. Finally, the most prominent difference between learners and native speakers was their attitude towards the metaphorical expressions that were only available in English. All groups of learners seemed to reject these metaphorical expressions, in sharp contrast to the native speakers. Also, only the most proficient learners with fair exposure to an English-speaking environment could read these expressions without any processing difficulties; the least proficient learners showed significant processing difficulties when reading these metaphorical expressions, and the relatively more advanced learners still demonstrated minor difficulties.

Although I examined Chinese learners of English exclusively in Chapter 7, similar results, to show the difference between native speakers and second language learners in terms of their reaction to metaphorical expressions, were also observed in studies by Türker (2016b), and it seems to be a universal pattern that learners react differently from native speakers in terms of conventional metaphorical expressions. This phenomenon is mostly in line with the studies on idioms reviewed in Chapter 3; learners showed a lower degree of acceptability and delayed reaction to figurative expressions, such as idioms and conventional metaphorical expressions, when compared to learners' reactions to literal expressions and native speakers' reaction to figurative expressions. In respect of all the studies that examined learners' performance on figurative expressions, I have assumed that a full mastery of these expressions is indicated if native-like performance by learners is observed. Here, performance could include acceptability judgement, reading patterns, answers to relevant questions and explanations. To be more specific, in the case of the experiments in Chapter 7, to show that a learner has acquired all three types of metaphorical expressions, one is expected to accept all of the metaphorical expressions available in their L2 (including the expressions shared between their L1 and L2, and the expressions exclusively available in their L2), processing them in a similar manner to processing literal expressions without processing difficulty; at the same time, one is also expected to reject those expressions not available in English and to show some processing difficulty when reading those expressions. The discrepancy between the expected and the actual results for learner participants indicates that the learner participants under observation had not, as yet, fully acquired the metaphorical expressions. If one observes a clear difference between learners and native speakers, it is then natural to consider whether cross-linguistic influence may have an impact on the acquisition of metaphorical expressions and, if any, how cross-linguistic influence may function in the learning process positively or negatively.

In the process of acquiring shared metaphorical expressions, it is possible for a learner to transfer knowledge of these expressions from L1 to L2; such a transfer will not lead to any evident error in L2. More importantly, I expect that the effect of such a transfer, on the acquisition of these shared metaphorical expressions, is comparable to the effect of a transfer of literal expressions, because they are designed to be shared between the two languages. In the actual process of acquisition, as shown in Section 7.2.6.3, traces of positive transfer were identified in around 30 per cent of the judgements made by intermediate and low-advanced learners, showing that learners actively adopted transfer when they acquired the shared metaphorical expressions. However, the borderline between the outcome of cross-linguistic influence and the results of full mastery of knowledge is rather delicate in the classification of cross-linguistic influence. Since a learner shows positive transfer in a transferable condition, the result of the transfer can easily be converted to the mastery of relevant knowledge, especially if L2 materials are received which later confirm that the transfer is 'valid'. The effect of the transfer will then disappear once the result of transfer is confirmed as 'valid' in L2, when the learner no longer relies on transfer to judge or process the shared metaphorical expressions. It is expected that the results for judgement and production will remain the same, and positive transfer will gradually 'fade out' after a learner fully acquires the metaphorical expressions. This expectation is confirmed by the results and the identification of cross-linguistic influence in the judgement task; while the degree of acceptability of the shared metaphorical expressions remains statistically the same across the four groups with different proficiency levels, more proficient learners show more confidence in their judgements, and the estimated percentage of instances of cross-linguistic influence on the shared metaphorical expressions declines as proficiency increases. Such change is a good indication that learners gradually convert the result of positive transfer to actual knowledge of the language and the influence of transfer, at the same time, likely 'fades out' from their performance.

As stated earlier, the transfer of shared metaphorical expressions is a form of positive transfer and the outcome of that transfer is equivalent to a full mastery of relevant knowledge. Compared with negative transfer, it is reasonable to assume that a learner is more likely to translate positive transfer into knowledge of lexical items, and such positive transfer will lead to and 'be replaced by' full mastery of knowledge, even at an early stage of acquisition. Positive transfer, especially in a classroom setting, is more likely to be reinforced by: (1) positive feedback from instructors and native speakers; and (2) similar input received by learners. This assumption is confirmed by the results in Table 7.6; after the identification of traces of transfer, the estimated percentage of instances of transfer of the shared metaphorical expressions is lowest among all three types of expressions within each group of learner participants. Whilst the intermediate and low-advanced learners still rely heavily on transfer for their judgements of L1-specific and L2-specific metaphorical expressions, the percentage of instances of transfer for shared metaphorical expressions is generally lower among the two groups of participants. Considering that it cannot be the case that the shared metaphorical expressions are generally seen as less transferable by learners when they begin acquisition than the L1-specific and L2-specific metaphorical expressions, there should be an evident decline in the transfer of shared metaphorical expressions at the beginning of acquisition. This may lead to two correlated arguments: (1) transfer of the shared metaphorical expressions will be even more significant before a learner reaches intermediate level, and possibly at beginner level, and (2) compared with other expressions, shared metaphorical expressions are more easily acquired at an early stage of L2 acquisition because the learner can effectively convert the content of the transfer to knowledge that has been fully mastered.

Interestingly, although more proficient learners showed a more confident mastery of shared metaphorical expressions, as the level of confidence was rather high in their judgements, they did not give a higher acceptability score to the shared metaphorical expressions, and they never accepted the shared metaphorical expressions to the same extent as the native speakers. It seems that the perception of the degree of acceptability of shared metaphorical expressions is 'fossilized' at a later stage of acquisition. When the performance of the native participants is used as a benchmark and that benchmark suggests that the literal expressions and shared metaphorical expressions should both be highly acceptable, learners cannot reach native-like levels to eliminate the difference between the literal expressions and shared metaphorical expressions in terms of the degree of acceptability.

In contrast with the case of shared metaphorical expressions, the transfer of both L1-specific and L2-specific metaphorical expressions is negative; it will cause 'non-nativeness' in both reception (including judgements and reaction time) and production. However, the transfer of the two types of expressions are drastically different in terms of the development of learners. The L1-specific metaphorical expressions do not exist in the learners' L2, so a transfer of those expressions should be regarded as 'transfer to nowhere'. Any instance of the transfer of L1-specific metaphorical expressions will lead to errors related to L1-specific metaphorical expressions, especially the acceptance or production of word-to-word translations of L1-specific metaphorical expressions. Such types of transfer can be easily suppressed by learners though. The result displayed in Table 5.4 shows that the transfer of L1-specific metaphorical expressions is rather significant when the learners are less proficient, but with a rise in the level of proficiency, the percentage of instances of transfer of L1-specific metaphorical expressions shows a drastic decline, from nearly 60 per cent among the intermediate learners to around 20 per cent among the high-advanced and overseas learners. At the same time, more feedback sentences, focusing on MS expressions, are found as the proficiency level of learners rises. It can thus be concluded that there is still a significant impact on intermediate learners from the transfer of MS expressions, but the influence of such negative transfer is not long-lasting.

The decline in the influence of transfer on L1-specific metaphorical expressions can be attributed to several factors, most importantly an increased exposure to L2 and, possibly, the instruction received by learners. Since L1-specific metaphorical expressions are not available in the learners' L2, learners will never encounter such expressions in the input, something that will become more obvious to them when their exposure to L2 increases. Under such circumstances, learners are likely to suppress the use of the L1-specific metaphorical expressions in L2 because they believe that those expressions are not possible. At the same time, the misuse of an L1-specific metaphorical expression is easily noticed by both learners and instructors. When teaching Chinese learners of English, it is common for an instructor to emphasize that errors and misuses caused by so-called 'Chinglish' should be avoided (Ma 2009). I appreciate that, even if a specific L1-specific metaphorical expression is not explicitly mentioned, learners will be advised by their instructors to avoid direct translation of conventionalized L1 expressions to L2 in a word-for-word fashion, or by idioms or metaphorical expressions. At a higher proficiency level, where learners are able to distinguish expressions shared between their L1 and L2 and those only available in L1, they can then avoid the L1-specific metaphorical expressions but maintain the shared metaphorical expressions in their use. It may then be expected that, due to both the learner's own caution and the emphasis made by the instructor, the misuse of word-for-word translations of L1-specific metaphorical expressions will significantly decrease as L2 proficiency increases.

After discussing the realization of transfer of the shared and L1-specific metaphorical expressions, I will compare the two types of transfer, because both involve the transfer of certain linguistic elements from L1 (positively or negatively), and both become less evident as learners become more proficient. When the learners reach intermediate level, traces of transfer of the shared metaphorical expressions become less obvious than for L1-specific metaphorical expressions. Transfer of the shared metaphorical expressions has already largely disappeared after the learners have passed the beginner threshold, probably due to 'replacement' by actual knowledge, while transfer of L1-specific metaphorical expressions is still clearly observable when they reach low-advanced level (corresponding to B2 in the CEFR). At a later stage, traces of transfer of L1-specific metaphorical expressions rapidly drop to the same level as shared metaphorical expressions, and highly proficient learners are able to perform in a native-like way in terms of acceptability scores for the L1-specific metaphorical expressions and feedback sentences targeting MS expressions. These results suggest that, while positive transfer remains at a low level among learners above intermediate level, negative transfer in 'transfer to nowhere' conditions can be successfully suppressed by more proficient learners, which corresponds to my expectations. The suppression of negative transfer of the L1-specific metaphorical expressions, however, does not sufficiently indicate that the meanings of the L1-specific metaphorical expressions cannot be accessed by advanced learners when they are forced to comprehend those expressions in their L2. In the reading experiment, by the time the learner participants had answered the comprehension questions related to the L1-specific metaphorical expressions, they already understood those expressions and answered the questions correctly. This means that the learners were still able to access the meanings of the L1-specific metaphorical expressions when they were required to do so, suggesting a compound organization of a bilingual lexicon.

Cross-linguistic influence also affects the acquisition of metaphorical expressions that are only available in learners' L2. I have predicted that cross-linguistic influence would have a negative impact on the acquisition of those L2-specific metaphorical expressions. At that time, I supposed that such an impact would be temporary among less proficient learners and later disappear among the more proficient learners. This prediction is only partially correct in that cross-linguistic influence does have a negative impact, but the results show that the impact is not temporary, but persistent. While native speakers generally accepted all L2-specific metaphorical expressions and processed them without significant difficulty, none of the learner groups showed full mastery of the L2-specific metaphorical expressions. Less proficient learners hesitated to accept the L2-specific metaphorical expressions, and more proficient learners entirely rejected them. All learners, except those from the overseas group, experienced processing difficulty when reading the L2-specific metaphorical expressions. As for traces of transfer of the L2-specific metaphorical expressions, as shown in Table 7.6, learners at all levels of proficiency relied heavily on transfer to judge L2-specific metaphorical expressions; more than one-third of the judgements of MT expressions made by the intermediate learners were influenced by their L2-specific metaphorical expressions, and this proportion reached more than

50 per cent for the high-advanced learners. The persistence of such a negative influence on the judgement of L2-specific metaphorical expressions distinguishes it from the transfer of shared and L1-specific metaphorical expressions.

Here, I would like to suggest that the distinction between the transfer of MT expressions and that of other metaphorical expressions is due to the difference in the content being transferred from L1 to L2. As observed before, the transfer of shared and L1-specific metaphorical expressions always involves the transfer of individual linguistic elements. Although the transfer of L2-specific metaphorical expressions corresponds to what Kellerman refers to as 'nothing to transfer', something is, indeed, being transferred from L1 to L2 in the process; what is transferred is the observation that 'X, a linguistic element, is not possible in L1'. This observation is part of the learners' knowledge of their L1 and, when it comes to the L2, they extend that knowledge to form the belief that 'since X is not possible in L1, it should not be possible in L2 either', and thus naturally they assume that the presence of X is 'wrong' in L2. Transfer of such observations means that some L2-specific metaphorical expressions are difficult to acquire, exactly as the results of the judgement task in Section 5.2 and the results of the reading task in Section 6.2 suggest. Transfer of 'nothing' to L2-specific metaphorical expressions or, to be more precise, the failure of acquisition of L2-specific metaphorical expressions, shows a stronger cross-linguistic influence on acquisition than a transfer in the context of shared and L1-specific expressions.

While the cross-linguistic influence on the shared and L1-specific metaphorical expressions becomes less evident as proficiency rises, the cross-linguistic influence on L2-specific metaphorical expressions seems to become even more significant. This is because it is more difficult to become aware of 'the belief that there is no such linguistic element' than the transfer of 'something'. Unless the availability of L2-specific metaphorical expressions is explicitly pointed out in L2 exposure, learners will have little opportunity to know and use those expressions, since it is less likely for them to realize the existence of those expressions. In the case of guided acquisition, the instructors hardly have the opportunity to 'correct' the use of those expressions; if students can express the intended meaning without using L2-specific metaphorical expressions, then there is no imperative to introduce these expressions to the students. Here, I would like to posit a deadlock in terms of the acquisition of the L2-specific metaphorical expressions. On the one hand, the lack of relevant knowledge of L2-specific metaphorical expressions is such that learners do not to use them since they do not have other sources that introduce them. On the other hand, when learners rely on cross-linguistic influence to judge expressions, they constantly transfer 'the belief that there is no such linguistic element' to their L2, which leads to the rejection of the L2-specific metaphorical expressions and a lack of knowledge of those expressions. A deadlock is clearly reflected in the results of the judgement task and the sentence correction component; advanced learners confidently rejected the L2-specific metaphorical expressions (see Section 7.2.6.2), and then substituted them for other expressions that are (possibly) available in both their L1 and L2 (see Table 7.12 for examples).

One further question regarding the transfer of the three types of metaphorical expressions is how a learner perceives its subjective transferability. While the objective transferability of a linguistic element depends entirely on the availability of that element in a learner's L1 and L2, learners will always hold their own perception of subjective transferability, which may differ from actual objective transferability. It was observed that a number of less proficient learners still accepted some metaphorical expressions that were not objectively transferable from L1 to L2, while at the same time, some learners chose to reject metaphorical expressions that were objectively transferable from L1 to L2. Both phenomena show that some learners may perceive subjective transferability in a different way from the objective transferability of the metaphorical expressions, which requires a valid explanation.

Based on the estimated percentage of traces of transfer across the groups of learners (see Table 7.6 and the trend therein), an assumption can be made about how learners establish their own sense of intuition to distinguish between the expressions they would like to transfer and those they do not want to transfer. As suggested in Section 2.3, subjective transferability should be seen as a continuum, and a learner can always adjust the subjective transferability of a linguistic element throughout the process of acquisition. A learner will have a relatively low L2 proficiency at the beginning of the acquisition process and may believe that every L1 expression has a similar subjective transferability. The 'default' degree of subjective transferability of every element should, therefore, be neutral on the continuum, rather than being set to 'fully transferable' or 'not transferable at all'. With more understanding of L2, adjustments will have to be made to the subjective transferability of each expression based on the linguistic materials the learner has been exposed to; subjective transferability of different linguistic elements will vary at that stage, which will lead to the two observations made in the previous paragraph.

Finally, it should be noted that, although the metaphorical expressions are generally less acceptable and more difficult to process than the corresponding literal expressions and the effects of cross-linguistic influence are prominent in the judgement and reading time of metaphorical expressions, literal paraphrasing was extensively used in the sentence correction section, but this does not sufficiently or necessarily indicate that the ability to use metaphorical expressions in L2 is suppressed. The learner participants, especially the more advanced groups, were able to find corresponding metaphorical expressions in L2 to replace L1-specific metaphorical expressions as well as create new metaphorical expressions in L2 to express the intended meaning, despite the fact that cross-linguistic influence could also be observed in the metaphorical expressions they created. In particular, the percentage of alternative metaphorical expressions in the feedback sentences was similar across different groups of learners and the native group, indicating that learners are similarly productive when they apply metaphorical expressions, even if they are using their second language.

8.3 Factors influencing the transferability and transfer of metaphorical expressions

While cross-linguistic influence has had a prominent impact on the acquisition of metaphorical expressions, and the said impact changes according to the cross-linguistic availability of metaphorical expressions, it is still worth noting that other factors may also impact the transferability of metaphorical expressions. Starting from Chapter 3, I have discussed the possible influence of several factors on transferability and the outcome of acquisition of metaphorical expressions, including markedness and learners' knowledge. As reported in Chapter 7, while the learners' state of knowledge has a more significant impact on the transferability of metaphorical expressions, the influence of the degree of markedness of metaphorical expressions is not as prominent as the influence of metaphoricalness.

While Jordens and Kellerman loosely define markedness in second language acquisition, it is possible to measure the degree of markedness of a metaphorical expression using a separate lexical evaluation task, which roughly corresponds to the measurement given by Jordens and Kellerman (1981). However, while different from their assumption, I suspect that (binary) metaphoricalness may still play a role in the transfer of metaphorical expressions, and it is less likely to fully separate (binary) metaphoricalness and markedness in a continuum. The influence of markedness on the transferability of a combination of shared and

L1-specific metaphorical expressions is reported in Section 7.2.6.3.2, for both are metaphorical expressions available in L1. It shows that the degree of markedness of a metaphorical expression does not influence the subjective transferability of that expression; that leads to the question of whether the degree of markedness plays a role in that setting. I then further compared the influence of markedness and the influence of binary metaphoricalness on the transferability of shared metaphorical expressions and corresponding literal expressions (i.e. the literal expressions that make use of the same critical lexical item). The two types of expression are both shared between L1 and L2, and, therefore, both are objectively transferable; the only differences between the two types of expressions are their degree of markedness in the first language and their metaphoricalness. The results show that the influence of markedness in this experiment is minimal, but the influence of metaphoricalness is more prominent. A metaphorical expression is less transferable than a literal expression, while a less marked expression is not necessarily more transferable than a more marked expression if they are shared by L1 and L2. I argue that, if a meaning is identified as 'non-literal' by a learner, it is seen as less readily available in L2, even if that meaning is available in both L1 and L2, and the transfer of the meaning does not lead to any errors.

This outcome seems to contradict Jordens and Kellerman's comparison between metaphoricalness and markedness. Jordens and Kellerman suggest that the subjective transferability of a meaning is not influenced by the abstractness or metaphoricalness of that meaning, but only by its degree of markedness; however, the results show a totally different story. Note that LB and shared metaphorical expressions are designed to have the same degree of acceptability in L1 and the same availability in both L1 and L2; thus, it is expected that the two types of expression should have the same degree of objective transferability, as well as the same degree of acceptability by learners, even in their L2. However, as shown in the comparison between the shared metaphorical expressions and their literal counterparts, the acceptability perceived by learners and the subjective transferability of the two types of meaning are significantly different. This result may indicate that metaphoricalness is essentially the factor influencing the subjective transferability of a meaning, which means that Jordens and Kellerman fail to distinguish the effects of metaphoricalness and markedness in their proposal. Alternatively, such a contradiction may be caused by some methodological limitation in the measurement of the degree of markedness of expressions. I will leave it to the reader to seek improvements in the possible methodologies that might capture the degree of markedness better.

The second factor on cross-linguistic influence that I aim to illustrate in this book, namely a learner's knowledge of L2, seems to be the one with the most straightforward and consistent influence. The current study follows the tradition of previous research and measures a learner's knowledge of L2 using a separate proficiency test, and then compares the learner's reaction to metaphorical expressions with a general proficiency level. It is shown that when learners become more proficient in their L2, they transfer less knowledge in their judgement of the shared and L1-specific metaphorical expressions and process the shared and L2-specific metaphorical expressions with less hesitation. However, some aspects of the acquisition of metaphorical expressions remain fossilized, even if the learner reaches a higher proficiency level. As with the discussion in the last section, the most significant fossilization happens with L2-specific metaphorical expressions; even highly proficient learners rely on transfer to judge L2-specific metaphorical expressions, which creates a great obstacle for learners to achieve native-like judgements for negative transfer. The fossilization of subjective transferability of the L2-specific metaphorical expressions leads to a reconsideration of the concept of 'knowledge' in the study of cross-linguistic influence. Knowledge of metaphorical expressions in L2, which is crucial for the discussion of cross-linguistic influence in this book, does not always develop alongside progress in L2 acquisition. Most of the factors relevant to an improvement in L2 general proficiency, including the length of guided acquisition, seemed to correlate with only part of the acquisition of metaphorical expressions. From a combination of the acceptability score and the estimated percentage of traces of transfer, the rejection of L1-specific metaphorical expressions increases as L2 proficiency rises, until the learner eventually gives up transferring unacceptable expressions from L1. At the same time, learners do not realize what has not yet been acquired. A 'blank' is left in the mental lexicon where the L2-specific metaphorical expressions are, since there is nothing available for transfer. Even if a learner has encountered the L2-specific metaphorical meaning of a lexical item in non-guided acquisition before the experiment, or is able to infer the metaphorical meaning from the context under the time pressure, as is observed in the processing task, that learner may still not find it possible to integrate that metaphorical meaning into L2 knowledge. Without exposure to frequently used expressions in daily life, as in the case of overseas students, or explicit teaching of these expressions in guided acquisition, the 'blank' will not be automatically filled, but will simply be left in L2 as it is in L1.

The gap between L2 general proficiency and improved knowledge of metaphorical expressions can provide some insights into research on both second language acquisition and language pedagogy. In investigating learners' knowledge of L2 and the constraints of cross-linguistic influence, there are some situations in which general proficiency in L2 cannot be a universal indicator of L2 knowledge, especially when the target of investigation is rather specific and sometimes absent from the content of language instruction. In these situations, general proficiency does not strictly match the knowledge of that target element of investigation, which may lead to a misinterpretation of the result. The lack of knowledge of metaphorical expression instruction, even at a higher proficiency level, indicates that the meaning and use of metaphorical expressions should be emphasized to second language learners when they acquire vocabulary. As a crucial part of daily language use, knowledge of metaphorical expressions is as important as other figurative expressions (e.g. idioms), while the meaning can be inferred from the literal meaning of a lexical item, which makes it more accessible to learners. Meanwhile, researchers and language instructors should not expect learners to access metaphorical meanings autonomously; it is necessary for instructors to provide some well-formed L2-specific metaphorical expressions as a part of the course material, or encourage learners to derive the meaning of metaphorical expressions from the context using figurative thinking.

8.4 Learning and teaching metaphorical expressions in a second language

As shown in the discussions above, a development of L2 knowledge does not always guarantee a development of the knowledge of metaphorical expressions in a second language. The following are the most important concerns for non-researchers working on second language acquisition, including learners and teachers; how can we learn and teach metaphorical expressions better in a second language? Can we get rid of the fate that the development of knowledge of metaphorical expressions is always behind the development of general knowledge of L2 vocabulary? The final subsection of the whole book addresses the issue of teaching metaphorical expressions, mainly resulting from the outcome of current research.

The very first issue, when thinking of teaching metaphorical expressions, is how we treat these expressions in L2 vocabulary knowledge. That said, we should consider whether language instructors should and would introduce the definition of 'metaphorical expressions' in a second language, or even in languages generally. According to the definition of conventional metaphorical meanings, these meanings are already highly conventionalized and even can be found in dictionaries and, theoretically, both instructors and learners can directly treat these conventionalized metaphorical meanings as a type of word meaning. In this sense, instructors can teach the conventional metaphorical meanings and relevant metaphorical expressions simply by teaching the literal meanings of these words. There is no need to further elaborate the concept of 'conceptual metaphors' or 'metaphorical expressions'; learners can and will learn the literal and metaphorical meanings separately, as if they were acquiring homonyms like 'bank'. That means the link between the metaphorical and literal meaning of a word is intentionally broken by the instructors, and, as shown in the results, learners may face difficulties in recovering the links without explicit instruction.

Alternatively, we can also put metaphorical expressions in a different basket to literal expressions, even if they are conventionalized and have their own place in dictionaries. This approach is more relevant to the history of these meanings; they were once 'live' metaphorical expressions that always required pragmatic enrichment, but have been gradually conventionalized to be relatively stable word meanings. In this way, it is probably inevitable that the concept of metaphor be introduced in second language teaching, which could be very different from the concept of (literary) metaphor in literature classes of primary and secondary schools. However, it is still possible to connect between the concept of a literary metaphor in one's first language and the concept of a conceptual metaphor when students learn it on a second language course. As mentioned before, this option will largely avoid the consequence of breaking the connection between literal and metaphorical meanings.

Then we can consider a second issue in the design of teaching; how much emphasis should instructors put on the concept of metaphors when they teach these expressions? Of course, instructors can theoretically introduce all aspects of the Contemporary Metaphor Theory to students (if they have enough hours to do so), and guide them through the common conceptual metaphors and their linguistic realizations. This would definitely help students to understand and use conventional metaphorical expressions in a second language and, probably, could also help them to deal with other 'new' conventional metaphorical expressions that they have not yet learned in the classroom. This, however, may not be applicable to younger students or beginners. First, their cognitive skills may not be mature enough to understand complicated theories like CMT, so teaching them CMT as a full theory may cause confusion, especially if they learn about literary metaphors at the same time. Second, younger students and beginners need to learn different aspects of a second language rather than mere vocabulary, so they probably do not have that much time in which to learn CMT systematically. Last, but not least, younger students or beginners may have a smaller L2 vocabulary; even if they can understand CMT, they may not be able to explore the metaphorical meanings of different words under the guidance of CMT, just because their vocabulary size cannot support the learning procedure. We can see that teaching CMT in order to improve the knowledge of metaphorical expressions is a less feasible option for students in primary and secondary schools; nevertheless, it can be used for more advanced learners or students at a tertiary level of education. For example, this approach can be utilized for language courses at university level, summer schools on foreign languages and, probably, self-learning materials for more proficient learners.

Another option is to bypass the theoretical arguments of CMT and go directly into the teaching after some shallow explanation of what 'metaphor' is. After all, second language teachers and learners may want to focus on the language itself rather than refer to the complicated theories behind it. Teachers could simply explain to students that metaphorical meanings are a kind of meaning that is closely related to, yet different from, the literal meanings of lexical items, while contents such as conceptual metaphors and the historical development of a metaphorical expression are omitted. Instructors could then teach students about individual metaphorical expressions as well as their connections to the literal meanings of the same lexical items while, at the same time, providing additional exercises for them just so they can become more familiar with the relationship between literal and metaphorical meanings of a lexical item. Compared with the previous approach, this one provides a clearer target on the acquisition and use of metaphorical meanings of different words in a second language, and students can also feel free to explore further contents about theories of metaphor since they have already been given the keyword 'metaphor'. This is a more approachable method for both younger learners and lower level learners with a fair vocabulary size.

While we can choose to stress the concept of 'metaphor' to different extents, it is also possible to skip the concept of metaphor when teaching and learning metaphorical expressions. That said, instructors do not need to give the metaphorical meanings of a lexical item 'a label' to teach them, but simply let the students come across the expressions and ask them to deduce the meanings on their own. This proposal is motivated by the idea of fostering metaphorical thinking (Littlemore & Low 2006) in second language acquisition, as well as native speakers' attitudes towards literal and conventional metaphorical expressions. We have already seen at the beginning of this book that native speakers of a language may not explicitly feel 'a sense of metaphoricalness' when they see a conventional metaphorical expression (although we have also seen that native speakers tend to rate metaphorical expressions as 'more abstract' than literal expressions). If native speakers do not pay special attention to the degree of metaphoricalness of an expression, then it is possible that instructors do not need to let learners know about it either.

Based on the disadvantages of classroom learning in terms of the acquisition of vocabulary, one major obstacle for learners in acquiring word meaning is that they have a relatively weak ability to infer the meaning of a given lexical item from a context. Such a disadvantage also keeps learners from acquiring metaphorical expressions autonomously after they have acquired the literal meaning of a lexical item. In return, instructors can cultivate their learners' ability of word meaning inferencing by asking them to read and to infer the meaning of metaphorical expressions. A possible strategy starts by simply presenting the literal meaning and metaphorical meanings of different lexical items in some valid contexts (preferably in sentences or short paragraphs rather than individual collocations) and asking learners to deduce the literal and metaphorical meanings of specific words after reading these sentences/paragraphs. Similarly, after they have experienced some use of metaphorical expressions in their second language, the instructors could then ask the learners to extend their knowledge of lexical meanings to make their own metaphorical expressions, depending on the context, and, at the same time, point out to them which is more conventionally used in their second language and which sounds more deviant and probably should be avoided. This approach could help classroom learners form a more autonomous learning strategy when acquiring metaphorical expressions.

Among all these possibilities, I would like to find one that is most suitable to the sustainable development of knowledge of metaphorical expressions; that means, I not only expect the learners to learn metaphorical expressions in their second language classes, but I also expect them to 'pick up' other metaphorical expressions in daily exposure and actively produce metaphorical expressions, whether conventional or novel (but, nevertheless, valid in their second language). I expect, at least, that learners at near-native level will show a native-like pattern when they judge and process metaphorical expressions; learners should be able to accept metaphorical expressions that are available in their second language and directly access these metaphorical meanings when they read these expressions. When contrasting the targets and actual performance by second language learners, it can be easily noticed that learners: (1) are not familiar with the category of metaphorical meanings in general; (2) do have some ability to transfer their knowledge of shared metaphorical expressions, but such ability is rather limited, which may be due to their lack of awareness of the availability of these expressions; and (3) are particularly weak when reading the metaphorical expressions only available in their L2. Considering that, I would like to propose an integration of some theoretical knowledge of metaphor and more extensive training on the use of metaphorical expressions in contexts. It is better to teach students some shallow concepts of metaphorical expressions, particularly a brief history of the evolution of metaphorical meanings, or, as a minimum, explicitly show them that there is a conceptual link between the literal meaning and the metaphorical meaning of a single lexical item. At the same time, instructors can introduce individual metaphorical expressions through both explicit teaching and a series of reading and comprehension tasks.

As shown in the experiment results, more advanced learners can gradually understand and share metaphorical expressions better, but may still encounter persistent difficulty when reading and understanding metaphorical expressions that are exclusively available in their L2. In the practice of teaching metaphorical expressions, L2 metaphorical expressions can be divided into two large categories based on their cross-linguistic availability. For shared metaphorical expressions, it is easier for learners to understand their mechanism and, probably, the relationship between the literal and metaphorical meanings, so instructors could teach these expressions by introducing the link between literal and metaphorical expressions and let the learners themselves derive the metaphorical interpretations of these expressions in reading and writing tasks using the theoretical knowledge and their knowledge of metaphorical expressions in their L1. For metaphorical expressions that are exclusively available in the L2, it is better to explicitly teach the expressions and meanings alongside an illustration of theoretical arguments. After the initial instruction of these expressions, learners can then be asked to participate in extensive reading tasks, which will help them to infer the metaphorical meaning within a given context.

Different from research on metaphorical expressions in cognitive semantics, the metaphorical expressions appearing in teaching materials need not be organized in different categories or based on different conceptual metaphors.

Instead, in language courses for general purposes, such as second language courses in secondary schools and for non-language major students, metaphorical expressions should be introduced according to their frequency and complexity (e.g. how difficult is it to understand the target concept/source concept in the learners' everyday experience). For example, under the same category of conceptual metaphor ARGUMENT IS WAR, it would be easier for younger learners to understand 'attack someone's idea' rather than 'shoot down someone's opinion', since the action of shooting may not be readily available for younger learners, while 'attack' is relatively more frequent than 'shoot down' when describing arguments. It should be noted that, when instructors prepare for the content about metaphorical expressions, the essential object is to let the learners know about these expressions and encourage them to use them accurately; therefore, a frequency-based investigation on different metaphorical expressions is recommended prior to the instruction. Nevertheless, metaphorical expressions can be organized into different themes or even different conceptual metaphors if they are to be taught in language courses for specific purposes – such as a course of English for Academic Purposes (EAP). In a course focusing on Business English, for instance, introducing business-related metaphorical expressions with the support of a systematic knowledge of conceptual metaphors is preferable to teaching individual expressions (see Holme 2004 for examples).

After talking about how to introduce metaphorical expressions into second language classrooms and defining what should be introduced, the last issue I would like to discuss in this subsection is the timing; when should metaphorical expressions in second language courses be introduced. Ideally, the earlier people start teaching and learning metaphorical expressions (i.e. teaching and learning the metaphorical meaning and the literal meaning of a lexical item at the same time), the better the outcome will be. However, teaching metaphorical meanings, especially through extensive reading or theoretical arguments of metaphor, may be more complicated, both cognitively and linguistically. I have already stated that a complex theory of metaphor may not be suitable for younger learners who do not have a basic understanding of metaphor in general. Moreover, it can be more difficult for early learners with a limited vocabulary to accomplish tasks like extensive reading and deducing the meanings of metaphorical expressions from collocations. In order to let learners acquire metaphorical expressions in a sustainable way, they should have an intermediate vocabulary size of at least three thousand words and be able to understand a number of concrete and abstract verbs and nouns. Considering all these factors, it is then more feasible to introduce metaphorical expressions when learners reach B1 level in CEFR, or at an equivalent proficiency level. Again, for courses such as English for Specific Purposes (ESP), metaphorical expressions falling within the scope of the courses can be taught together with other vocabulary, even at the beginning of the courses.

The discussions above can be seen as an attempt to propose some strategies of teaching metaphorical expressions in a second language that takes both cognitive semantics and second language acquisition into consideration. While there is rich literature on teaching metaphorical expressions, which propose metaphorical thinking based on the cognitive semantic view of metaphor, most of them aim to propose a more independent teaching methodology that requires language teachers to have a solid background of theory of metaphor or cognitive linguistics (see Holme 2004; Littlemore & Low 2006, and others). On the other hand, few of them attempt to provide a teaching strategy based on the current curriculum of second language. Compared with those proposals, the discussions above are more manageable by teachers with a general knowledge of a second language and can be easily added into a curriculum. By integrating the teaching and learning of metaphorical expressions into other tasks that are frequently used in second language classrooms, these suggestions aim to make metaphorical expressions more accessible to both teachers and students and, generally, more acceptable to learners regardless of their linguistic background and major.

8.5 Summary and loose ends

In this book, I have mainly discussed the acquisition of three types of metaphorical expression according to their cross-linguistic availability. Although I mainly use Chinese learners of English to inform the discussions, it is possible to extend the discussion, as well as the research and teaching methodology, to the three types of metaphorical expression in any language pair: shared metaphorical expressions; L1-specific expressions; and L2-specific metaphorical expressions.

While this book has a similar purpose to that of other studies (see García et al. 2015 for a summary) on the acquisition of figurative language in a second language, it provides a more detailed picture in that field, including in the following aspects: (1) a comparison between the acquisition of literal and metaphorical meanings of a same set of lexical items; (2) an analysis of different realizations of cross-linguistic influence on metaphorical expressions; (3) an analysis of the factors influencing transferability and their impact on the acquisition and processing of metaphorical expressions, following work by Jordens and Kellerman (1981); (4) an attempt to place the metaphorical meanings of a lexical item in a bilingual mental lexicon; and (5) an attempt to explain how metaphorical expressions are accessed by L2 learners. It shows that, while cross-linguistic influence is observed in the acquisition of metaphorical expressions and expressions with different availability are acquired according to distinct patterns, metaphorical expressions are nevertheless treated as 'secondary' by Chinese learners of English in a classroom setting; these learners experience persistent difficulty in mastering metaphorical expressions. This result might provide pedagogical insights for both instructors and learners, which can be seen as an essential part of the improvement of "metaphoric awareness" proposed by Littlemore and Low (2006).

It has been pointed out in Section 8.3 that, although the factors influencing transferability are investigated here, the concepts involved are slightly different from Jordens and Kellerman's original proposal, thus any difference between the results here and that proposal may be caused by variances in concepts and the measurement of those factors. In future research, it might be possible to compare the acquisition of metaphorical expressions between learners with the same L1 but different L2s, or between learners who have acquired both an L2 and an L3, to see if the psychotypological distance collectively perceived by a group of learners of three languages has any impact on the acquisition of metaphorical expressions in general. Also, a further examination might be conducted to evaluate how much knowledge of conceptual metaphors (as per Lakoff & Johnson 1980) is involved in the acquisition of metaphorical expressions by L2 learners who have no theoretical background of cognitive semantics, and whether the conceptual metaphors themselves are transferable between languages. A comparison might also be drawn between child L1 and adult L2 acquisition of metaphorical expressions, to discover why highly advanced L2 learners still treat metaphorical expressions as 'secondary' while native speakers do not.

Appendix 1

Instruction and sentences used in the acceptability judgement task

Instruction for the acceptability judgement task:

Please imagine the following scene: your school/university now has an English writing club and you are an active member in it. Every week you need to write your own compositions and hand them to your teachers/advisors; at the same time you will get some paragraphs from other students in the writing club, and you can point out the problems with their writing. The whole procedure is anonymous, so you will not know whose composition you are reading and marking, and the author of the composition will not know who the marker is either.

Please feel free to point out any parts in the sentences that make you feel awkward or uncomfortable, and describe your feeling of acceptability by giving a score between 0 and 10 (0 for not acceptable at all, and 10 for totally acceptable; if you are not sure how to do it, you can refer to the examples below). If you believe that there is a better sentence, you can always write it down in the blank space below the score, so your peers will know more about the mistakes they have made. After doing so, please indicate how confident you are when you mark and correct the sentences. Please do not use a dictionary, just follow your intuition and make the judgement as quickly as possible.

The underlined lexical item is the designed critical lexical item in the sentence. Sentences are arranged in the alphabetical order of the critical lexical items.
    MB (metaphorical-both) sentences:

He attacked every weak point in my argument.
I admire him because he is the father of modern biology.
The sudden death of his mother hit him hard and he cried for a long time.
Don't worry. There is always a market for good plans.

When he was young, the <u>seeds</u> of his great thoughts have been already planted.
When Judy came back after four years, she finally felt the <u>warmth</u> of her family again.
If she focuses on reading instead of <u>wasting</u> her time, she will be a better student.
He is very knowledgeable and I never <u>won</u> an argument against him.

LB (literal-both) sentences:

When everyone was asleep, the enemies <u>attacked</u> the village.
Lisa was happy when she got her birthday gift from her <u>father</u>.
The car <u>hit</u> me hard in the accident and my leg was broken.
I really enjoy taking a walk in the flower <u>market</u> in the morning.
Growing vegetables from <u>seeds</u> may take some time, but it can save a lot of money.
I sat back, enjoying the <u>warmth</u> of the sun on a Sunday afternoon.
He <u>wasted</u> a lot of money on this useless machine.
It is unlikely that the United States will <u>win</u> the Football World Cup this time.

MS (metaphorical-source) sentences:

Sally always <u>bites</u> the words and phrases whenever she writes an article.
Sophie lost her golden <u>bowl</u> after her boss decided to shut down the company.
Martin <u>broke</u> the crime and received an award from the police.
He <u>ate</u> some loss when he started his own business.
The teacher forced the <u>fire</u> in her heart down, and didn't let it break out.
The mother held a belly of <u>gas</u> because her son failed in the exam.
This incident might influence the fame of our brand, so we'd better handle it at a low <u>pitch</u>.
Justin often <u>sings</u> an opposite tune when we discuss the homework.

LS (literal-source) sentences:

Sometimes I <u>bite</u> my nails when I become very nervous.
The shiny golden <u>bowl</u> in the cupboard belongs to my elder brother.
Laura found that a stranger <u>broke</u> her door and entered her room.
My sister is very picky and always refuses to <u>eat</u> vegetables.
Now some modern cars can use both <u>gas</u> and electricity as power sources.

The brave boy saved his dog and helped put out the <u>fire</u>.
When people want to sound more attractive, they will choose to speak at a low <u>pitch</u>.
I heard someone <u>singing</u> a beautiful song in the corridor.

MT (metaphorical-target) sentences:

The idea is too stupid. He won't <u>buy</u> it.
They <u>exploded</u> his last theory, so he felt really disappointed.
My mother said that these books would be <u>food</u> for thought.
The first two paragraphs prepare the <u>ground</u> for the main argument of the article.
I <u>see</u> what your problem is, and I believe that I can solve it in a moment.
I tried really hard, but just couldn't <u>swallow</u> his claim.
What he said left a really bad <u>taste</u> in my mouth.
Clare has a <u>wealth</u> of ideas and she always makes successful plans.

LT (literal-target) sentences:

He <u>bought</u> an old wooden clock on the Internet.
Someone just <u>exploded</u> a balloon suddenly and the loud sound scared everyone.
We cannot survive for long without enough <u>food</u> and drink.
Bob found his wallet lying on the <u>ground</u> near his bike.
I can <u>see</u> the boy playing with his classmates in the garden.
You can put the pills in your mouth and <u>swallow</u> them.
I lost my sense of <u>taste</u> because of the heavy cold, but I believe I will be better soon.
Peter inherited his family's <u>wealth</u> after the death of his father.

Appendix 2

Instruction, sentences and questions used in the self-paced reading task

Instruction for the self-paced reading task:

In this experiment, you will read some English sentences and provide judgements according to the contents of the sentences. Before each sentence, a '+' mark will appear on the screen to indicate the position of the first word of that sentence.

The first word of that sentence will appear after you press SPACEBAR, and the next word will appear when you press SPACEBAR again, when the previous word will disappear. You will read all the sentences in this way. Please be as natural as you can be when reading, and understand the content of each sentence as quickly as possible.

After finishing a sentence, you will see a question, please use the keyboard to provide your judgement of that question according to the content of the sentence. The key with a 'Y' sticker means 'Yes', and the one with an 'N' sticker means 'No'. Please respond to all questions as quickly as possible.

The underlined lexical item is the designed critical lexical item in the sentence. The comprehension questions are not included in the appendix. Sentences are arranged in the alphabetical order of the critical lexical items. A comprehension question (CQ) is attached after each critical sentence.

MB (metaphorical-both) sentences:

The famous doctor <u>built</u> an argument in his article in the book.

CQ: Did the doctor only describe some facts in his article?

The pretty girl <u>changed</u> her mind before she went to the party.

CQ: Did the girl have a different idea when she went to the party?

The honest woman <u>cleared</u> her thoughts and told her story to people.

CQ: Did the woman refuse to talk about her story?

    The busy musician <u>found</u> some time to take a very quick rest.

CQ: Did the musician have no time to rest?

    The wise gentleman <u>gave</u> an idea to the students in the classroom.

CQ: Did the gentleman ask his student to provide an idea?

    The little boy <u>grabbed</u> the chance and ran into the house quickly.

CQ: Did the boy use his chance effectively?

    The happy lady <u>lit</u> the passion in the mind of her daughter.

CQ: Did the lady have no influence on her daughter?

    The busy musician <u>played</u> a part in the creation of the song.

CQ: Did the musician contribute to the song?

    The famous doctor <u>saved</u> his time by making a very compact schedule.

CQ: Did the doctor waste a lot of time?

    The honest woman <u>showed</u> the solution to the question from the professor.

CQ: Did the woman explain the solution to a question?

    The pretty girl <u>spent</u> some time on computer games with her friends.

CQ: Did the girl play computer for some time?

    The young man <u>won</u> Anne's heart by writing a very sweet poem.

CQ: Did the man attract Anne with his own poem?

LB (literal-both) sentences:

    The famous doctor <u>built</u> a balcony for his home near the city.

CQ: Did the doctor construct a balcony?

    The pretty girl <u>changed</u> her clothes before she went to the party.

CQ: Did the girl wear different clothes when she went to the party?

    The honest woman <u>cleared</u> her room and put everything into her suitcase.

CQ: Did the woman leave something in her room?

The busy musician <u>found</u> some food to make a very simple dinner.

CQ: Did the musician get some food?

The wise gentleman <u>gave</u> some money to poor people on the street.

CQ: Did the gentleman send food to poor people?

The little boy <u>grabbed</u> the knife and killed the crazy dog quickly.

CQ: Did the boy killed the dog with a knife?

The happy lady <u>lit</u> the fireplace in the bedroom of her house.

CQ: Did the lady start a fire in the fireplace?

The busy musician <u>played</u> the drums as a kid for several years.

CQ: Did the musician learn violin as a kid?

The famous doctor <u>saved</u> his wife by performing a very important procedure.

CQ: Did the doctor cure his wife effectively?

The honest woman <u>showed</u> a video about the story of her family.

CQ: Did the woman play a song about her family?

The pretty girl <u>spent</u> some money on new clothes for her dolls.

CQ: Did the girl use money to buy snacks?

The young man <u>won</u> that prize by writing a very sweet poem.

CQ: Did the man get that prize by composing a song?

MS (metaphorical-source) sentences:

The poor teacher <u>bit</u> her words when she was writing an article.

CQ: Did the teacher choose her words carefully in her writing?

The young man <u>broke</u> the crime and received an award from police.

CQ: Did the man fail to solve the crime?

The naughty student <u>chewed</u> his tongue while his classmates discussed their homework.

Appendix 2

CQ: Did the student keep quiet when his classmates were working?

The rich manager <u>ate</u> some loss when he started his own business.

CQ: Did the manager get profit at the beginning of his business?

The old chef <u>fried</u> some stocks when he was not at work.

CQ: Did the chef buy and sell some stocks?

The naughty student <u>raised</u> his heart when he walked on the ice.

CQ: Did the student feel anxious when he walked on the ice?

LS (literal-source) sentences:

The poor teacher <u>bit</u> her nails when she was worried about something.

CQ: Did the teacher paint her nails when she was nervous?

The young man <u>broke</u> the door and brought the sleeping baby outside.

CQ: Did the man open the window of that room?

The naughty student <u>chewed</u> his gum while his classmates discussed their homework.

CQ: Did the student have some chewing gum?

The rich manager <u>ate</u> some fruits because they were healthy for him.

CQ: Did the manager have fruits in his diet?

The old chef <u>fried</u> some rice when he was not at work.

CQ: Did the chef cooked some rice?

The naughty student <u>raised</u> his hand when the teacher asked a question.

CQ: Did the student stay still when his teacher asked a question?

MT (metaphorical-target) sentences:

The happy lady <u>bought</u> an idea because it sounded clever to her.

CQ: Did the lady reject the idea?

The rich manager <u>drove</u> his business all the way to the top.

CQ: Did the manager run a successful business?

The poor teacher <u>lost</u> her temper and shouted at her students angrily.

CQ: Did the teacher keep calm to her students?

The young man <u>paid</u> some attention to the question from his colleagues.

CQ: Did the man ignore the question from his colleagues?

The wise gentleman <u>saw</u> the problem and gave a piece of advice.

CQ: Did the gentleman understand the problem correctly?

The naughty student <u>spilled</u> the secret when he entered the meeting room.

CQ: Did the student tell the secret to other people?

LT (literal-target) sentences:

The happy lady <u>bought</u> a wallet because it looked lovely to her.

CQ: Did the lady sell a wallet?

The rich manager <u>drove</u> his motorbike all the way to his house.

CQ: Did the manager take a taxi to home?

The poor teacher <u>lost</u> her wallet and was locked outside her apartment.

CQ: Did the teacher fail to open the door?

The young man <u>paid</u> some money to the owner of the store.

CQ: Did the man give some money to the shopkeeper?

The wise gentleman <u>saw</u> a schoolgirl and gave a book to her.

CQ: Did the gentleman meet a girl?

The naughty student <u>spilled</u> the coffee when he entered the meeting room.

CQ: Did the student drink the coffee in the meeting room?

Appendix 3

Lexical property scores for the critical lexical items

Lexical property scores rated by Chinese native speakers:

Lexical item	Literal			Metaphorical		
	Concreteness	Coreness	Perceived frequency	Concreteness	Coreness	Perceived frequency
attack	5.82633	4.4274	3.891	−6.9819	0.117	4.5026
bite	5.8988	2.087	5.943	−7.81165	−1.884	−1.1004
bowl	6.0092	2.39	4.7666	−6.8566	−1.4369	6.7192
break	−0.16993	−0.6552	1.984	−5.10876	−1.4458	3.9426
build	5.3495	3.3191	6.031	−5.23283	1.3573	3.0036
change	5.57523	1.195	5.418	−5.86484	3.2018	4.9436
chew	6.0057	3.2796	6.209	−4.91618	−3.6048	−0.1124
clear	5.6995	2.0282	5.595	−6.53022	−0.9401	2.4036
eat	5.38031	3.2181	6.517	−8.78353	−2.5093	6.6968
father	6.04466	1.9245	6.164	−5.58029	−1.2006	4.6066
find	4.05575	0.4868	5.907	−5.85947	−0.8592	6.3327
fire	6.23508	2.7528	6.056	−8.21035	−2.3974	7.0574
fry	6.02597	2.0764	5.727	−6.45958	−5.1048	5.3813
gas	5.12229	−0.7983	2.474	−8.67792	−0.6749	6.6406
give	5.40671	3.1062	6.434	−3.20561	0.4415	6.7262
grab	6.41508	1.6994	4.0841	−7.94997	−2.5072	5.8297
hit	5.12113	3.1471	6.069	−7.61792	1.2321	6.675142
light	6.08868	3.6803	4.1991	−8.29239	−1.1863	2.5787
market	6.21625	1.7934	6.063	−6.49971	0.3762	4.7016
pitch	5.72485	1.6842	1.203	−7.39737	−3.4429	3.6176
play	5.85573	3.4017	5.135	−1.79351	2.0013	4.9402
raise	6.28033	2.2706	5.772	−7.63044	−2.1414	2.6486
save	−0.40462	3.4193	6.65	−0.85354	3.5412	6.2116

	Literal			Metaphorical		
seed	6.37895	3.1227	5.005	−7.49968	0.3855	3.6076
show	4.54543	2.2854	5.001	4.4079	3.4992	4.3366
sing	5.54837	3.7592	6.253	−6.84813	−4.0898	3.1596
spend	−1.29724	−0.5261	7.414	−4.78579	−0.3153	7.356
warmth	1.09021	4.2433	5.882	−7.99794	1.4557	6.683
waste	0.67763	2.4315	6.368	−3.68628	2.4929	7.2043
win (1)	1.8292	3.9843	6.009	1.62894	4.4171	6.2166
win (2)	1.8292	3.9843	6.009	−6.92766	0.5862	4.2896

Note: The metaphorical meanings of 'win' in the acceptability judgement task and the self-paced reading task are different. Therefore, two different metaphorical versions of 'win' were examined in the lexical evaluation task, (1) for the AJT version and (2) for the SPRT version. The literal meaning of 'win' in the two tasks are the same.

Lexical property scores rated by English native speakers:

Lexical item	Literal			Metaphorical		
	Concreteness	Coreness	Perceived frequency	Concreteness	Coreness	Perceived frequency
attack	6.96222	4.79165	4.985	−2.23299	0.58693	2.996
build	6.91029	5.39747	4.89668	−4.62748	1.32336	−0.09032
buy	6.33739	4.76017	5.987	−4.48432	−1.80827	2.71
change	4.93221	2.88143	5.04158	−4.07764	2.54343	5.98158
clear	5.39275	3.27493	2.993	−5.09954	1.33876	1.5079
drive	6.70816	4.28102	5.6482	−4.83117	0.41525	−0.4238
explode	7.08368	5.11843	1.656	−5.64038	0.32546	−4.691
father	6.80744	4.7553	6.012	−4.92316	0.98474	1.421
find	6.62536	3.33527	4.976481	−3.7023	−0.36685	4.877481
food	6.39517	5.07086	5.9007	−5.38246	−0.32865	0.5127
give	6.06869	4.89809	5.8439	−1.65167	1.4654	4.2022
grab	6.81795	4.27247	4.94641	−5.71287	1.36528	0.19141
ground	6.1521	4.69314	5.4369	−5.06949	−0.36672	0.1699
hit	6.59071	4.12384	4.5606	−4.43679	−0.66861	3.8786
light	5.5639	4.48074	4.4938	−5.13998	−0.49967	−1.8082
lose	6.17639	4.71474	5.1463	−4.05251	−0.49139	4.9553
market	7.2007	3.96919	3.533	−3.67078	1.11089	1.8747
pay	6.17507	4.94483	5.5897	−3.86152	−1.95548	5.1707
play	5.32397	2.78393	5.5181	−0.67382	−0.26376	4.2395
save	4.85798	4.21603	4.0003	−2.54162	0.23236	5.0043
see	5.99858	5.11721	5.4772	−2.56472	−0.57465	5.8902

Appendix 3

	Literal			Metaphorical		
seed	7.26521	5.00998	3.927	−6.14803	1.11321	0.548
show	4.44655	4.6286	5.3984	3.4668	1.01337	4.6494
spend	5.93701	4.47464	5.5984	−2.48323	0.1064	5.8764
spill	6.75773	4.83644	5.0007	−5.08138	−0.53396	0.5307
swallow	6.98839	5.01018	5.3297	−5.88035	−1.2625	0.2547
taste	4.48032	4.49854	3.813	−5.15986	−0.25007	1.0436
warmth	4.93315	5.71586	4.1643	−5.34929	0.12458	2.10163
waste	1.3769	3.41856	5.928	0.20119	0.86042	5.989
wealth	4.64058	4.85016	3.813	−4.95126	1.04848	1.4649
win (1)	4.2081	4.04553	6.088	−0.4092	2.79053	4.3918
win (2)	4.2081	4.04553	6.088	−3.78974	0.95219	1.522

Note: The metaphorical meanings of 'win' in the acceptability judgement task and the self-paced reading task are different. Therefore, two different metaphorical versions of 'win' were examined in the lexical evaluation task, (1) for the AJT version and (2) for the SPRT version. The literal meaning of 'win' in the two tasks are the same.

Notes

3 Metaphorical expressions under cross-linguistic influence

1. While the described situation exists and native speakers can be seen as an optimal example, the actual performance of L2 learners may vary due to language aptitude, sociolinguistic factors or other reasons, and it is probable that L2 learners in certain sociolinguistic backgrounds are less effective when making the inference of metaphorical meaning. See Section 5.4 for a review of relevant studies.

5 Placing metaphorical expressions in a bilingual mental lexicon

1. In the experiments in Chapter 7, all the words investigated in the experiments were known to the learners in terms of literal meanings, since the literal meanings had already appeared in the learner's textbook. The status of the metaphorical meaning is unknown.
2. For the sake of simplicity, the literal concepts are treated as being fully shared between the L1 and the L2. However, as pointed out by Pavlenko (2009), there may be language-specific literal concepts.

Bibliography

Aristotle (1961). *Aristotle's Poetics*, trans. S. H. Butcher (Vol. D27), New York: Hill and Wang.

Athanasopoulos, P. (2015). Conceptual representation in bilinguals: the role of language specificity and conceptual change, in J. W. Schwieter (ed.), *The Cambridge Handbook of Bilingual Processing*, 275–92, Cambridge, UK: Cambridge University Press.

Bamgbose, A. (1982). Standard Nigerian English: Issues of identification, in Braj Kachnu (ed.), *The Other Tongue: English across Cultures*, 99–111, Champaign, IL: University of Illinois Press.

Bard, E. G., Robertson, D., and Sorace, A. (1996). Magnitude estimation of linguistic acceptability. *Language*, 72 (1): 32–68.

Bardel, C., and Lindqvist, C. (2006). The role of proficiency and psychotypology in lexical cross-linguistic influence. A study of a multilingual learner of Italian L3 (pp. 123–45). Presented at the Atti del VI Congresso di Studi dell'Associazione Italiana di Linguistica Applicata, Napoli, Italy.

Barsalou, L. W. (1983). Ad hoc categories. *Memory & Cognition*, 11 (3): 211–27.

Barsalou, L. W. (1987). The instability of graded structure: Implications for the nature of concepts, in U. Neisser (ed.), *Concepts and Conceptual Development: Ecological and Intellectual Factors in Categorization*, 101–40, Cambridge, UK: Cambridge University Press.

Beardsley, M. C. (1962). The metaphorical twist. *Philosophy and Phenomenological Research*, 22 (3): 293–307.

Black, M. (1962). *Models and Metaphors: Studies in Language and Philosophy*. Ithaca, NY: Cornell University Press.

Blais, M.-J., and Gonnerman, L. (2013). Explicit and implicit semantic processing of verb–particle constructions by French–English bilinguals. *Bilingualism: Language and Cognition*, 16. https://doi.org/10.1017/S1366728912000673.

Blum, S., and Levenston, E. A. (1978). Universals of lexical simplification. *Language Learning*, 28 (2): 399–415.

Boers, F., and Lindstromberg, S. (2008). *Cognitive Linguistic Approaches to Teaching Vocabulary and Phraseology*. Berlin; Boston: De Gruyter Mouton. https://doi.org/10.1515/9783110199161.

Bortfeld, H. (2003). Comprehending idioms cross-linguistically. *Experimental Psychology*, 50 (3): 217.

Bowdle, B. F. and Gentner, D. (2005). The career of metaphor. *Psychological Review*, 112 (1): 193–216.

Brysbaert, M., and Duyck, W. (2010). Is it time to leave behind the Revised Hierarchical Model of bilingual language processing after fifteen years of service? *Bilingualism: Language and Cognition*, 13 (3): 359–71.

Carrol, G., Littlemore, J., and Gillon Dowens, M. (2018). Of false friends and familiar foes: Comparing native and non-native understanding of figurative phrases. *Lingua*, 204: 21–44. https://doi.org/10.1016/j.lingua.2017.11.001.

Carston, R. (2002). *Thoughts and Utterances: The Pragmatics of Explicit Communication*. Oxford: Blackwell.

Chiappe, D. L., and Kennedy, J. M. (1999). Aptness predicts preference for metaphors or similes, as well as recall bias. *Psychonomic Bulletin & Review*, 6 (4): 668–76.

Chiappe, D. L. and Kennedy, J. M. (2001). Literal bases for metaphor and simile. *Metaphor and Symbol*, 16 (3–4): 249–76.

Chiappe, D. L., Kennedy, J. M., and Chiappe, P. (2003). Aptness is more important than comprehensibility in predicting recognition bias and preference for metaphors and similes. *Poetics*, 31: 51–68.

Cieślicka, A. B. (2006). Literal salience in on-line processing of idiomatic expressions by second language learners. *Second Language Research*, 22 (2): 115–44.

Cieślicka, A. B. (2008). Hemispheric differences in processing salient and nonsalient meanings of L1 and L2 fixed expressions. Lenguaje Figurado y Motivación: Una Perspectiva Desde La Fraseología, ed. MÀ de La Granja, 111–27.

Clahsen, H., and Felser, C. (2006). How native-like is non-native language processing? *Trends in Cognitive Sciences*, 10 (12): 564–70.

Danesi, M. (1986). The role of metaphor in second language pedagogy. *Rassegna Italiana Di Linguistica Applicata*, 18 (3): 1–10.

De Groot, A. M. B. (1992). Bilingual lexical representation: A closer look at conceptual representations. *Orthography, Phonology, Morphology, and Meaning*, 94: 389–412.

Deignan, A. (2005). *Metaphor and Corpus Linguistics*. Amsterdam: John Benjamins.

Dufour, R., and Kroll, J. F. (1995). Matching words to concepts in two languages: A test of the concept mediation model of bilingual representation. *Memory & Cognition*, 23 (2): 166–80.

Ellis, R. (2005). Measuring implicit and explicit knowledge of a second language: A psychometric study. *Studies in Second Language Acquisition*, 27 (2): 141–72.

Fauconnier, G. (1994). *Mental Spaces: Aspects of Meaning Construction in Natural Language*. Cambridge University Press.

Fauconnier, G., and Turner, M. B. (2008). *Rethinking Metaphor* (SSRN Scholarly Paper No. ID 1275662). Rochester, NY: Social Science Research Network.

Finkbeiner, M., Forster, K., Nicol, J., and Nakamura, K. (2004). The role of polysemy in masked semantic and translation priming. *Journal of Memory and Language*, 51 (1): 1–22.

Frege, G. (1991). *Collected Papers on Mathematics, Logic, and Philosophy* (1st edn). Oxford, UK; New York: Wiley-Blackwell.

Frisson, S., and Pickering, M. (2001). Obtaining a figurative interpretation of a word: Support for underspecification. *Metaphor and Symbol*, 16: 149–71.

Fu, Q. -J. (2012). Digit Span (Version 1.3.2). Los Angeles: TigerSpeech Technology. University of California Los Angeles. Retrieved from https://itunes.apple.com/us/app/digit-span-test/id834048597?mt=8.

García, O., Cieślicka, A. B., and Heredia, R. R. (2015). Nonliteral language processing and methodological considerations, in A. B. Cieślicka and R. R. Heredia (eds), *Bilingual Figurative Language Processing*, 117–68, Cambridge University Press.

Gentner, D., and Bowdle, B. F. (2008). Metaphor as structure-mapping, in R. W. Gibbs (ed.), *The Cambridge Handbook of Metaphor and Thought*, 109–28, Cambridge, UK: Cambridge University Press. Retrieved from https://www.scholars.northwestern.edu/en/publications/metaphor-as-structure-mapping.

Gibbs, R. W. (1995). *The Poetics of Mind: Figurative Thought, Language, and Understanding*. Cambridge, UK; New York: Cambridge University Press.

Gibbs, R. W. (2017). Metaphor, language, and dynamical systems, in E. Semino and Z. Demjén (eds), *The Routledge Handbook of Metaphor and Language*, 56–70, New York: Routledge.

Gibbs, R. W., and Colston, H. L. (2012). *Interpreting Figurative Meaning*. Cambridge, UK; New York: Cambridge University Press.

Gibbs, R. W., and Nayak, N. P. (1989). Psycholinguistic studies on the syntactic behavior of idioms. *Cognitive Psychology*, 21 (1): 100–38.

Gildea, P., and Glucksberg, S. (1983). On understanding metaphor: The role of context. *Journal of Verbal Learning and Verbal Behavior*, 22 (5): 577–90. https://doi.org/10.1016/S0022-5371(83)90355-9.

Giora, R. (2002). Literal vs. figurative language: Different or equal? *Journal of Pragmatics*, 34 (4): 487–506.

Glucksberg, S. (2001). *Understanding Figurative Language: From Metaphors to Idioms*. New York: Oxford University Press.

Glucksberg, S., Gildea, P., and Bookin, H. B. (1982). On understanding nonliteral speech: Can people ignore metaphors? *Journal of Verbal Learning and Verbal Behavior*, 21 (1): 85–98. https://doi.org/10.1016/S0022-5371(82)90467-4.

Glucksberg, S., and Haught, C. (2006). On the relation between metaphor and simile: When comparison fails. *Mind & Language*, 21 (3): 360–78.

Glucksberg, S., and Keysar, B. (1993). How metaphors work, in A. Ortony (ed.), *Metaphor and Thought* (2nd edn), 401–24, Cambridge, UK: Cambridge University Press.

Grant, L., and Bauer, L. (2004). Criteria for re-defining idioms: Are we barking up the wrong tree? *Applied Linguistics*, 25 (1): 38–61.

Grice, H. P. (1967). *Logic and Conversation* (William James Lectures). Harvard.

Grice, H. P. (1989). *Studies in the Way of Words*. Cambridge, MA: Harvard University Press.

Haspelmath, M. (2006). Against markedness (and what to replace it with). *Journal of Linguistics*, 42 (1): 25–70.

Heredia, R. R., García, O., and Penecale, M. R. (2007). The comprehension of idiomatic expressions by Spanish-English bilinguals. *48th Annual Meeting of the Psychonomic Society*, Long Beach, CA.

Holme, R. (2004). *Mind, Metaphor and Language Teaching*. Basingstoke: Palgrave Macmillan.

Irujo, S. (1986a). A piece of cake: Learning and teaching idioms. *ELT Journal*, 40 (3): 236–42.

Irujo, S. (1986b). Don't put your leg in your mouth: Transfer in the acquisition of idioms in a second language. *TESOL Quarterly*, 20 (2): 287–304.

Irujo, S. (1993). Steering clear: Avoidance in the production of idioms. *IRAL – International Review of Applied Linguistics in Language Teaching*, 31 (3): 205–20.

Jarvis, S. (2009). Lexical transfer, in A. Pavlenko (ed.), *The Bilingual Mental Lexicon: Interdisciplinary Approaches*, 99–124, Bristol: Multilingual Matters.

Jegerski, J. (2013). Self-paced reading, in J. Jegerski and B. VanPatten (eds), *Research Methods in Second Language Psycholinguistics*, 20–49, New York: Routledge.

Jiang, N. (2000). Lexical representation and development in a second language. *Applied Linguistics*, 21 (1): 47–77.

Jiang, N. (2004). Semantic transfer and its implications for vocabulary teaching in a second language. *The Modern Language Journal*, 88 (3): 416–32.

Jiang, N. (2007). Selective integration of linguistic knowledge in adult second language learning. *Language Learning*, 57 (1): 1–33.

Jones, L., and Estes, Z. (2005). Metaphor comprehension as attributive categorization. *Journal of Memory and Language*, 53: 110–24. https://doi.org/10.1016/j.jml.2005.01.016.

Jordens, P. (1986). Production rules in interlanguage: Evidence from case errors in L2 German, in E. Kellerman and M.S. Smith (eds), *Crosslinguistic Influence in Second Language Acquisition*, 91–109, Pearson College Division.

Jordens, P., and Kellerman, E. (1981). Investigations into the 'transfer strategy' in second language learning. *Actes du 5e Congres de IAILA*, 195–215.

Kaplan, D. (1989). Demonstratives, in J. Almog, J. Perry and H. Wettstein (eds), *Themes from Kaplan*, 481–563, Oxford: Oxford University Press.

Kecskés, I. (2000). A cognitive-pragmatic approach to situation-bound utterances. *Journal of Pragmatics*, 32 (5): 605–25.

Kellerman, E. (1979). Transfer and non-transfer: Where we are now. *Studies in Second Language Acquisition*, 2 (01): 37–57.

Kellerman, E. (1983). Now you see it, now you don't. *Language Transfer in Language Learning*, 54 (12): 112–34.

Kolers, P. A. (1963). Interlingual word associations. *Journal of Verbal Learning and Verbal Behavior*, 2 (4): 291–300.

Kövecses, Z. (2005). *Metaphor in Culture: Universality and Variation*. Cambridge, UK: Cambridge University Press.

Kövecses, Z. (2017). Conceptual metaphor theory, in E. Semino and Z. Demjén (eds), *The Routledge Handbook of Metaphor and Language*, 13–27, New York: Routledge.

Kroll, J. F., and De Groot, A. M. B. (1997). Lexical and conceptual memory in the bilingual: Mapping form to meaning in two languages, in A. M. B. De Groot and J. F. Kroll (eds), *Tutorials in Bilingualism: Psycholinguistic Perspectives*, 169–99, Mahwah, NJ: Lawrence Erlbaum Associates.

Kroll, J. F., and Stewart, E. (1994). Category interference in translation and picture naming: Evidence for asymmetric connections between bilingual memory representations. *Journal of Memory and Language*, 33 (2): 149–74.

Lado, R. (1957). *Linguistics across Cultures: Applied Linguistics for Language Teachers*. Ann Arbor: University of Michigan Press.

Lai, V. T., Curran, T., and Menn, L. (2009). Comprehending conventional and novel metaphors: An ERP study. *Brain Research*, 1284: 145–55.

Lakoff, G. (1987). *Women, Fire*, and *Dangerous Things: What Categories Reveal about the Mind* (new edn). University of Chicago Press.

Lakoff, G., and Johnson, M. (1980). *Metaphors We Live By*. Chicago: University of Chicago Press.

Lakoff, G., and Turner, M. (1989). *More than Cool Reason: A Field Guide to Poetic Metaphor*. Chicago: University of Chicago Press.

Laufer, B. (2000). Avoidance of idioms in a second language: The effect of L1-L2 degree of similarity. *Studia Linguistica*, 54 (2): 186–96.

Leezenberg, M. (2001). *Contexts of Metaphor*. Amsterdam: Elsevier.

Leung, Y.-K. I. (2005). L2 vs. L3 initial state: A comparative study of the acquisition of French DPs by Vietnamese monolinguals and Cantonese–English bilinguals. *Bilingualism: Language and Cognition*, 8 (1): 39–61.

Libben, M. R., and Titone, D. A. (2008). The multidetermined nature of idiom processing. *Memory & Cognition*, 36 (6): 1103–21.

Link, P. (2013). *An Anatomy of Chinese: Rhythm, Metaphor, Politics*. Cambridge, MA: Harvard University Press.

Liontas, J. (2002). Context and idiom understanding in second languages. *EUROSLA Yearbook*, 2 (1): 155–85.

Littlemore, J. (2010). Metaphoric competence in the first and second language. *Converging Evidence in Language and Communication Research (CELCR)*, 13: 293.

Littlemore, J., and Low, G. (2006). *Figurative Thinking and Foreign Language Learning*. Basingstoke: Palgrave Macmillan.

Liu, D. (2002). *Metaphor, Culture*, and *Worldview: The Case of American English and the Chinese Language*. Lanham, MD: University Press of America.

Ma, Q. (2009). *Second Language Vocabulary Acquisition*. Bern; New York: Peter Lang.

Matlock, T., and Heredia, R. R. (2002). Understanding phrasal verbs in monolinguals and bilinguals. *Advances in Psychology*, 134: 251–74.

McElree, B., and Nordlie, J. (1999). Literal and figurative interpretations are computed in equal time. *Psychonomic Bulletin & Review*, 6 (3): 486–94. https://doi.org/10.3758/BF03210839.

Meisel, J. M. (2011). *First and Second Language Acquisition: Parallels and Differences*. Cambridge, UK: Cambridge University Press.

Miller, G. A. (1969). A psychological method to investigate verbal concepts. *Journal of Mathematical Psychology*, 6 (2): 169–91.

Mitchell, D. C. (2004). On-line methods in language processing: Introduction and historical review, in M. Carreiras and C. Clifton (eds), *The On-Line Study of Sentence Comprehension: Eyetracking, ERPs, and Beyond*, 15–32, New York: Psychology Press.

Nacey, S. (2014). *Metaphors in Learner English*. Amsterdam: John Benjamins.

Odlin, T. (1989). *Language Transfer: Cross-Linguistic Influence in Language Learning*. Cambridge, UK: Cambridge University Press.

Papadopoulou, D., Tsimpli, I., and Amvrazis, N. (2013). Self-paced listening, in J. Jegerski and B. VanPatten (eds), *Research Methods in Second Language Psycholinguistics*, 50–68, New York: Routledge.

Pavlenko, A. (2009). Conceptual representation in the bilingual lexicon and second language vocabulary learning, in A. Pavlenko (ed.), *The Bilingual Mental Lexicon: Interdisciplinary Approaches*, 125–160, Bristol: Multilingual Matters.

Pragglejaz Group. (2007). MIP: A method for identifying metaphorically used words in discourse. *Metaphor and Symbol*, 22 (1): 1–39.

Quillan, M. R. (1966). *Semantic Memory* (No. SCIENTIFIC-2). Cambridge, MA: Bolt Beranek and Newman.

Recanati, F. (2004). *Literal Meaning*. Cambridge, UK: Cambridge University Press.

Ringbom, H. (1978). What differences are there between Finns and Swedish-speaking Finns learning English? *Papers and Studies in Contrastive Linguistics Poznan*, 8: 133–45.

Ringbom, H. (2006). The importance of different types of similarity in transfer studies, in J. Arabski (ed.), *Cross-Linguistic Influences in the Second Language Lexicon*, 36–45, Clevedon: Multilingual Matters.

Roncero, C. (2013). *Understanding Figurative Language: Studies on the Comprehension of Metaphors and Similes*. Concordia University. Retrieved from http://oatd.org/oatd/record?record=oai%5C%3Aspectrum.library.concordia.ca%5C%3A977747.

Rutherford, W. E. (1982). Markedness in second language acquisition. *Language Learning*, 32 (1): 85–108.

Sanders, L. D., and Neville, H. J. (2003). An ERP study of continuous speech processing: I. Segmentation, semantics, and syntax in native speakers. *Cognitive Brain Research*, 15 (3), 228–40.

Sanford, A. J., Sturt, P., Moxey, L., Morrow, L., and Emmott, C. (2004). Production and comprehension measures in assessing plural object formation, in M. Carreiras and C. Clifton (eds), *The On-Line Study of Sentence Comprehension: Eyetracking, ERPs, and Beyond*, 151–68, New York: Psychology Press.

Siyanova-Chanturia, A., Conklin, K., and Schmitt, N. (2011). Adding more fuel to the fire: An eye-tracking study of idiom processing by native and non-native speakers. *Second Language Research*, 27 (2), 251–72.

Sjöholm, K. (1976). A comparison of the test results in grammar and vocabulary between Finnish-and Swedish-speaking applicants for English. *Errors Made by Finns and Swedish-Speaking Finns in the Learning of English. Abo, Finland: Department of English, Abo Akademi (ERIC Document Reproduction Service No. ED122628)*.

Sperber, D., and Wilson, D. (1995). *Relevance: Cognition and Communication* (2nd edn). Cambridge, MA: Harvard University Press.

Spolsky, B. (1985). Formulating a theory of second language learning. *Studies in Second Language Acquisition*, 7 (3): 269–88.

Stern, J. (2000). *Metaphor in Context*. Cambridge, MA: MIT Press.

Sweetser, E. (1990). *From Etymology to Pragmatics: Metaphorical and Cultural Aspects of Semantic Structure*. Cambridge, UK: Cambridge University Press.

Titone, D., Columbus, G., Whitford, V., Mercier, J., and Libben, M. (2015). Contrasting bilingual and monolingual idiom processing, in R. R. Heredia and A. B. Cieślicka (eds), *Bilingual Figurative Language Processing*, 171–207, Cambridge, UK: Cambridge University Press.

Traugott, E. (2004). Historical pragmatics, in L. Horn and G. Ward (eds), *Handbook of Pragmatics*, 538–61, Oxford: Blackwell Press.

Türker, E. (2016a). Idiom acquisition by second language learners: the influence of cross-linguistic similarity and context. *Language Learning Journal*: 1–12.

Türker, E. (2016b). The role of L1 conceptual and linguistic knowledge and frequency in the acquisition of L2 metaphorical expressions. *Second Language Research*, 32 (1): 25–48.

UCLES. (2001). *Oxford Quick Placement Test*. Oxford: Oxford University Press.

Van Hell, J. G., and De Groot, A. M. B. (1998). Conceptual representation in bilingual memory: Effects of concreteness and cognate status in word association. *Bilingualism: Language and Cognition*, 1 (3): 193–211.

Vega-Moreno, R. E. (2007). *Creativity and Convention: The Pragmatics of Everyday Figurative Speech*. Amsterdam: John Benjamins.

Wehmeier, S. (2000). *Oxford Advanced Learner's Dictionary* (6th edn). Oxford; New York: Oxford University Press.

Wittgenstein, L. (1953). *Philosophical Investigation*, trans. G. Anscombe, Oxford: Blackwell.

Wong, S.-L. C. (1983). Overproduction, under-lexicalization and unidiomatic usage in the make causatives of Chinese speakers: A case for flexibility in interlanguage analysis. *Language Learning and Communication*, 2: 151–63.

Xia, M. (2017). Psychotypology of Chinese learners of English and its influence on the acquisition of metaphorical expressions: An offline study. *Cambridge Occasional Papers in Linguistics*, 10: 237–55.

Xia, V., and Andrews, S. (2015). Masked translation priming asymmetry in Chinese-English bilinguals: Making sense of the Sense Model. *Quarterly Journal of Experimental Psychology*, 68 (2): 294–325.

Yu, N. (1998). *The Contemporary Theory of Metaphor: A Perspective from Chinese*. Amsterdam: John Benjamins.

Zhang, D. (2008). *A Study of Cross-Linguistic Transfer of Metaphor in SLA* (Master of Arts). Liaoning Normal University, Dalian.

Index

ability
   cognitive 16
   of inferencing 8, 15, 92, 93, 188
   learners' 104, 107, 112, 124, 128
   native speakers' 114
   pragmatic 16, 103, 104, 113
   of using metaphorical expressions 182
abstract
   -but-core 50
   concept 62
   (conceptual) domain 56, 59, 75
   entity 22
   meaning 49, 74–82, 99, 102
   sense 61
   word 74–82
abstraction
   in creating metaphorical meanings 62
abstractness 49, 93, 126, 183
acceptability 133, 166, 183
   degree of 10, 103
   of metaphorical expressions 102–3, 175–83
   judgement task (AJT) 45, 97, 109–13, 113, 124, 125, 127, 134–8, 142–4, 152, 158, 170–1
   score 138–41, 143, 148, 150, 151, 177, 179, 184
acquisition
   and cross-linguistic influence 3, 30
   of figurative language 9, 29, 39, 43, 66, 73, 103, 174, 191
   of idioms 40–3
   of L2 phrases/expressions 36, 38
   of metaphorical expressions 6, 8–11, 25, 26, 29, 32, 38, 40, 44–6, 50, 53, 72, 92, 99–115, 118, 129, 130, 133, 144, 149, 171, 173–80, 190–2
   of vocabulary 34–5, 181
ad hoc concept 18–19
alternative
   metaphorical expressions 153–6, 182

   as a type of reaction to metaphorical expressions 151–2
ambiguity resolution 61, 66
aptness 63
approximation 37–8. *See also* semantic overextension
availability
   of metaphorical expressions 93–4, 121–2, 135–6. *See also* cross-linguistic availability
avoidance 31, 41, 45, 118
awareness 168, 173, 189
   metaphoric 192

baseline
   literal expressions as a 7, 124, 135, 158
   native speakers as a 94–5, 109, 121
behaviourism 30
bilingual 35, 41–2, 69, 82
   (mental) lexicon 4, 9–10, 66, 72, 73–9, 82–6, 88–9, 93–4, 99, 102–3, 107, 115, 179, 192
   sequential 82–3, 99
   speaker 29, 33, 55, 87
   vocabulary 3
Blending Theory 14, 22–5, 75

Career of Metaphor 64
character 19–20. *See also Dthat; Mthat*
Chinese 1–2, 22, 25, 31, 78, 113, 118, 121, 135–6, 155–6, 162, 174
   learners of English 10, 89–90, 113, 133–4, 174–92
Chinglish 92, 153, 178
classroom 1, 4, 10, 25, 52, 74, 89–92, 93, 99, 101, 123, 186–92
close-ended task 112
cloze 128
cognate 32–3, 35, 76–7
   non- 32–3, 35, 38, 76–7
cognitive

effort 19, 65
linguistics 191
semantics 13, 14, 16, 22, 23, 25, 26, 89, 123, 189, 191, 192
collocation 1, 5–7, 19–31, 36, 43, 45, 60, 61 104–6, 113, 117, 129, 188, 190
compositional meaning 4, 14, 20–1, 68, 70
compositional semantics 14
comprehension 18, 29, 38, 40, 41, 63, 65, 70, 85, 90, 99, 113, 129, 189
questions 10, 117, 160, 161, 166–8, 170, 179
concept 11, 16, 23, 24, 27–35, 43, 44, 47, 49, 52, 57–9, 66, 71, 72, 74, 83–7, 89–99, 101, 104–9, 116, 147, 194, 196, 197, 199, 200, 202
mediation 83–5, 94–8
conceptual
broadening 17, 19, 64
Conceptual Metaphor Theory (CMT) 14, 22–6, 56, 57, 58, 62, 75, 102, 187
domain 23, 24, 56, 59, 75, 80, 81
feature 75–7, 79, 81
loosening 64
mapping 23, 44, 81
narrowing 17, 19
representation 75–7, 79–81
concordancer 104, 105
concrete
-but-peripheral 50
concept 56, 62, 80
(conceptual) domain 59, 75, 80
entity 22, 77
meaning 49, 75, 77, 80, 81, 99, 102
word 74, 75, 77, 80
concreteness 49, 50, 75, 77, 79–81, 126, 127, 136, 159
confidence 30, 52, 71, 110, 112, 137–9, 142–4, 176, 177
constraints 90, 91, 185
context 6, 8, 14, 16–20, 23, 24, 26, 36, 38, 39, 43, 45, 57, 59–61, 62, 67, 69, 73, 75, 76, 79–81, 91, 92, 93, 98, 104, 105, 106, 108, 111, 112, 113, 116, 117, 123, 124, 138, 151, 159, 171, 180, 184, 185, 188, 189
context-sensitivity 23
contextualist 8, 79

contextual
inference 8, 112
information 14, 16, 20, 57, 70, 91, 94, 109, 117, 124, 158, 159
contrastive analysis (CA) 30–1
conventional
metaphor 21, 24, 57, 65
metaphorical expressions 1, 3–5, 7, 9, 13, 15, 16, 19, 23–6, 44, 55, 60, 63–7, 70, 71, 106, 112, 123, 174, 175, 188. *See also* conventionalized metaphorical expressions
metaphorical meanings 7, 19, 20, 74, 95, 186. *See also* conventionalized metaphorical meanings
conventionality 59, 63
conventionalization 3, 14, 24, 64
conventionalized
metaphorical expressions 5, 20, 25, 55, 59, 61, 64, 70, 102. *See also* conventional metaphorical expressions
metaphorical meanings 4, 6, 33, 71, 73, 79, 93, 186. *See also* conventional metaphorical meanings
coreness 49, 50, 126, 127, 136, 146, 147, 159
corpus/corpora 104–6, 108, 124, 135
correction 139, 151–6
sentence task 112–14, 122, 124, 137
creativity 105, 113, 155, 156
critical
lexical item 7, 8, 123–5, 129, 134–6, 154, 157–9, 174, 183
region 118, 161
cross-domain mapping 80
cross-linguistic 25, 27, 40, 44, 48, 69, 70, 79, 130
availability 53, 74, 171, 182, 189, 191
influence 3, 9, 11, 29–53, 77, 80, 81, 89, 91, 92, 99, 102, 105, 107, 108, 112, 114, 121, 123, 143, 144, 146, 149, 150, 175, 176, 179–82, 184, 185, 189, 191, 192. *See also* transfer
variability 4
variation 4, 22
cross-linguistic comparison 46, 48
curriculum 91, 191

data adjustment 138, 139, 160, 161
data normalization 160

Index

Distributed Conceptual Feature Model (DCFM) 75–82, 85, 88, 102. *See also* Distributed Feature Model (DFM)
Distributed Feature Model (DFM) 75, 81. *See also* Distributed Conceptual Feature Model (DCFM)
decomposability 69–70
developmental
   view of bilingual lexicon 81–4
digit span task 130, 139, 157, 160, 161
direct access view 57, 59, 61
discourse 1, 23, 166
   completion task 40, 43, 104, 106–8, 112, 125
Dthat 19

education
   primary 91
   secondary 91
   second language 10, 25
   tertiary 187
English 1–2, 25, 33–7, 41, 45, 49, 68, 69, 86, 113, 122, 123, 135, 136, 139, 140, 142, 143, 153, 155–7, 159, 161, 162, 168, 174
   for Academic Purpose (EAP) 190
   for business purpose 123, 190
   learners 36–7, 40, 43, 44, 49, 68, 69, 116, 155. *See also* Chinese learners of English
   native speakers 2, 43, 60, 68, 113, 122, 136, 141, 142, 152, 159, 166, 174
   proficiency 134, 157
   as a second language 1
   -speaking environment 2, 41, 134, 157, 166, 175
   for specific purposes (ESP) 191
   teaching in China 90–1
event-related Potential (ERP) 65
experimental instruments 104–19
experiments 134–8, 157–61
explicature 17, 18, 64
exposure 41, 42, 52, 74, 90–3, 128, 134, 139, 157, 161, 166, 174, 178, 180, 184, 188
eye
   -movement 120
   -tracking 60, 68, 116, 118, 120, 131

factors
   influencing cross-linguistic influence 45–53, 182–5
false friends 31, 35–8, 53
familiarity 59, 63, 69
feature
   conceptual 75–7, 79, 81
feature-based 81
feedback 44, 110, 112, 138, 139, 150–6, 176, 178, 179, 182
filler 125, 136, 138, 158, 159
figurative 5, 9, 16, 29, 32, 34, 38–45, 55, 59–62, 65–71, 73, 90, 93, 94, 98, 99, 103, 106, 115, 116, 120, 131, 171, 174, 175, 185, 191
figurativeness 39, 42, 68, 69
formulaic 23, 39, 90
fossilization 184
frequency 31, 36–8, 46, 47, 49, 59, 63, 104, 105, 123, 126, 127, 136, 139, 159, 161, 190

Graded Salience Hypothesis 58–60
grammar-translation 90
grammaticality 40, 111

hearer 15–18, 20, 56
hierarchy of difficulty 166
high-advanced (high-adv) 134, 140, 141, 142, 143, 145, 152, 156, 157, 164–6, 168–70, 178, 180
homonyms 7, 86, 186
homophones 86
hyperbole 17

identification of trace of transfer 143–5
idiom 4, 5, 9, 29, 36, 39–45, 47–9, 53, 55, 66–70, 90, 106, 116, 122, 153, 175, 178, 185. *See also* idiomatic
idiomatic 5, 35, 40, 67–70, 94, 124. *See also* idiom
implicature 13–15, 17, 24, 56, 74
indeterminacy 143
indexical expression 19. *See also* character; *Dthat*
indexicalist view of metaphor 8, 16, 19, 20
information
   encyclopaedic 18
input 30, 42, 90–3, 97, 166, 176, 178

instruction 4, 41, 42, 52, 85, 90, 103, 104, 122, 133, 137, 138, 178, 185, 186, 189, 190. *See also* pedagogy; teaching
instructors 4, 39, 43, 92, 133, 173, 176, 178, 180, 185–90, 192. *See also* teachers
interlanguage 31
intermediate (Int) 128, 134, 136, 140–2, 145, 147, 156, 157, 163, 164, 166, 168, 169, 176–9, 190
interpretation task 112–14
irony 58

judgement 30, 40, 45, 51, 52, 53, 57, 70, 71, 83, 92, 97, 108, 109–13, 122, 124, 125, 126, 127, 134–9, 141–7, 149–52, 157, 158, 166, 170, 171, 174–6, 177, 179, 180–2, 184. *See also* acceptability judgement task

knowledge 2, 3, 8, 9, 11, 15, 16, 22, 25–7, 30, 33–6, 38, 40, 41, 46, 50–53, 71, 74, 79, 87, 90, 92–4, 96, 102, 105–9, 112–14, 124, 128, 131, 144–6, 149, 150, 153–5, 175–8, 180–2, 184, 185, 187–92
   assumed 50–3

L1 16, 27, 29–31, 33, 35, 36, 38, 40–3, 45–9, 51, 53, 67–70, 74, 76–80, 82–8, 91–8, 102–7, 112–14, 121, 127, 135, 143, 144, 147, 149, 150, 155, 156, 175, 178, 180, 181, 183, 184, 189, 192
   L1-specific 45, 88, 92, 94, 97, 98, 114, 150, 154, 161, 170, 176, 177, 178, 179, 180, 182, 183, 184, 191
L2 16, 26, 27, 29–33, 35–46, 48–53, 66–70, 73, 74, 76–88, 90–9, 102, 103, 105–9, 112, 114, 121, 123, 127, 133, 143, 144, 147, 150, 153, 155–156, 166, 170, 175–85, 187, 189, 192
   L2-specific 45, 88, 94, 96, 97, 98, 99, 176, 177, 179, 180, 181, 184, 185, 191
L3 35, 192
language
   acquisition 1–4, 9, 10, 20, 23, 26, 29, 40, 42, 46, 47, 50, 51, 66, 88, 89, 91, 109, 121, 128, 171, 182, 185, 188, 191

comprehension 18, 85
processing 3, 66–9, 85, 98, 99, 115, 120
use 1, 2, 7, 8, 22, 47, 63, 80, 126, 155, 185
user 2, 4, 5, 13, 24, 26, 42, 57, 58, 63, 87, 126
language-neutral 38, 76, 153, 154
language-specific 3, 10, 33, 34, 39, 40, 87, 94, 143, 151, 153
late-Wittgenstein 75, 79
lemma 32
lexeme 32
lexical
   evaluation survey 125–7, 136, 146, 159, 182
   item 4–8, 10, 15–22, 24, 26, 29, 32–7, 39, 40, 42–5, 49, 53, 61, 67, 71–7, 79–83, 85–93, 95, 99, 101–3, 105, 116, 117, 121, 123–5, 129, 131, 134–6, 143, 154–9, 173, 174, 176, 183–5, 187–92
   semantics 14, 22, 24, 59, 61, 73, 74, 90
lexicon 4, 9, 10, 59, 61, 62, 66, 72–7, 79, 81–9, 91, 93–5, 97, 99, 102, 103, 107, 115, 171, 174, 179, 184, 192
Likert scale 110, 127, 136–9
literal
   concepts 20, 34, 81, 87, 94–7, 99
   expressions 3, 5, 7, 9, 16, 20, 26, 38, 39, 44, 48, 55, 65, 68, 74, 89, 93–5, 99, 106, 107, 124, 125, 135, 139–42, 148, 153–5, 158, 162, 163, 168, 173–5, 177, 182, 183, 186, 188
   meanings 5–8, 15, 16, 18–21, 24, 26, 42–4, 56, 57, 59, 60, 62, 67, 68, 70–73, 75, 79–81, 86, 87, 91–3, 95–9, 102, 103, 117, 123, 124, 126, 155, 173, 174, 185–90
literal-both (LB) 135, 136, 140–2, 147, 148, 158, 162–5, 167–9, 183
literal-source (LS) 135, 136, 140, 142, 158, 161–9
literal-target (LT) 135, 136, 140–2, 158, 162–70
literal-first hypothesis 56, 67, 99, 162
literalness 17, 18, 30, 31, 59, 60, 68, 136
logical form 17
low-advanced (low-adv) 134, 140–2, 145, 156, 157, 163–5, 168, 169, 176, 179

magnitude estimation 110–12, 127
mapping 22, 23, 24, 34, 44, 62, 77, 80, 81, 86, 89
markedness 9, 46–50, 53, 59, 102, 126, 136, 146–8, 159, 173, 182, 183
masked priming 116
maxims 14, 15, 56
maze task 118–20, 124, 125, 129
medium language 91
mental lexicon 10, 59, 61, 62, 72, 73, 74, 75, 77, 79, 81, 82, 83, 85, 87, 89, 91, 93, 95, 97, 99, 107, 171, 174, 184, 192
metalinguistic 30, 51, 52, 109
metaphor 1, 3, 4, 6, 8, 13–15, 19–26, 34, 43, 49, 56–8, 62–6, 70, 73, 79, 90, 94, 101, 103, 104, 105–7, 109, 111, 113, 115, 117, 119, 121, 123, 125, 126, 127, 129, 131, 155, 173, 186, 187, 189–92
  Aristotelian view of 80
  conceptual 4, 6, 14, 22, 23, 25, 26, 56, 58, 94, 104, 186, 187, 189, 190, 192
  Gricean view of 13–17, 21, 22, 24, 55, 58
  Identification Paradigm (MIP) 105, 106, 124, 156
  linguistic 23, 25, 63, 65
  literary 3, 22, 186, 187
  post-Gricean view of 16–20, 23
metaphorical
  competence 67
  concept 34, 43, 44, 84, 89, 91, 97, 99, 104, 106, 107, 109
  expressions 1–11, 13–27, 29, 30, 32–4, 36, 38–40, 42–6, 48, 50, 52, 53, 55–74, 76–8, 80–2, 84, 86–94, 96–9, 101–31, 133–6, 138–56, 158, 159, 161–3, 165–8, 170, 171, 173–92
  interpretation 8, 24, 43, 57, 79, 189
  knowledge 106
  mapping 22, 23
  meanings 2, 4–10, 13, 15–21, 24, 26, 32–4, 36, 42, 43, 45, 49, 56–62, 70, 71, 73–5, 77, 79–82, 86–99, 102, 103, 115–17, 123, 124, 126, 129, 131, 155, 156, 159, 162, 163, 170, 173, 174, 184–92
  metaphorical-both (MB) 135, 136, 140–53, 158, 161–70

metaphorical-source (MS) 135, 136, 140–7, 149–52, 154, 158, 160–70, 178, 179
metaphorical-target (MT) 135, 136, 140–5, 149–52, 158, 161–71, 179, 180
  utterances 15, 17, 18
metaphoricalness 6–8, 49, 50, 65, 102, 125, 126, 136, 146–8, 159, 161, 173, 182, 183, 188
metaphoric extension 34
metonymy 17, 58
minimal-literal (m-literal) 20, 21
mis-paraphrase 153–5
Modified Hierarchical Model 87–9, 94
monolingual 79, 115
Mthat 19, 20
mixed-effect 138, 147
multi-word 4, 6, 36, 39, 45, 66, 116

native
  language (NL) 29, 69, 114, 122
  -like 3, 30, 37, 66, 69, 70, 92, 93, 108, 144–6, 148, 165, 166, 170, 173–5, 177, 179, 184, 188
  speaker 1–3, 8, 9, 11, 15, 16, 26, 30, 31, 36, 37, 41–3, 47, 55–8, 61, 65–71, 91–5, 98, 102, 105, 109, 112–6, 121–3, 125–7, 131, 133, 134, 136–141, 143, 144, 147, 152, 154–7, 159, 160, 162, 163, 165, 166, 170, 171, 174–7, 179, 188, 192
n-back 130
near-native 188
near-paraphrase 154
non-acquisition 83
non-cumulative 116, 118
non-guided 52, 92, 184
non-idiomatic 41
non-literal 3, 4, 20, 21, 44, 55, 56, 67, 148, 183
non-literalness 21, 22
non-native 3, 44, 165
non-native-like 30
non-nativeness 38, 177
non-transfer 145, 146, 149
non-words 119, 120

offline 10, 43, 63, 70, 71, 73, 97, 109, 113, 115, 123–5, 133, 171

online 10, 55, 63, 70, 71, 73, 97, 109, 112, 115, 119, 123–5, 127, 129, 130, 133, 160, 171
open-ended 112
ostensive phenomenon 16, 17
overproduction 36–8
overseas 128, 134, 140–3, 145, 156, 157, 164–6, 168–70, 178, 179, 184
Oxford Quick Placement Test (OQPT) 134, 149, 150, 157, 160

paraphrase 38, 41, 45, 114, 122, 153–6
pedagogy 103, 114, 173, 185. *See also* instruction; teaching
pen-and-paper 109, 112, 127, 128, 137
perception 22, 25, 30, 32, 47–9, 71, 111, 126, 177, 181
performance 3, 10, 66, 70, 76, 81, 85, 93, 108, 121, 130, 133, 134, 144, 145, 148, 157, 170, 173, 175–7, 189
peripheral 36, 37, 47, 49, 55, 78, 146
peripheral-ness 126
phrasal verb 4, 9, 39, 43, 44, 55, 66–9, 71, 116
picture-naming 129
p-literalness 22
primary-literal (p-literal) 20, 21
polysemy 24, 34, 77, 79, 86
pragmatic enrichment 13, 17–19, 186
pragmatics 3, 4, 15, 16, 23, 24, 55
priming 68, 77–9, 115, 116
Principle of compositionality 4, 26
processing 3, 9, 10, 15, 16, 18, 40, 43, 55–71, 77, 80, 83, 85, 93–5, 98, 99, 102, 115–18, 120, 123, 124, 131, 135, 156, 158, 161–3, 165, 166, 168, 170, 174, 175, 179, 184, 192
    cost 62, 163
    difficulty 57, 66, 117, 118, 131, 170, 174, 175, 179
    pattern 9, 15, 55, 59, 60, 64, 65, 66, 69, 71, 93, 99, 102, 165, 166, 174
    speed 58, 59, 63, 64
production 10, 29–31, 36–8, 40, 41, 43, 51, 52, 70, 71, 90, 92, 106–8, 112, 114, 121, 122, 129, 131, 150, 153, 155, 176, 177
proficiency 9, 10, 32, 41, 51–3, 68, 76, 83–5, 90, 95–9, 108, 128–30, 133, 134, 136, 137, 139, 141–3, 146, 148–50, 152, 154–7, 161, 166, 168, 170, 173, 176–81, 184, 185, 191
    test 128, 137, 184
prototype 81
proverbs 9, 67
psycholinguistic 9, 15, 23, 47, 55, 58, 61, 62, 71, 85
psychotypology 35, 46, 47, 160

questionnaires 108, 109, 112, 137

reaction time 66, 68, 71, 76, 85, 103, 108, 109, 123, 160, 166–70, 177
reading
    pattern 68, 69, 116, 130, 162, 163, 165, 170, 175
    time 57, 63, 66–8, 99, 108, 116, 117, 158, 160–5, 182
real-time 65, 69, 80, 85
receptive 3, 10, 105–9, 112–14, 121, 124, 125
Relevance Theory 17–19, 58, 64
restructuring 88
retrieval 10, 16, 66, 70, 74, 85, 90, 95–8, 163
Revised Hierarchical Model 83–9, 91

second language 1–4, 8–10, 13, 15, 16, 25, 26, 29, 30, 32, 33, 36, 40, 45, 46, 48, 50, 51, 55, 65, 66, 71, 73, 83–5, 88, 89, 91, 93, 101, 102, 104, 106, 109, 112, 114–6, 118, 120, 121, 128–130, 133, 171, 173–5, 182, 185–191
    acquisition 26, 29, 40, 46, 50, 51, 66, 88, 91, 109, 121, 128, 171, 182, 185, 188, 191
    learner 16, 29, 45, 46, 55, 65, 66, 71, 73, 83, 93, 115, 116, 118, 171, 175, 185, 189
secondariness 3
segment 116, 117, 159, 161–6
self-learning 187
self-paced reading task 115–20, 124, 125, 129, 133, 156, 158–60, 170, 171
semantic
    domain 5, 115
    extension 37, 38
    memory 75, 79
    overextension 35, 37, 38. *See also* approximation
    transparency 42, 48, 49, 53

semantically opaque 39, 40, 42, 43, 47, 48, 124
semantics 3, 4, 13, 14, 16, 18, 22–6, 40, 58, 59, 61, 62, 73, 74, 89, 90, 123, 189, 191, 192
semi-fixed 5–7
Sense Model, the 77–9, 82
sentence completion task 43–4, 106–9, 112–13
simile 62–4
speaker 1–3, 8–11, 14–17, 26, 29–31, 33, 36, 37, 41–4, 47, 55–8, 60, 61, 65–71, 75, 87, 91–5, 98, 102, 105, 109, 112–16, 121–3, 125–7, 131, 133, 134, 136–41, 143, 144, 147, 152, 155–7, 159, 160, 162, 163, 165, 166, 170, 171, 174–7, 179, 188, 192
speech 15, 36, 58, 77, 119, 123, 125
spill-over
    area 119, 159
    effect 118–20, 159, 161
standardization 111. *See also* z-score
stimuli 65, 115, 117–19, 124, 125, 161
strategy 9, 10, 25, 38, 45, 50–3, 64, 69, 90, 98, 99, 102, 120, 144, 149–51, 153–6, 188, 191
superordinate 34
subordinate 34

target language (TL) 31, 89, 90, 92, 98, 113, 114, 119, 135, 167
task-specific effect 70
teachers 91, 122, 185, 187, 191. *See also* instructors
teaching 10, 25, 90–2, 99, 102, 108, 115, 121, 173, 175, 177–9, 181, 183–7, 189–91. *See also* instruction; pedagogy
tenor 62–4
traces
    of transfer 143–50, 176, 178, 179, 181, 184
transfer 24, 29, 31–41, 43, 45, 46, 48–53, 68, 69, 80, 83, 87–9, 91–3, 103, 107, 108, 114, 121, 143–50, 156, 155, 156, 175–84, 189. *See also* cross-linguistic influence
    concept 33, 34, 37, 88
    lemmatic 29, 32–9, 53, 88

lexemic 32, 35
lexical 32, 35, 37, 38, 83
    negative 35, 37, 41, 51, 92, 114, 121, 145, 149, 176, 178, 179, 184
    positive 35, 41, 51–3, 108, 144, 148, 149 176, 179
    theory 41, 48, 68, 69
transferability 10, 39, 40, 45, 46, 48–50, 66, 80, 81, 102, 103, 126, 135, 147–50, 181–4, 191, 192
    objective transferability 45, 181, 183
    subjective transferability 45, 46, 48–50, 147–9, 181, 183, 184
transference 80
translation 33, 36, 37, 40–5, 75–86, 88, 89, 91, 92, 103, 104, 106, 107, 114, 118, 135, 136, 170, 177, 178
    equivalents 33, 36, 37, 40, 45, 75–83, 86, 88, 89, 91, 92, 103, 136
    near- 86, 88
    task 41–4, 76, 77, 79, 80, 84, 90, 106
trimming 160, 161
truth-conditional 13, 14, 16
typology 47

underdeterminacy 18
underproduction 36–8, 45
Underspecification Hypothesis 60–2
universality 4, 22
utterance 14, 15, 17–19, 31, 56, 71

variability 4, 111, 121, 122, 149
variation 2, 4, 22, 29, 47, 125
vehicle 62–4
vocabulary 3, 9, 32, 34, 45, 71, 83–6, 90, 103, 104, 108, 121, 123, 128, 129, 171, 185, 187, 188, 190, 191

window (in reading task) 116, 119, 159
word association 83–5, 95–7
word-concept 86, 89
word form 33, 73, 74, 76, 82, 84–8, 93, 95–8, 167
word-processing 98
working memory capacity 129–31, 139, 161, 185
wrapping-up effect 118, 159

z-score 111. *See also* standardization

www.ingramcontent.com/pod-product-compliance
Lightning Source LLC
Chambersburg PA
CBHW052038300426
44117CB00012B/1881